I Pay You to Listen, Not Talk!

A Psychiatrist's Fifty-Year Odyssey

Nathan Schnaper, M.D.

PublishAmerica

Baltimore

First printing

ISBN: 1-59286-304-3
PUBLISHED BY PUBLISHAMERICA, LLLP
www.publishamerica.com
Baltimore

Printed in the United States of America

To my grandson, David, for sixteen years of Wednesdays

Acknowledgments

Writing can be fun, but not all the time. It all begins with an idea that, like a volcano, erupts suddenly and continues to flow, sometimes bursting forth with renewed energy, sometimes smoldering with inactivity. Why the urge, the inspiration to write? Ego? Perhaps. Exhibitionism? Possibly. I believe it is the need to create, in a sense, "to have a baby." (The proof comes later when would-be editors tamper with, criticize, or reject "the baby," thereby incurring the wrath of the possessive "parent.")

As the writing proceeds, it is indeed fun, even exciting; the process has the seductiveness of a mistress. As with other similar liaisons, however, a change gradually takes over; soon it becomes the master, taking full control. One feels driven to work at it; at times even awakening in the middle of the night just to add a clever word, change a sentence, "It will only take a minute." Sure, and two hours later you are back in bed and still sleepless. And it suffices to simply curse the words, "writer's block." The writing *per se* becomes more important than publishing.

Fortunately, the process is softened by the help of those who in some way have made the work less of a task and more of a creative, self-fulfilling experience. To them I express my sincere appreciation.

First, to Ms. Margaret Gallagher, the uncanny decipherer of my scribbling, who was with me all the way, revising and revising the text. Her suggestions were always cogent, and her patience unflappable.

To the many students, interns and Fellows, who through the years rewarded me by asking for "more stories" and more insight into the theoretical and philosophical concepts of psychiatry and oncology. They frequently urged me to "write a book," which I treated with a smile and an attempt at humility. (Fueling the latent "smoldering" of my urge to write.) Whether one-on-one or in the classroom, they made teaching a joy.

Special People:

To Mark Hyman, the skilled and caring writer, who was my Moses as he guided me toward the "promised land," (publication).

To Huell "Skip" Connor, a long-time and dear and generous friend.

To Ronald Shapiro, a most talented friend, counselor, and personal champion.

To Dianne Lash, who arranged order out of random words.

To Lou Panos, the well-known journalist, who gave me warm words of encouragement.

And to the publishers who spared me the effort of building a new scaffold from which I might build new thoughts. Following are those publishers who gave kind permission to reprint portions of articles to which I previously contributed.

Schnaper, N: The Sick Doctor—The Worst Patient. *Medical Insight*. Insight Publishing Company, Inc., New York, Dec. 1973.

Schnaper, N: "Management of the Terminally Ill Patient and His Family." In: *Psychiatric Foundations of Medicine*, Vol. 6. Ed. Balis, JV, McDaniel, E, et al. Butterworth-Heinemann, Woburn, MA, pp. 231-249, 1978.

Schnaper N, Hahn, AP and DeVries, RA: Psychosocial Roles in the Cancer Drama. *American Journal of Medical Sciences*, Vol. 276. Charles B. Slack, Inc., N.J., Lippincott, Williams & Wilkins, Philadelphia, pp.:248-261, 1978.

Schnaper, N: Jason Retrieves the Golden Fleece or a Psychiatrist's Excursion Into General Medicine, or How I Ordered the Captain Off His Ship. *Maryland State Medical Journal*. 30:59-60, 1981.

Schnaper, N and Wiernik, PH: The Hospice: Old Wine in New Bottles? *Maryland State Medical Journal*. 32:102-104, 1983.

Schnaper, N, Kellner, TK: "Emotional and Psychologic Aspects of Cancer Management." In: *Comprehensive Textbook of Oncology*. Moosa, AR, Robson, MC and Schimpff, SC Second Edition, Vol. 2, pp. 1789-1975, 1991.

PREFACE

Patients in psychotherapy possess the talent to keep their therapists honest and humble. Enter Stanley. Stanley had been a patient of mine for almost three years. He had come to therapy seeking relief from his overwhelming anxiety. He was making good use of therapy, and as time went on, I became quite fond of him, as I felt Stanley did for me. Matter of fact, the therapy had become somewhat looser and more directive on my part. One day, Stanley began the session by telling me what he had done over the weekend. I leaned forward, feigning annoyance, and grouched, "Damn it, Stanley, if I've told you once, I've told you a hundred times and you never listen. You did the same damn thing all over again!" Stanley leaned forward in his chair, shook his finger in my direction and yelled, "Well let me tell you something, *I pay you to listen! I'm not supposed to listen! I'm supposed to talk and you're supposed to listen!*" Startled, we looked at each other in disbelief, and began laughing spontaneously. I ran into Stanley two years or so after we had terminated therapy. Jokingly, he said to me, "The only thing I remember about therapy was *that* funny incident." Good teacher, that Stanley.

Having been thoroughly admonished by Stanley, why am I now "talking" instead of listening? Indulge me. It is true that we, as individuals, are different. But it is also true that we are, for the most part, similar even in our very differences. So much so that we, as individuals, are able to identify with the ups and downs, the shocks and relief of others. Witness hearing about or viewing on television, earthquakes, airplane crashes, missing children—it's as if it is emotionally happening to us. And then, the sigh of relief, "There but for the grace of God go I." Sometimes humor enters the equation, typified by the familiar "slipping on a banana peel" joke. The clown slips on the banana peel, we hold our breath (we identify with him), he falls; it's not us, we laugh.

The above is an attempt to explain why I decided to "talk," to record these stories. The vignettes are about us, as in every life there is a story waiting to be told. The reader and the patient become *us* through the privilege of shared conversation. The patients tell their own stories in their own voices, the reader interacts mentally and emotionally with them, "been there, done that." Although some stories are, of necessity, brief in their telling, they nonetheless offer recognizable direction and the reader can flesh out the account from his or her own life experiences.

This is not quite an autobiography, and not necessarily a memoir, but rather a sharing of some of the reminiscences these patients and others have so generously provided for me. This journey has not been without personal experiences, however; some separate from those of the patients and others intertwined. My journey, that is, my career, begins with my time in World War II, then immediately into medical school, internship, then psychiatric residency leading to nearly fifty years as a psychiatrist. The last forty years have been weighted time-wise in the care of the critically ill, for the most part in the discipline of oncology. I relate only those experiences I feel are relevant to the telling of the patients' stories. Except for a brief personal history, the words herein are not about me, but told through me. They are about special people who, despite carrying heavy emotional burdens, were remarkable in their giving.

So, what follows are those stories harvested along the way. All are essentially true, but with identities, reconstructions and details carefully disguised. At times, for the purpose of clarity, an example is represented by a composite of stories. Some are funny, some tragic, some comi-tragic, some poignant—all warm and utterly human. In addition to the vignettes, there are essays. Some short, some long. Some philosophical, some tutorial. Regardless, each reflects the kindness of patients though those years. They have offered me insights upon which I have built the essays. If they are not convincing to the reader, then I should have been more attentive to what they were trying to tell me.

For their gifts of kindness, generosity, and above all, for their patience toward me, I am in their debt.

Nathan Schnaper

CONTENTS

INTRODUCTION

There are eight chapters in this book. So, how come the first and last are about me? Succinctly put, the stories told by patients and others did not evolve out of some black hole or void; or like living in some relationship-free bubble. They are defined by their physical and emotional interactions with another being. Fortunate for me, I was the one they were using as a sounding board and voice for their thoughts, ideas, and most significantly, their feelings.

Neither the storyteller nor I are two-dimensional. All of us, during any interaction, any event, social or otherwise, bring our prior experiences, our personalities with us. Even if we try to hide our personalities, it does not happen. We relate behaviorally and emotionally with and to others *with and without* awareness.

So what am I saying? That I presented myself to them as I am, without effort or intent to influence or mold their stories. All of our meetings provided each of us with a mutual as well as an individual experience. My hope is that the reader, by learning something of my personal life, will understand where I come from, and what has motivated me to do the work that has kindled my interest in sharing the experiences of others. It is my further hope, that by sharing the words that follow, the reader might find them educational, yet entertaining.

As you will come to see, not only patients, but also many others whose paths I have crossed, have been generous with their time, their patience, and their kindness. I am humbled. And yes, I am very fortunate as well as grateful.

I.

BEGINNINGS

Introduction

I have to begin somewhere, so here it goes: a chronology.

Not a minute-to-minute biographical counting off, but rather an overview—a background—of events in my early life. Those events that, through my family, my teachers (some educators, some not), and others have inexorably taken me into the business I am in. Events, in their own special voices, speaking to my future, but not as yet sharing their secrets with me.

My early exposure to those subtle influences may have determined my career: How I came to the World of Psychiatry, and then, to the World of Cancer.

Nature or nurture? We'll see. Your guess is as good as mine.

A Chronology: I Was Born...

Independence Day was past, and the next day was over. Then it was July 6, 1918, and I was born. This blessed event took place on the second floor above my father's East Baltimore shoe store at the hands of the local midwife. The poor thing, having done battle with me, then struggled to make out the birth certificate. Not knowing how to spell in English, she did the job phonetically: NTEN SHAPPER. She did get my parents almost right.

My parents were Jewish immigrants from Russia, like so many others. Pop came first, in 1902, from Hamburg, Germany, directly to Baltimore and never left until his death in 1941. Mom and my oldest brother, Bernie, emigrated later, but first his story. Pop was a soldier in the Russian Army. The Sino-Japanese war was approaching the horizon, so he "went over the hill," he deserted. Eventually, and somehow, he arrived in Germany then on to Baltimore.

Mom was not his first wife. He first had married Mom's older sister, arranged by a *shadgan*, a matchmaker, as per Jewish custom. She and their child died in childbirth, so he married her sister—also per Jewish custom. Mom, then just fifteen years old, had been living a lifestyle that was relatively soft, catered to by the hired help. (In my memory lingers a fragment of a story told to me by Mom or Bernie of Mom and little Bernie having fun being pushed in chair sleds by the servants.) Her life in Baltimore was to be the opposite, hard, poor, and suffering. Her father was a financially comfortable dairy farmer, the family an educated one. Early on, one sister, an engineer, came to the United Sates, took in the American ambience and returned to Russia. Another sister, a doctor, perhaps influenced by the engineer's experience, refused to emigrate.

At age sixteen, Mom gave birth to Bernie and four years later, she and Bernie, accompanied by one of Pop's younger brothers, joined Pop in Baltimore. I did not know Mom's parents or any of her relatives. Not so with Pop's. I knew his parents and Pop's three younger brothers and a sister, Pop being the oldest. The males in my father's family, including his father, were tailors. (Pop's first job in Baltimore was in a clothing factory.) Jewish holidays brought the family together, usually at our house, with food and joy—how was I to know we were poor? (I thought everybody had their mothers put cardboard in their shoes when the soles got holes.) Although my grandparents did not live with us, they lived with their daughter, my aunt, they would stay with us during the holidays. I recall my grandfather with his long white beard and soft manner. Grandmother was typically grandmotherly, and what little Yiddish I know came from trying to communicate with her. Everyone treated them deferentially; me, I regarded them with awe. Their quiet dignity permeated every gathering.

Nostalgia grips me as I recall two of the many Passover Seders. (I never finished a Seder in those days, I would fall asleep after two glasses of wine and dinner.) I was probably five or six. It was customary to bring friends, non-Jewish or Jewish to the Seder—as the Passover story reminds us, "We were strangers in the land of Egypt." Bernie brought a friend and his wife, owner of a jewelry chain. Grandfather (*"Zaidy"*) and Grandmother (*"Bubby"*) usually sat together at the head of the table, eating from the same plate, the same bowl. The jeweler was so impressed with the regal couple dressed in white, that he sent them rings in gratitude for having met them.

At another Seder, the meal was finished as was the short prayer of thanks, and we were ready for the usual two hours of song. My brother Moe, age 19, quietly asked to be excused, as he had a date. Mom frowned, Pop shook his head. But Zaidy said softly, "Let him go. Tonight we celebrate freedom, not only as slaves, but also as children of slaves. Tonight he is free to go."

Pop was heavy-set, spectacled, with the yellow-stained fingers of a heavy smoker, an easy-going guy. He was a registered Republican and friends with many local politicians. Mom, who always smelled soapy clean, was short and plump. The round steel-rimmed glasses accented her role as the disciplinarian—although usually it took only that tight-lipped "look." Here's an example of the "look" in action. In synagogue I would soon get bored and ask my father if I could go out and play with the other children. He would say okay. The women sat upstairs, and as I walked up the aisle, I fought the need to look up to the balcony. Of course, I looked and there was Mom's frown, the "look." Somehow, despite the tremendous guilt, I was able to leave and have fun.

Here's another example of their interactive approach to parental discipline. Mom had many teacher-parent meetings, anywhere from one to sometimes three a week. She usually was summoned by a note from the teacher carried home by me. I did not threaten teachers, nor did I ever shoot up the class, rather I would talk, move around, and generally be disruptive (attention deficit disorder? Possibly). So, my father would come home, and Mom would say I had been bad and needed to be punished. She never took my side, intuitively she knew the teachers were always right. Acting according to the script, he would remove his belt, I would bend over, he would hit me on the buttocks, I would cry loudly, and Mom would yell, "What are you trying to do—kill him?" That was it, over until the next time.

The Brothers

My three brothers had preceded me. Benjamin ("Bernie") was eighteen years older and I really did not become aware of him until my adolescence. I remember he was a large man, an impeccable dresser, and he always wore a vest regardless of the weather. He had worked in circulation at the *Baltimore Post*, a tabloid-size newspaper, but just prior to his death, he was administering a clothing manufacturing plant that was a gift from a notorious criminal to his mother as he departed for jail. At age 49, he was lunching at Globus, a popular downtown delicatessen. He fell off his chair, having suffered a massive heart attack. He was rushed the three blocks to University Hospital's emergency room, only to be pronounced dead on arrival. At that time I was a psychiatric resident at Sheppard Pratt Hospital. A medical school classmate was working in the emergency room and called me. I rushed to the hospital, even though it must have been two or more weeks before I fully comprehended his message.

Two memories come to mind, each competing to be first. One day I entered the house, returning from my day at high school to hear Bernie shouting. My fears were compounded by the fact that he was yelling at my mother in Yiddish. What was he saying? His face was red as he pointed to the hall cabinet. My tiny mother stood there looking perplexed at this huge man, but she was surprisingly calm. Suddenly, the light went on for me. Bernie had his own private collection of whiskeys in the cabinet: scotch, vodka, blends, liquors, etc. (My father, in contrast, kept only one bottle, a blend, an ounce of which he gulped as he sat for dinner.) Apparently my mother had been cleaning, and seeing the partially filled bottles, consolidated them into two bottles, which provoked the explosion. Mom? She just heard him out and that was that.

The other recollection of Bernie is that of my first encounter with roast turkey, or any turkey for that matter. Oh, we had chicken occasionally for Friday nights, less occasionally a capon for the special Sabbath dinner. I was about seventeen when Bernie became engaged to Hilda, who would eventually become his wife. He was joining Hilda's family for Thanksgiving dinner and took me along. There it was! Turkey with all the trimmings, fancy as anything. It was good. I cannot recall the next time I ate turkey, perhaps years. I eat it all the time now, usually in sandwiches.

The next brother, Martin ("Moe"), was twelve years my senior and everyone's favorite until he died at the age of seventy-two. Unlike my other brothers, Moe was a sloppy dresser, not unclean, just nothing hung right. He was a wine and whiskey salesman at the end of his life, and his customers, friends, and I mourn him to this day. His customers in Baltimore's Little Italy regarded him as their "mayor." When Moe was three, polio struck. Mom nursed him, carrying him daily to the doctors and hospital. After years, the disease quieted, leaving him with a weak left arm, a slight limp, and Mom forever feeling guilty.

How do I know this? Her three other sons had to go further in education, or else. Bernie achieved a bachelor's degree in science by going to Johns Hopkins at night. He never used his degree. Brother Isidore attended law school at night. But Moe, she allowed him to quit school after the eighth grade. And also, through the years when he was a traveling salesman, she would never say "no" to his pleas for money, despite her own financial constraints.

As it was with Bernie, I did not know Moe until my adolescence, when I was fourteen. During those years he would occasionally take me on overnight business trips. They were fun; it seemed as if I was a "world traveler," despite never being more than seventy-five miles from home. (It was not until I was nineteen that I traveled more than one hundred miles from home. A summer job between college years as a boy's camp counselor took me to Binghamton, New York.)

A teenage recollection: Moe had been married to Rose for about six months. (What a great person she was, independent, warm, told off-color jokes. After Moe died, she kept a large picture of him in the bedroom. She would recount the day's events to it at bedtime.) It was a Sunday morning, the usual Sunday Jewish family breakfast, lox, bagels, onions, and cream cheese. He showed up and Mom asked where was Rose. He mumbled that they had argued. Mom told Moe, "Go bring her, or go home. You belong with her, not here." He left; I do not recall whether he brought her. I think it was the first time Mom said "no" to him. More importantly, their marriage was a long and successful one.

Moe, an inveterate hypochondriac, was dedicated to his heart symptoms.

Oh, true, he did have two heart attacks, but he would not make even minor decisions unless his doctor was consulted and had given approval. For the last fifteen years of his life, he would telephone his brothers and his children every evening at dinnertime. (He was ahead of his time; today we have telemarketers for that.) I once asked him if he was checking on our health or letting us know he was alive—this was met with frowning displeasure. All of us knew when the telephone rang at dinner it was Moe—and we would groan, "Damn, it's Moe." Now, a telemarketer at dinnertime calls and we wish it was Moe.

There are times now, even after all these years, that I encounter someone, and they will ask if I am "Moe Schnaper's brother, the doctor he talked about all the time." And they add, "What a helluva nice guy." I agree.

Then there was Isidore ("Izzy"), who is twenty-three months older than I. There was much sibling rivalry between us, although we went to different junior and senior high schools. But we were together enough to fist fight and thus provoke Mom to scream that she would pull her hair out if we did not stop. His friends were older than mine and so essentially we went in different directions. He was neat and I was not. He was a club person, while I played sports (although not any more). During college and subsequently over the war years, we saw little of each other. He handled the correspondence and problems at home and inevitably became the one our parents depended upon. A hardship deferment during World War II was justifiably his lot.

My father, after his shoe store was lost to fire, became an insurance salesman. Perhaps he was taught a lesson because he had no insurance to cover the fire. Along with law school at night, Izzy worked part time selling insurance with Pop. After Izzy completed law school he decided to actively work full time in our father's business rather than practice law. Izzy hustled, he made himself available at all times, selling not only insurance, but more importantly, selling service. He was very much into it when Pop died. Izzy unfortunately soon found out that a lot of Pop's business was in the form of insurance policies for his friends. Pop had paid the premiums, and they ended up as unpaid loans. Within a few years after Pop died, the "dead wood" was cleaned out. Izzy has been a highly successful independent insurance agent, selling casual, life, and all types of insurance.

He continued to work for some sixty years. This despite relentless bouts of cardiac failure—in and out of the hospital. On New Year's eve, 2002, a month after his last visit to his office, at age 86, he quietly slipped off to a better place.

We will no longer be able to try and meet weekly for lunch or "phone visit"—our routine.

And so, another brother moves on, leaving me, the "baby" of the four sons, not only the legacy of their lives, but also the task of trying to fill their "hand-me-down" shoes, much like the hand-me-downs that were passed from one brother to another when we were kids. What goes around comes around.

My Childhood

I was a blond-haired child in a dark-haired family. I would hear people, friends of my parents, comment about the "tow-head," saying, "Where did the *'shagetz'* (gentile boy) come from?" Later, via therapy, I realized why it was so necessary for me to cling to my Jewishness, and to continue Hebrew studies beyond Bar Mitzvah, which my brothers chose not to do—perhaps it was an unconscious effort on my part to achieve a sense of belonging. A significant and possible contribution to my insecurity was a separation from my mother in infancy. When I was an adolescent, I was told my mother became ill soon after my birth and she was hospitalized for six months to a year. (Her diagnosis? TB? Post-partum depression?) During that time, a family friend who had just given birth to a daughter was my wet nurse. Our two families remained friends for years, then I drifted apart sometime after my college days and following the death of my parents. When we do cross paths, the greetings are always most cordial.

Here are some more childhood recollections, albeit brief. I was born and lived in East Baltimore for seven years. My father's shoe store was on the first floor and we lived on the second. Then came the fire and we moved "uptown" to a predominantly blue-collar neighborhood. Only one memory fills the time before we moved. I was about four, and the tin ceiling of the store was being replaced. Sheets of tin were stacked edge-wise next to a scaffold. Naturally, I climbed the platform, fell off, and a tin sheet sliced the edge of my chin, missing my neck by only an inch or so. The blood, the emergency room; what a fright for everyone but me. I was too dumb, but the scar remains to this day. Another time, somewhat later, I visited another emergency room. This time I was at an aunt's house and we children were running up and down the stairs. I chose to slide down the banister, my tongue hanging out—you can finish this story.

When I was seven, we moved uptown. My friends were of various religions, Jewish, Catholic and Protestant. Mr. Tony and Miss Jenny and their children were our next-door Italian neighbors. Mr. Tony gave me my first and subsequent haircuts. His son, Giuseppe ("Joe"), was my age and taught me the necessary Italian, "Come here," "What do you want," and a number of dirty words and songs. And Joe wasn't the only person I learned from—I think one of his sisters and I took turns at "I'll show you mine if you'll show me yours." Having grown up around four other males, I probably thought she was hiding hers.

We played "ball," usually hitting a small stick called a "caddy," with a long one, made from a broom handle and running bases. Occasionally we would steal into the Avalon movie house. We also hung out at a large field beyond our row houses. Mom would call us to come in at dusk. She would call, "Bernie, Moe, Izzy," and then me. I always waited for my name just to prolong the inevitable going inside.

But it was not all play. There was school, and for a while I had a part-time job selling newspapers. I would hop on a stopped streetcar with several copies of the *Post* (or *News American*) and hawk them for two cents, jumping off at the next stop. Then this routine was followed in reverse. Mom, who was not enthusiastic about my jumping off streetcars, stopped this after about six months.

At school, Miss Yost was a tall, wiry, chisel-faced teacher who collected stray dogs. This *was* the fourth grade and she was tough, no nonsense. I did not give her any problems. No sir. When she spotted a stray roaming about the schoolyard, she would gesture to me and I would bring it in to the classroom and hold it for her. This was my assigned task, and it paid off. Later, when my name came up as a candidate for an accelerated junior high school, she shot down the opposition. They felt my deportment, as well as my spelling, "were bad." Both are still true.

Horror! Even now this next memory chokes my breath and jerks my eyes into a wide-open stare. Fortunately, my mind dictates that its visits be infrequent. It was a hot summer night. In those days doors were not locked, and we could, and did, sleep in the park. This night was shatteringly different. I awakened to hear the murmuring bustle of people disturbing the silence of the night air. Quickly, I realized the house was empty, that my family had joined the neighbors huddled nervously together in the street. The sky was lit up as if day had burst forth prematurely. All faces and eyes were pointed beyond the end of the street toward the field bordering the railroad tracks. They were focused on a huge wooden cross ablaze in shameful bitterness. I, terrified like the rest, stood there frozen with my mouth open, taking in the tableau never to be forgotten. Later, I found out that it was the work—no, not work, a desecration by the Ku Klux Klan. This was its response to the Catholic community building its first neighborhood church, St. Ambrose, a wooden structure. After a fire in the 1940s it was replaced by a lovely stone edifice.

Now, quickly to a pleasant, salivating recollection: the smell of *gefulte* fish cooking, the perfume of the gods. Mom would mix all the ingredients, raw fish, onions, seasonings, and more. I would stick my finger in the bowl, scoop up some and eat it. Delicious. Did I know I was eating sushi? Mom was a good cook for all the traditional Jewish foods—and she had never cooked until she came to America. I don't know how she learned, but what a baker! Every Friday, Mom would bake two three-layer yellow cakes with chocolate icing. Then before going to bed as a teen, I would eat a quarter of one with half a quart of milk. Wonderful! The next morning, the cakes would be as flat as pancakes and hard as rocks. But on Saturday mornings I would enjoy dunking chunks in milk. My father used to brag about how wonderfully efficient my mother was as a cook: "She makes two three-layer cakes every week, with no butter and one egg!"

Family life was the traditional orthodox Jewish way. Father was the seeming head of the house, but Mother was the real boss. He sat down at dinner and was served first, Mother standing and serving. Except on Friday nights, she would eat after we had finished. This play of "Who's in charge?" was very real to me. When it was time to get my Bar Mitzvah suit (my first), Uncle Dave, the tailor, took me to a closeout store. He then modified the suit to fit. One evening as dinner was about to begin, Mom said, "Go put on the new suit Poppa bought you." (Huh?) I did, and I was told to thank him. I did. Smart, it was Mom's way of letting Pop think he was head of the household.

Yes, they argued, sometimes heatedly, but in Russian or Yiddish. Early on, Bernie and Moe were exposed to a bilingual household. Izzy and I were not. We were to be "Americans," and so our parents spoke English, reserving their native tongues for their arguments. Pop, with his early start in America, did pretty well with English. Mom took classes at night at the local school, always carrying her hardback, marble-colored notebook.

My Bar Mitzvah. *Mazel Tov.* When we moved uptown, there was no synagogue, so Pop and Uncle Dave founded one on Park Heights Avenue, across from the Avalon Theater. It was a wooden building and Izzy and I were Bar Mitzvahed there. In time, it was replaced by a brick and stone structure. Today, it houses an African-American church.

My party was in the synagogue after the service. Two bottles of whiskey, pickled herring and flat bread, then a festive dinner at home. Sure, I got presents, the usual Bar Mitzvah gifts of the time, several fountain pens ("Today you are a man"), some belts, and of course, the new suit.

While the Bar Mitzvah is a rite of passage to manhood, some say a person is never truly grown until his parents are gone. Why was there no premonition with Pop? It was a brisk Sunday in November 1941, prior to the Pearl Harbor attack. I was already in the Army and buoyed by a day off, had hitched a ride into Baltimore from nearby Fort Meade. The family had moved to a second-floor apartment in the Liberty Heights, Reisterstown Road area. Up the stairs I went, through the doorway and into the living room. The telephone was ringing and so I picked it up. The male voice asked, "Is this the home of Harry Schnaper?" "It is." "This is the city morgue, will someone come and identify him?" I was too shocked to ask for details. I kissed Mom, took Izzy aside, and whispered the news to him. We left, not telling Mom why.

Pop had taken a streetcar to visit a friend that Sunday morning. After leaving his friend, he went to a bus stop; there he collapsed, dying immediately. The funeral was impressive, the hearse stopping at Pop's synagogue while they opened the doors in honor and respect for him. Me? I drank whiskey in isolation for most of the *shiva* (mourning) period, even though compulsive drinking was not, and is not, my thing. Finally, Bernie, in a business-like voice, said, "I'll buy you all the booze you want. If this is what you're going to do with the rest of your life, so be it." And he left the room. That was the end of my binge. "Good-bye, Poppa."

Sadly, there was a premonition with Mom. From time to time she would complain of severe chest pain. Her physician gave her pills. Little did we know, she was having severe cardiac angina. Despite the angina, she lived alone and independently for seven years after Pop died. And there was a quaint courtship. A widower, a neighbor, would join her every afternoon for cards—canasta. His children and my brothers and I encouraged Mom to accept his proposal, but she relished her independence.

It was during my senior year in medical school. Could Mom have been any prouder that her baby son was on the verge of becoming a doctor? In retrospect, I conjecture that my becoming a doctor was a long-cherished dream of hers—cruelly she didn't live to see that dream become a reality. So close. She called me on Christmas Eve, complaining of abdominal pain. Sensing trouble, I went to her apartment. Scared, I called a surgeon, who in those days made house calls, to come and examine her. He diagnosed an acute gall bladder and called for an ambulance to take her to the hospital. Early the next morning I was on a streetcar going to the hospital when the tears began. It was not a premonition; I *knew* she was dead. But she wasn't, quite. Lying there, oxygen mask notwithstanding, she seemed so calm, so beautiful, even young. Soon it was over. No more hard life for Mom. In some peculiar way, I felt that although she was missing the pride and joy of my medical school graduation, God had given her an even greater gift—peace.

Perhaps, unconsciously, learning about the illness Mom suffered when I was an infant had something to do with my career choice. Maybe it was an unconscious wish to "heal" her and help her through the later years of illness and pain. The autopsy did reveal that she had had at least two previous coronaries. So it was that Pop died at sixty-one and Mom died at sixty-one, but not at the same time, nor together.

I married in 1944. How that happened requires some background. Upon entering the Army in 1941 I was sent to Fort Meade, just outside Baltimore. There, I reported to the Fort Meade Hospital to work as a laboratory technician: My responsibility was to perform clinical pathology tests on patients' blood, as well as on other body fluids.

Immediately after Pearl Harbor, the laboratory was visited by a group of doctors from the Johns Hopkins Unit. They were mobilizing to go overseas and there, in some country as yet unknown, to establish a hospital. They offered me the job of non-commissioned officer in charge of the lab and the task of organizing it—planning and ordering supplies, etc. I accepted; the lure of uncertainty, of exploring the unknown, was irresistible.

Shortly thereafter, the unit came together at a camp in Cape Cod, Massachusetts. Several days later, I was given a letter of credit, and was dispatched to Baltimore to purchase anything that I felt necessary to outfit a hospital lab. For four days I shopped; instruments, glassware, chemicals, etc. No limits, the price was no object. That was a sense of power. Evenings were spent at my home.

Late one afternoon, having spent lots of free money, I stopped at a deli near my home. I recognized the attractive young woman standing near the counter as a neighbor, and we chatted. That led to a movie and to a walk in the local park the next night. That was it, no kissing, no hanky-panky, just two pleasant "dates." The next day I went back to Cape Cod, and soon was off to San Francisco, then, with destination unknown, an eleven-day boat ride with 5,000 military companions ended—surprise!—Australia.

Some months after landing, I received a chiding letter from my brother

Isidore. "Mom wants to know what you did to this girl. She comes over to the house every day in tears." I responded that I did nothing beyond conversation and had felt no need to correspond with her.

Jumping ahead some two years plus; I'm still in Australia. My commanding officer, knowing of my interest in medical school, saw an opportunity to send me on thirty-day leave to the United States. There, I was to seek entrance into one of the government-paid medical education programs. Repeated visits to the Washington bureaucracy were unsuccessful.

One afternoon, returning from Washington and entering my house, I saw, to my surprise, sitting in the sun porch, the same young lady. We exchanged cordial greetings and she informed me that Mom had invited her to dinner. No big deal. So, we spent some evening time together, pleasant, not particularly romantic. I had yet to hear from the Army about their plans for me.

It was summer and we took walks in the park. Then, one evening, *it* happened. We approached my house and there was Mom and my lady friend's mother sitting out front, waiting to greet us. The two mothers thought we should get married. We did: Hell, why not, there was a war on.

There are two children, the fruit of this union. A daughter, now a prominent breast cancer surgeon, and a son, an academic in medicine with recognized research and administrative skills. Happily, they have had children of their own.

The midwife who delivered me came back to haunt me years later. It was 1960 and Bermuda beckoned. But wait, to leave the country I had to have a birth certificate or a passport. The best the Maryland Bureau of Vital Statistics could come up with was a birth certificate that read: NTEN SHAPPER. I was not about to use this to get me back into the United States, so I applied for a passport. Denied. Why? Maybe the birth certificate was mine; it had the same birth date and parents, but who is NTEN SHAPPER? Finally, the immigration officials suggested I write an affidavit about the family and bring my oldest living relative with me to the post office for a scheduled visit. Uncle Dave, alert in his late eighties, vouched for me. Nonetheless, I was queried as to names of siblings, dates of parental citizenship. The examiner stood behind the counter holding some papers. During the questioning he would glance down at them, perhaps to verify Uncle Dave's and my answers. He did provide an interesting and somewhat curious bit of information. Did we know that Pop, Mr. Harry Schnaper, had stood for and twice passed for U.S. citizenship? The second time in 1913?

Finally, the passport was granted in the name of Nathan Schnaper. And I did enjoy Bermuda.

How I Came to the World of Psychiatry

Everything I know about psychiatry I learned from my mother: "You never throw away your dirty water until you get clean water," and its natural partner, "You never go *from* something, you go *to* something."

Not only Mom's counsel, but also her demeanor inspired. I am sure she unwittingly set the stage for my career as a psychiatrist. There she sat in the kitchen, kind of Buddha-like, this little roly-poly figure, her round, wire-rimmed glasses shooting rays, intently listening to the *angst* of the neighbor ladies. It was as if I was watching a parade of pilgrims to the oracle. I do not recall her giving advice, just offering a sympathetic ear. (See—she didn't talk. Mom just listened. And, *she* didn't get paid!)

There were times, however, when she physically intervened. Manny, an Al Capone-like bootlegger, and his wife, Maude, lived next door. He was Jewish, she was a fiery tempered, red-haired Irish colleen who towered over him by some eighteen inches. They were kind to my brother, Izzy, and me, giving us small gifts and rides in their Austin convertible. They were not kind to each other when they drank. Their violent, china-throwing, physical battles and loud, profane screams pierced our rowhouse walls as if they were paper, which they might as well have been. There went my little mom, in the middle of the night, clad only in her nightgown. A Jewish Joan of Arc, she charged into the midst of their war, placing herself between them. They would never dare to touch her. Somehow her chastising penetrated their drunkenness and quiet returned, until the next time.

Through the years, many of my patients had the good fortune to benefit from Mom's insights. (Occasionally, I generously would give Mom due credit).

I had a most unhappy high school experience. My school, Baltimore Polytechnic Institute, was a technical one, it gave advanced training so that upon graduating from the "A" course, the student could enter an engineering college as a sophomore. I did not choose this school, the Department of Education chose for me. Mathematics was the backbone of the curriculum. If a student failed any three topics in any three semesters and failed to pass makeup exams, the student was mandated to repeat the year in which the third failure occurred. This I accomplished in my second year, failing two

29

freshman algebra and one sophomore geometry semester. (Later through my psychotherapy sessions, I discovered that it did not require any effort on my part, as I had no awareness that I was unconsciously dictating the failure.) My father came to talk with the principal, who suggested I transfer to the "B" course or to another school. Tearfully, I pleaded with my father to let me go to my brother's school. (His school had mostly Jewish students, mine had few.) Pop ignored me and was firm, which surprised me as I was convinced my mother was the boss. He asked the principal if I was capable of doing the "A" work. He replied that I was. My father announced that I was to repeat the year. I did, completing all the makeup work and eventually graduating with not great, but adequate grades, and the sense that I was awakening from a bad dream.

What I did not tell my parents—or anyone else—was why I was so miserable there and why I feel I was unconsciously dictating my own failure. Simply put, I was a Jew. There were frequent epithets, "goddamn Jew" and weak attempts at slurs referring to my antecedents. My tormentors would walk behind me and throw erasers, chalk, and other things at me as we left class. Many times, I would challenge one or another of this particular group, or they would challenge me, to a fight in back of the school. Routinely, I would be beaten, by the whole group if I was foolish enough to be winning a one-on-one battle. Of course, I would go home bloody, shirt torn, and my mother would cry, "What am I raising, a gangster, what!?" I could never tell her why I was in the fights. I think I was too embarrassed, too ashamed; somehow I was disappointing her.

Thus ended two years of unhappy adolescent struggling, thanks to failing, my unknowing achievement. Not that the next three years—my repeated sophomore year, junior and senior years—were happy; they were not. But now, at least, since I was among a different group of kids, I could pay some attention to my studies, which were punctuated by only an occasional epithet flung in my direction. Grudgingly, I must admit, the schooling at Poly was first class. The study habits and discipline taught there served me well in college and medical school. And, I have two good thoughts to soften this experience. One boy, of the same elevated socioeconomic background of the crowd, did what he could to defend me. Unfortunately, he was successful only when I was lucky enough to have him around. The second thought is, not once since then have I been the object of anti-Semitic words or actions. Thankfully, my experience has been just the opposite.

A segue. I attended Washington College, and although at the time most of the students were not Jewish, acceptance of Jews was, and is, to this day, complete. How did I get there, you ask? I took an exam. Back up. After high school, with no money for college, I got a job clerking in a drugstore, sixty hours a week for eleven dollars. A year later, Bernie told me a state senatorial scholarship would be awarded to the winner of a competitive exam to be given at the main post office. It was a four-year, tuition, room, and board scholarship at Washington College on Maryland's Eastern Shore. I had never heard of the college nor had anyone else. But I took the exam and won the scholarship, and spent four wonderful, carefree years there. (When I informed the owner of the drugstore, he suggested I turn the scholarship down, offering me the incentive of a raise to thirteen dollars a week.)

The idea of being a doctor had always been in my head. Why? Perhaps, it was my unconscious response to Mom's illness during my early years. Certainly it was not to cure people or to be all-powerful. Rather, I think, it was curiosity. I was always curious about everything, but perhaps I thought that somehow being a curious doctor would solve the mystery of how babies were made.

So, in 1939, my junior year at Washington College, I applied to the University of Maryland School of Medicine and was accepted. My interview by the medical school Dean consisted of one question, "Do you see your way clear financially for four years?" "I do," I lied. Frantic efforts by Bernie and my father for loans were to no avail. I requested a deferment of admission for "personal family reasons." The Dean, fortunately, granted me an indefinite entrance postponement. Back I went for the senior year of college, took education courses and after graduation, I got a job as a high school science teacher—a baby sitter for the most part. The Selective Service for World War II selected me early. Teachers, however, were deferred. But then came the promise from the government, enlist for one year and be free of an indefinite military commitment. I did. Ten months later, Pearl Harbor and the Army convinced me I should stay another four and a half years. Then, at last—medical school. And from there, to training in psychiatry and for the many opportunities to deliver Mom's counsel.

I would be remiss to not pay due homage to two relevant others, who, albeit unknowingly, colluded in mapping my future in psychiatry: Dr. Frederick G. Livingood and Dr. Henry M. Fox.

It was while at Washington College that I put my toe in the ocean of psychology, metaphorically speaking. The Chairman of the Psychology Department was a short, gnome-like, bespectacled man, Dr. Livingood. His gentleness, his kindness, and his wisdom soon blotted out all perception of his disfigurement not only for me, but for all the students and faculty. He was kind to me and nourished my interest in psychology by suggesting I take over his class in abnormal psychology from time to time. Of course this mandated that I do considerable preparation—Dr. Livingood's way of ensuring I learn more than just what he was teaching. He also encouraged my interest in hypnosis by asking me to lecture and demonstrate the procedure for the class. Indeed, Dr. Livingood was a most generous and positive influence for me.

Another powerful, guiding influence was Dr. Fox, who was my mentor during World War II while I served in the Army in Australia. He taught by hands-on observation; no reading. Although he was a captain and I was an enlisted man, he treated me as a colleague, even including me as a co-author on an article for a prestigious psychiatric journal, published during the war.

How fortunate and blessed for me! Mom, Dr. Livingood and Dr. Fox, all great teachers and *patrones*.

I would respectfully add that there is another factor that nudges many of us into the psychological or psychiatric field. We unconsciously choose this area of work to get psychotherapy for our emotional problems or to avoid it. Those who avoid personal therapy use their patients to act out their neuroses. For example, a therapist having marital problems may subtly encourage patients to divorce without being aware they are doing this. (A therapist with a high divorce rate in his or her practice bears testimony to this.)

Those who seek therapy for themselves increase their self-awareness, and it allows them to delve into their emotional "blind spots." The result benefits not only the therapist but his or her patients as well. Through the years of supervising psychiatric residents, I have always strongly urged them to seek personal therapy—any school of psychiatry or psychology—just do it.

Most important is the work itself. Voyeuristic it certainly is. *But*, patients generously and with great trust lift up the window shade, part the curtains, and permit us the sacred privilege of looking into their lives. And, we cannot, dare not, violate this trust. There is obvious fascination. No matter how ordinary or how prominent the person, there is always a story waiting to be told. Sometimes dramatic or pathetic, sometimes happy or sad, and sometimes even epiphanies for both the patient and the therapist. And, always, there is gratitude to the patient for the gift of sharing.

And to the World of Cancer

Do you know how it feels when you call a patient's home to ask about his health, only to have the wife tell you she has just returned from the funeral mass? Terrible. But that's the price of working with patients who bear a painfully finite prognosis. That's the trade-off for the pleasure of meeting and remembering the intimate experiences shared with another vibrant person.

Have I ever done combat with cancer? No. Anyone in my family have cancer? No. My family tree bends reluctantly to the harsh winds of heart disease. So, how did I come to labor in the vineyards of something as heavy as cancer—with its emotional pull upon the patient, the family, and their caregivers and caretakers?

Coming events cast their shadows before them. How could I know? It was 1949; graduation from the University of Maryland School of Medicine sent me on to the required internship. During my rotating internship in the Public Health Service, it was my turn to immerse myself into six weeks of exposure to cancer patients. The U.S. Public Health Service Hospital (USPHSH) in Baltimore had been taken over by the newly created National Institutes of Health (NIH). The sojourn of the NIH at the USPHSH would last until the concrete NIH edifices in Bethesda were completed. This internship included all the "Institutes": heart, neurology, cancer, etc. Each intern rotated through all services.

The establishment of the National Cancer Institute and other institutes as branches of the NIH was visionary. It was designed to be the cutting edge of research into citizens' health. This has paid off; current research within the institutes, and funding for research outside of the NIH has produced medical-scientific understanding and discoveries beyond expectations.

At the USPHSH, the enthusiasm for research permeated all the institutes—from which I profited experientially. The institute's apprenticeship to the creative ideas of the doctors interested in treating cancer patients has been keenly evident to me. Therapy was not today's standard basic approach; treatment was limited to surgery, radiation, or both. Radiation was experimental, utilizing either X-ray or cobalt. Chemotherapy was soon to be experimental.

Dr. Ezra Greenspan headed the medical side of the USPHSH Cancer Unit. (Today, he is considered to be the grandfather of chemotherapy, and has been the long-time president of the National Chemotherapy Foundation.) Hortense, an attractive, stereotypical Latin-type, tanned, black shining eyes, and long hair, had Hodgkin's disease. As an experiment and with her permission, Dr. Greenspan administered ACTH, a crude steroid medication. He granted me the honor of doing the legwork, administering, monitoring, and taking notes. I relished it. After I left the service, I continued to follow her progress until the end of the year. She lived for two years.

Was this powerful experience preparing me for my life's work? Was I committed to the field of cancer even then, but not know it? Thinking back now, I have to believe I had already internally made my decision.

The story resumes again in 1954 after finishing my residency. The University of Maryland Medical School and Hospital had functioned without a Department of Psychiatry prior to 1952. There had been a token glance in the direction of psychiatry; a dry, one-hour Wednesday lecture, poorly attended. But in 1952, Dr. Jacob Finesinger left Harvard and arrived at the University of Maryland. He had received a gift of a new building and was eager to organize a program that would interact with the other medical disciplines. I joined him, as did others in 1953. He was a well-known, highly respected psychiatrist with Groucho Marx eyebrows. His idea of psychotherapy was to be verbally passive, except we noted that he did "communicate" by wiggling his bushy eyebrows. He vigorously denied he deliberately used this "technique" of therapy.

I wasn't aware of it until many years later, but my faculty assignment inexorably molded me into the field of cancer. Serendipity. Dr. Finesinger called three of us to meet with him. To facilitate collaboration with the other school departments, he assigned each of us to a specific area. Dr. Kent Robinson to OB-GYN, Dr. William Magruder to Medicine, and me to Surgery. Surgery!? Yes, Surgery. Each of us had to spend half our time in our designated area, encouraging rapport. The rest of the time we spent in psychiatry.

Jake also put me in charge of setting up a six-week program for the students. During the summer, I told him my ideas every week. Repeatedly, and frustratingly for me, he would smile and liltingly chant, "Good, let it dance around in your head for awhile." Fall came and the students arrived, and I, annoyed by his lack of direction and apprehensive of implementing my ideas, began the program. Jake never did give me the verbal okay, but he was always very supportive.

The other disciplines expressed varying degrees of interest in Jake's experiment. Not so with Surgery. It has only been in recent years that surgeons—and some other medical disciplines—have acknowledged the role of psychiatrists. Every morning, I made seven o'clock rounds with the Chief Resident, then off to the eight o'clock and nine o'clock lectures by the senior surgical faculty. I lived this life for eight years. Friendship with the residents was quick and easy—our ages were not too far apart. It was not so easy with the senior faculty. Oh, yes, they were polite. Somewhere in the third year they acknowledged me as a psychiatrist, even asking for an occasional consult. After the fifth year I was viewed more as a colleague ("one of the guys") rather than as a psychiatrist. The last years I participated in Grand Rounds, hosting a patient management conference.

Now, on to cancer and me. In those days, cancer therapy was surgery. That was it. Chemotherapy was peeping over the horizon. Patients complaining of pains, weight loss or lumps were treated with the scalpel. Women who had the misfortune to grow a breast lump would suffer the massive, radical Halsted mastectomy. Sometimes the other breast was removed as prophylactic protocol. Did the women know they had cancer? They did not say, nor did their surgeons say. But they must have known because they would awaken after the operation with their chests swaddled in wrap-around bandages. Reconstruction? What reconstruction? Padded bras and hard prostheses were available. As a rule, patients were not told the diagnosis. (A rule prevalent even today in many foreign countries.) Today, in the United States, informing the patient is part of the compulsory legal consent form. I sat on early panels debating the pros and cons of "telling." I have always felt that those who were not told knew anyway, if only because of the bandages. Those who had been told inadvertently would experience shock and then enter into a blessed denial, and thereby, retain hope.

Here's a relevant anecdote, not without irony. Jake, during the days of "telling" or "not telling" strongly believed the patient should be told, compassionately, but told nonetheless. The day came when Jake suffered the fate current at that time: exploratory abdominal surgery, colon cancer, close the wound, period. His surgeon, Dr. Robert Buxton, Chief of Surgery, believed that patients need not be told the diagnosis. He consulted with me, as he was aware of Jake's conviction otherwise. I demurred. So he told Jake's

35

wife, Grace.

From that time on, until his death a year later, Jake repeatedly would say, "I know what I have. Grace knows what I have. The children know what I have. And that's good." Jake never used the word "cancer" again, a word that he had used so frequently given the fact that he was an authority on the topic. He had established a reputation at Harvard as an expert in understanding the family dynamics of patients with cancer.

I visited Jake at his home a few weeks prior to his death. During the visit, Grace brought him two white tablets and a glass of water. He smiled to me, "I have a kidney infection," and swallowed the pills. The next morning I commented to Dr. Buxton that it was bad luck that Jake now had a kidney infection. Bob wrinkled his brow, "A kidney infection? He doesn't have a kidney infection. Those were Demerol pills for his pain." Dear Jake, like all of us, was practicing a useful denial, not recognizing "cancer" by word or symptom.

The surgeons functioned in the confines of an "old boy" network. Not only with each other, but with their patients as well. They socialized with them, fished with them, operated on their family members and even their extended families. As the years went by, it gradually, ever so slowly, dawned on me that there was a fixed, consistent pattern of behavior among the surgeons toward their patients. The surgeons would open the patient's abdomen, explore it, find evidence of metastatic cancer, close the abdomen and that was that. This was routine. If the cancer could be cut out, good. If not, stitch up the incision so as to hide the deadly spread inside and await the inevitable outcome.

But, there's more. Noting one surgeon's behavior after a fruitless procedure on and an ominous prognosis for his friend, something perplexing occurred to me. After the surgery, the surgeon would pop his head, not his body, into his friend's room, say, "Hi," and leave. The resident would then assume the responsibility of the patient's care. This pattern was repeated not only by this surgeon, by the others as well.

What was going on? These were dear and close friends. Was there alienation? No. Were the surgeons uncaring and insensitive? Not more so than most, if not all, physicians who must maintain a clinical distance from the patient. My interest was piqued.

Over the years, some thoughts slowly evolved. There are some physicians who are uncomfortable working with cancer patients and so choose to practice in other disciplines. Perhaps there are reminders of ill relatives who died. No value judgment intended, but these surgeons were working daily with patients who had an up-front potential of a severe prognosis.

I would conjecture that first, the surgeons' close relationship with the friend-patient reminded them of their own mortality. This, possibly, was in the doctor's awareness. Secondly, on a deeper level, was the threat to the doctor's own omnipotence. Many patients regard their doctors as gods with the ability to perform magic. (Some doctors believe this as well. In today's managed care environment, however, patients are not so sure their doctors can perform magic.) Nonetheless, patients have expectations of their doctors and doctors have similar expectations of themselves. The crucial conflict is the result of the doctor's omnipotence clashing with the patient's dire prognosis. Doctors, ministers, industry CEOs, and others are motivated by their omnipotence, which demands they manage, if not control, other people's lives. They need to be all-powerful, to "cure" as a mandate of their chosen professions. This need is unconscious, and when it is sublimated, society benefits. When it is not sublimated, the failure of one's power to "cure" can elicit overwhelming anxiety. The doctors' defensive consequence is to avoid the patient, suppress his awareness of the patient and the patient's lack of future, or both.

The threat to omnipotence stems from the physician's unconscious fear that he is accountable for the death. *Subconsciously,* the doctor concludes, "Since I have the power to cure, I must also have the power to kill." The roots for such rationale are laid in childhood when the infant is, indeed, omnipotent. Infants cry or simply grimace, and parents respond immediately. As children develop and pass through the normal state of ambivalence toward people and objects in their environment, feelings of power are easily transformed into feelings of pain. Wishes are equated with deeds, for children believe that merely wishing the parent "away" (dead), such as when the parent is punishing the child, make it happen. Such imagined power frightens children, because they believe they will be held accountable, i.e., an eye for an eye. In time, however, if development proceeds normally, the sense of power and ambivalence is sublimated into healthy outlets. Much later, however, when some physicians are faced with the inevitability of their patient's death, they are overcome by unconscious guilt. Borrowing from the past, they are again, somehow responsible, and must separate emotionally before "the moment of truth."

And me? Was reaching for personal omnipotence the force that decided my career choice? If so, it wasn't in the hands-on sphere of physically attacking the patient's cancer. I would welcome the hope that it was in the service of alleviating the patient's emotional pain and suffering. Of holding the patient's hand during the meandering viscitudes of the course of his or her disease. That I might share the patient's fears and defenses as an emotional exchange, and not as an intellectual exercise. A conviction that the goal of medicine is the promotion of life, not its prolongation.

Another level of understanding of why one works with patients who face an uncertain fate is seeking to dispel the mystery of death. Perhaps to defeat, and if not defeat, at least to master it. To blunt the separation anxiety, death as the ultimate, irreversible separation. I concede all of these to be part of me.

So, here I am, still at it some fifty years later. How come? To the reasons above, I would add the following: It was a confluence of life experiences, some quite conscious, others not so. My identification with my mother, the psychotherapist to the neighbor ladies, pointing me to psychiatry. The clinical work during my internship, which exposed me to cancer patients and doctors, both as role models. The work in surgery as a psychiatrist and as a psychotherapist outside of surgery. All of these came together, ever so subtly, influences determining my career, my field of endeavor. And I was ready and receptive.

We have come a long way in the treatment of patients with cancer. Survival is now measured in years, not months. Hope cannot be denied. We do not know what might be around the corner, a new procedure, a new medication, a new view of cancer. Insulin, polio and the many other vaccines are examples that dictate that we not relinquish hope.

Both worlds—psychiatry and cancer—in my experience, share a similar history. In both disciplines, the therapeutic tools and armamentarium were, by today's perspective, crudely primitive. In the early treatment of cancer, open the body surgically, remove the offending part, close the wound. Period. So it was with my beginning exposure to psychiatric treatment, psychotherapy and psychoanalysis ("talking cures") for those with varying intensities of neuroses. While not barbaric, the treatment for the severely depressed and psychotic was, by today's standards, akin to the tricks of some witch doctor. Patients were put to sleep by barbiturates for twenty hours a day for thirty days; patients deliberately were overdosed with insulin to near death and rescued by intravenous glucose; isolation in seclusion rooms for those dangerous to themselves or others; cold, wet sheet packs, hydrotherapy, and electro-convulsive therapy (ECT, still in use today). Now, psychopharmacology offers hope and promise for the entire spectrum of mental illness.

I was fortunate to have borne witness to the creative and courageous progress so far by both disciplines. Fate has granted me the opportunity to not only be part of the splendor of the past forty-plus years, but also, even more, to share the pain, joy, and yes, the loss of so many courageous friends.

II.

THE ARMY
(WORLD WAR II)
MEDICAL SCHOOL AND
MEDICAL INTERNSHIP

Introduction

Having traveled this far through life's vicissitudes without any awareness that my ultimate career was being molded for me by these very same vicissitudes, it was now time for some disciplined education.

The educators were soldiers, nurses, doctors, patients, and others who taught me what it means to be a *real* doctor. It is here during my internship that the vista of my future labor in the psychiatric vineyards of cancer begins, an opportunity for new feelings, new ideas.

Again, without any planning or conscious direction on my part, my Army experience leading to and combining with that of medical school and internship, gradually solidified my career—and my future.

Kismet? A guardian angel? You read and decide.

Whatever—I'm not complaining.

World War II

Hello Psychiatry. During the Second World War, I was in Australia as a member of the Johns Hopkins Hospital Medical group. I was the noncommissioned officer in charge of the laboratory. When I had free time, I tried to spend it with the psychiatrists as I had an interest in being a psychiatrist even before I had been to medical school. Even though my time in the Army delayed my entrance to medical school by five years, I did profit from my experience.

Shortly after enlisting, I was assigned to the 118th General Hospital, the Johns Hopkins Unit, to serve in the Southwest Pacific. All the officers had been long-time faculty members at the Johns Hopkins Medical School, which contributed to the beneficial aspects of my Army stint. Always on the medical side, I was responsible for the laboratory overseas as well as in the States prior to going overseas. My confirmed acceptance to medical school was so widely known by the officers and staff that they would call me whenever they thought there was something of medical interest. And they relished having the opportunity to teach. I participated in autopsies and worked in pathology. It was much like going to medical school. Indeed, this was a very practical experience, more like an apprenticeship.

My interest in psychiatry led me to spend what time I could spare on the psychiatric wards. There were two psychiatrists, five huge open wards and two closed, or locked, wards. This was outside Sydney, Australia, and the hospital had a thousand beds. We received injured Army patients from Northern Australia and New Guinea. At that time, the Japanese were bombing Northern Australia. One psychiatrist, Dr. Henry Fox, a captain, went on to Harvard after the war. He was responsible for the seven inpatient psychiatric wards, and another, Dr. Richard Lambert, also a captain, did the outpatient consults throughout the hospital. Since there was such a tremendous load, Dr. Fox was pleased to have me. Wanting to learn, I asked, what could I read? He said, "You read nothing, you will just interview patients and observe." To which I gratefully said, "Okay."

He sent me to one of the wards that housed seriously disturbed patients to talk with the charge nurse. This I did, and she gave me a patient to interview, a tense young man with a thin face, fixed gaze, and short, prematurely gray hair. Our conversation took place in a little room that was about ten feet by six feet. I sat with a pad in hand and he sat opposite. Between us was a small folding table. Not looking at him, I was poised, ready to write. I asked him to state his military company, to which he replied, "You look like my Uncle Ed." I then asked him where he was from in the States, and he replied, "You look like my Uncle Ed." At that time, I did not have the knowledge or the good sense to ask about his Uncle Ed. Instead, I kept asking him other questions, thinking my assignment was to take a very careful history. But no matter what I asked, he responded, "You look like my Uncle Ed." Finally, I looked up at him as he insisted I looked like his Uncle Ed, and I must admit, on a visceral level, I became frightened. I went to the charge nurse and told her the patient kept saying that I looked like his Uncle Ed. She smiled and said, "Maybe you do." I said, "What's wrong with him?" She said, "He's a paranoid schizophrenic," and I said, "Thank you."

I went to Dr. Fox and told him about the experience, and whining, asked if I could read about it. He said, "No," that I couldn't read anything about it, and instructed me to get another patient. The next day, the patient I was assigned by the nurse was a sergeant, six feet, six inches tall, shiny black skin, very broad, an African-American man who was perhaps in his twenties. He was wearing a robe and pajamas. We went into another room, which again had this little table and a cot. He sat on the cot. He was very pleasant; I had my pad, and began to write, asking questions about his history. He told me how things were in New Guinea, and about being shot at, and then his voice began to quicken as he said, "Everybody up there was living outside of town, they are doing bad things." While he was repeating this, he had his right hand over his head, his fingers closed into a fist. He was shaking his hand back and forth as if he were shaking dice for a craps game. I kept asking questions, but he ignored me and continued to sermonize about "people living out of town." Then he fell on his knees with his back to me and began praying, all the while banging his fists on the cot without pause.

Again, not knowing why, I became frightened and quietly eased out of the room. I went to find the hospital corpsman, Louis, who was in charge of all the attendants in the disturbed ward. Louis was about five feet, three inches tall. I told him about the sergeant, Solomon, and about what he was doing. Without a word, Louis walked with me into the room. There was Solomon, still banging on the cot and praying to the Lord to save these people who were "living outside of town." Louis reached down, put his finger in the end of the sleeve of Solomon's robe, and twisted it around his finger, saying, "Come on, Solomon." Solomon stood up. Louis began walking, leading Solomon, who was still talking. I walked in awe behind the two of them, tall Solomon and short Louis. Louis took him back to the ward without any problem. Later, Louis told me that Solomon was a nice guy but schizophrenic. Again, back to Dr. Fox to ask him what I could *please* read to learn about this. Again he said, "No." And so, I had to learn through my own experience. You heard him, he had said, "*Observe.*"

For my last year in Australia, I left the lab and worked full time in psychiatry. During this time, I served on a patient psychiatric rating board and did research with Dr. Fox who published and graciously included me as an author. At the end of the year, five new psychiatrists joined us.

What I Learned. For me, the technique in psychotherapy is to go along with the mood of the patient rather than the content verbalized. For example, if a patient is saying that I look like his Uncle Ed, we need to know more about Uncle Ed. If a patient comes into the hospital and says, "I'm angry because my mother brought me to the hospital, telling me I was going to get ice cream and didn't tell me it was a hospital." We then talk about the promised ice cream because in that way we learn more about his relationship with his mother. So what we do in psychotherapy is go from the general to the specific. Everything is grist for the mill. For example, if a patient says, "I went downtown," we need to know "how come," not "why," he or she went downtown. We learn something as we go from the general to the specific. Again, the important thing is that mood is more significant than the content, although the content is very meaningful. If the mood reflects anger, happiness, sadness or whatever, that is what needs to be dealt with first.

Australia, Gonorrhea, and Shipping Out. In 1941 and 1942 in Australia, American soldiers were unwittingly contracting gonorrhea. At that time there was no suitable medication, no antibiotic. We had heard there was such a thing as "sulfa drugs," but we had not received any. However, at that time, with patients who had gonorrhea, treatment without drugs was not unlike the primitive treatment of cancer during the early years. The patients with gonorrhea had to line up at a trough and inject silver nitrate into their own urethras, then pass through an assembly line. Metal sounds, rigid rods, were then inserted into their urethras and quickly removed to prevent strictures.

Eventually we did get some sulfa. Patients who were not responding to sulfa, or who were sulfa resistant, were given either milk shots or typhoid shots in their arms or buttocks. Very high fevers were induced in an attempt to kill the bug, with resulting nausea and vomiting. We walked around the ward seeing these patients, many of whom wished they were dead. They did not die, but got pretty close to it. Dr. Josh Billings was assigned to this particular chore, and I would work with him, mopping foreheads and holding an emesis basin for the patient.

Fortunately, my return to the United States came about because there was a troop transport preparing to leave Sydney to return psychiatric patients to the States. There was a large number of patients diagnosed as suffering from various neuroses, including another twelve who were psychotic and would have to be isolated aboard ship. The doctor in charge of the patients had no interest in psychiatry and wanted someone to join him. Luckily, I was chosen by Dr. Fox and the Commanding Officer to be responsible for all the psychiatric patients, justifying my return to the United States. It was a forty-one day journey to San Francisco on a Liberty ship. The rationale for choosing me: Once there, I was to negotiate my entrance to the government program that was financing the training of doctors. Sadly, I was too late for that, and it would be a year before my formal training would begin.

Shortly thereafter, back in the States, I was given a direct commission as a second lieutenant in the Sanitary Corps as a laboratory officer. Not so fast. The Army bureaucrats discovered I had never experienced basic training. Remember? I had been inducted early into the Army and sent directly to Fort George G. Meade, outside Baltimore. There, I was assigned to the Fort Meade Hospital clinical laboratory to perform patient blood chemistry tests. Ten months later, I left, as I was invited to travel with the Johns Hopkins 118th General Hospital to the Southwest Pacific Area. I had had no basic training, no marching, no drills, no guns. I did, however, receive official drab green uniforms.

So what to do with this new lieutenant? Apparently, it's never too late for basic training, as I was sent to the Carlyle Barracks in Pennsylvania for six weeks to become a soldier. I did as ordered, and joined a drafted group of fresh-out-of-school doctors and dentists who were in need of a bath in military indoctrination. So we did partake of basic training: a late-morning stroll led by a pleasant, laid-back sergeant, lunch, afternoon bridge or other card games in the officer's club, capped off with the club's "happy hour," then dismissed for the day. I never knew basic training could be such a difficult routine. But soon enough, the fun was over, as all good things must end. I was assigned to a ten-week malariology research project in Panama. It turned out to be a ten-week course in tropical diseases. Great!

Panama. Hot, humid—so humid that the roll of stamps I had brought with me solidified into one soggy lump. (I will spare you the details of the relationship my socks had with my feet and my Army boots.) I was billeted at Fort Clayton, an Army base on the Pacific side of the Canal Zone, but was transported daily to an isolated village in eastern Panama occupied by San Blas Indians. What a culture shock! George W. Goethals had completed the Canal through his engineering skill; Walter Reed had proven that mosquitoes carry yellow fever; and William C. Gorgas, the sanitarian, cleaned out the Panamanian mosquito breeding areas and with it malaria, as well as yellow fever. But here it was—unbelievable! It was as if I had been caught in a time warp and precipitously deposited in an ocean-side pristine jungle. Fragments of coconut shells filled with water gave sanctuary to mosquito larvae. Wherever water pooled, in stone and wood crevices, clumps of leaves, there were mosquitoes and their progeny. We were fed Atabrine as anti-malarial protection.

The people were gentle and kind. The children were young and beautiful, despite their bulging bellies hiding the presence of large, malaria-infected spleens. With the onset of adolescence, however, came aging, their shiny skin became like leather, the light in their eyes seemed to slowly dim. These kind and gentle people were bound in by their primitive way of life. Perhaps my view is tarnished by my own cultural bias. Not so for them; they took pride in their friendliness, their seeming acceptance of the world and particularly of us, the intruders. They took pleasure in their attire, the women with their embroidered lace and white cotton dresses, beaded necklaces, nose and ear rings. Men wore embroidered shirts over their short pants, reminding me of the shirts worn by men in the Philippines. Both decorated their teak-like skins with painted designs. Their homes were on the beach; sand floors, bamboo and dried sugar cane formed the walls. Food was rice and huge sea turtles harvested for their meat and shells.

Our task was to collect mosquitoes and larvae to be studied later under a microscope and labeled. The information garnered went to an unknown Army laboratory.

The time spent in Panama nearly sixty years ago provided me with several meaningful experiences. The most moving experience was spending a long day with our group at a leprosarium in Sao Paulo. There was no fence to guard the property from without or within. The patients reflected varying degrees of illness and physical symptoms. The familiar deformities of leprosy were prevalent. Some patients were in wheelchairs, some on crutches and others just sitting or lying about. Therapy, for the most part, was meticulous hygiene and housing.

But what was remarkable and somewhat surprising in this leprosarium was that the patients would greet us with their eyes and their smiles. Even those blinded by the bacillus, sensing our presence, welcomed us with smiles. And, the doctors: A husband and wife team from Kansas. They were in their seventeenth year at Sao Paulo, evidently very comfortable in their element. Their compassion was obvious. The warmth between doctors and patients was mutual and freely shared. Patients in wheelchairs would dash ahead to open the doors for us as we walked. The doctors assured us that contagion is difficult. When they finished their rounds, they simply washed their hands with soap and water.

While in Panama, I also visited Gorgas Hospital, a veritable museum of tropical diseases, perhaps the greatest in the world. It housed a collection of the most rare and exotic of the human afflictions thriving in the tropical environment. Two days were hardly enough to take it all in. Today, the hospital is known as the Gorgas Community Hospital and has reverted to the Panamanian government. This is a result of the Carter-Torrijos Treaty, which took effect at noon on December 31, 1999. In all probability, the hospital is available primarily to the upscale socioeconomic community.

I also took a trip through the Panama Canal from Bilboa in the Gulf of Panama on the Pacific side to Cristobal and Colón on the Atlantic side. Having hitched a ride on a passing destroyer, I could barely contain my excitement, as the Canal seemed to create itself just in front of us bit by bit as we moved. It was an all-day (and more) trip. I cannot describe the magnitude of the Canal, but here's an overview. There are three sets of locks, two (Miraflores and Pedro Miguel) on the Pacific Ocean side, and one (Gatun) on the Atlantic Ocean side. To observe the operation of the locks is to experience wonder and appreciation for those heroic engineers and laborers. In between the locks is Gatun Lake, man-made, and there ships wait their turn to proceed in either direction to the respective locks. The entire Canal is a near miracle. Today, happily, there are many cruise ships that include this pleasurable experience in their tours.

It was a chance meeting on the flight returning from Panama to Miami on a military transport that fatefully directed me to Washington, D.C., and a reunion with Dr. Josh Billings. On the plane was Colonel B., who had been the infectious diseases officer of the 118th General Hospital in Australia, now a consultant for the Surgeon General of the Army. We chatted about this and that, and "do you remember" things, and "who was where." In a casual way, he informed me that Josh Billings was now the Deputy Surgeon General stationed in Washington, D.C.

One day after I had returned from Panama, I went to Washington en route to the Pentagon still pursuing medical school; several Army doctors with whom I had worked recommended I try this approach. As luck would have it, driving along the streets in Washington, D.C., I noticed a building displaying the sign, "U.S. Army Surgeon General." So, I entered the Surgeon General's office hoping to meet with Dr. Billings. (Bingo!) We met, and in the course of our conversation, which was warm and light, he asked where my next assignment was. When I told him that I didn't know, he said he would check. While on the phone to headquarters "to find out where Lt. Schnaper was assigned," his face froze, turning white. He hung up the telephone, beckoned me to follow, and introduced me to Gen. Hugh Morgan, the Surgeon General. Josh accented my malariology tour in Panama to General Morgan, who reassigned me to do schistosomiasis research in Swannanoah, North Carolina. I later learned that Dr. Billings was distressed to hear that I was to be sent to Fort Louis, Washington, for Far East duty. How different things would be today had I not met Colonel B. on the plane, had I not seen that "sign" in Washington, had I not met with Josh Billings, and had I instead gone overseas again. *Serendipity.*

Medical School

It seemed to come out of nowhere. Medical school had been put on the back burner of my mind; maybe one day, maybe this war will be over, who knows. But here I was in Swannanoah, North Carolina, doing research that included examining patients' stools for evidence of schistosome eggs. Occasionally, I was confronted by a familiar name on the specimen label—identifying one of my buddies from the 118th General Hospital. I had heard that some months after I had left the Unit, it moved on to the Leyte Gulf in the Philippines. And there in the rice paddies, soldiers were rewarded for their war effort with a gift from the swimming creatures lurking there. These whip-tailed burrowers had metamorphosed from the larvae that had lived in and dined so well in snails. The burning thought—it could have been me at Leyte. My good fortune humbles and scares me.

But I wander. It was October 1945, during my eighth month of duty in North Carolina. I was in the laboratory when the Commanding Officer alerted me that the point system of time and overseas credit needed for discharge for officers had been announced. I had plenty of points. More good luck for me: The Commanding Officer was a graduate of the University of Maryland School of Medicine and a native Marylander. He suggested I call the Dean in Baltimore—immediately—as the semester was under way. I did, and was delighted to hear that I could enter the school as soon as I could deliver a fifty-dollar deposit. I called home and brother Izzy fulfilled my obligations that very day.

Serendipity and more good luck. The Commanding Officer, almost as excited as I, his face puckish, his voice exuding conspiratorial and confidential tones, told me that he had the authorization to establish a separation center to process soldiers' discharge from the Army. He was in process of opening the center, preparing to start next month. He said, however, he would open it for only one day, the next day, *Yom Kippur*, to process my discharge! Rush, rush, physical examinations, signing papers—a whirling dervish in a mental blur. The next day I packed up by throwing and pushing clothes, things—whatever—and traveled on to Baltimore.

It was two days since I left Swannanoah, school already two months plus in progress, when I officially entered the freshman class of the University of Maryland School of Medicine. Three weeks later, I found time to get out of my Army uniform and into civilian clothes.

Medical school was pretty much routine, as medical schools go—except my senior year.

Baby Doctor. As seniors in medical school, we were required to do outside obstetrics. All the assigned patients had previously delivered one or more babies. This meant that for six weeks we were on call to do deliveries outside the University of Maryland Hospital, in the neighboring low socioeconomic area. This was challenging because for the first time we functioned as "real doctors." We wore white jackets and white pants and had to go out to the patient's house and deliver a baby. Earlier, in the third year, we had some inside hospital experience in obstetrics. Now, however, we were *doctors*, entirely on our own, which was a very ego-building and challenging thing. Unfortunately, this program has been discontinued in medical schools.

It was the rule that if you called the Chief Resident to bring in the patient by ambulance and the patient did not have a problem, you failed the course. (They were tough in those days.) I began the six weeks, at all times waiting in rotation to get a call; we had little sleep. In my early eagerness, I took cabs to the patients' houses, all within a two-mile radius of the hospital. I was financially burdened and a cab ride was a lot of money. After two, three, four deliveries and seeing that every time we seniors got to the patient we had to spend five or more hours before the baby came, I changed my routine. I began using the bus. And, by the fifth week, I chose walking. Sometimes I had the good fortune of coming up the street to the expectant mother's house and seeing someone outside hollering, "Come on, doc, come on, doctor, come on—the baby's here!" I must confess, I felt relieved and very happy to hear it.

Once I was sent to a house about three blocks away from the hospital—a storefront. When I got there, I found gypsies, and the woman was indeed in labor. About fifteen people, to me it seemed more like 150 people, crowded around me, men smoking cigars and puffing smoke in my face, and women talking, all within inches of me. I was trying to do a rectal examination on the patient with everyone frowning, even though it was done blindly out of sight under a blanket. I was sort of feeling my way with the crowd while becoming increasingly frightened. Finally, I went outside to a pay phone and phoned the Chief Resident. Hyperventilating and agitated, I told him the patient was bleeding, and I didn't understand why the patient was bleeding, and I had to have an ambulance bring her to the hospital. He said to me, "You damn sight better be right or else." At that point I was so frightened I did not care if I failed. The ambulance came and took her to the hospital. Then I whimpered and whined to the Chief Resident, telling him about the situation. He frowned, and after the noisy family and many friends came in, he begrudgingly said, "You did right." I passed the course.

By the time the sixth week arrived, all eight of us in this particular rotation were exhausted from lack of sleep. It was February and bitter cold. I had only a thin raincoat to wear when I responded to a call from outside the hospital. I went to the house and found a young woman, her belly huge, in bed. This was her third baby and her grandmother was sitting nearby in a rocking chair. The patient had a thin blanket over her and her grandmother, enveloped in a shawl against the cold, had spread newspapers under the young woman. There were newspapers stuffed optimistically into the holes in the windows. After about an hour there was still no activity on the part of the baby, so I crawled into bed alongside the woman, curled up next to her for warmth, and exhausted, fell asleep.

Suddenly I became aware of the grandmother shaking me gently and saying, quietly, "Doctor, the baby is here." I got up and there was the baby between the mother's legs. I did what was necessary and got ready to leave. Mother, baby, grandmother, and doctor did very well. Acceptance was the mood experienced by all parties. I kissed the grandmother and the mother on their cheeks and said, "Congratulations and thank you," and that was that.

Internship

What a Smile. In 1949 while I was interning at the Public Health Service Hospital, there was this patient who for all intents and purposes and medical statistics, was supposed to die, but did not. She taught me about living ingenuously. A 24-year-old woman admitted for a repair of an umbilical hernia. This was no big deal. As the intern, however, it was my responsibility to do a thorough examination, including a pelvic. This I did and discovered to my amazement that her vagina consisted only of a half-inch dimple, which had vaginal mucosal lining. I called the Chief Resident, who confirmed the examination. The Chief of Surgery, at the request of the patient and her husband, decided to construct a vagina. The technique consisted of a dissection into her perineal area. Strips of the remaining vaginal mucosa were pushed into the area of the dissection. The vaginal area then was filled with cold sea sponges, supposedly sterile, to keep the space open. It was hoped that in time the mucosal cells would grow and line the vaginal space.

There followed a period of morning rounds with my checking patients as per routine. One particular morning I came in and the patient had a broad smile showing a lot of clenched teeth. I commented that perhaps she was having a good day, and she said, "No, I am feeling stiff all over." I asked her to step out of bed and stand up. She did and stood only on her toes; her heels could not come down to the floor. Having just come out of medical school, I was shocked to consider that this patient was having these particularly unusual, ominous symptoms. Hoping I was thinking of the wrong diagnosis, I dashed into the scrub area of the operating room where the Chief of Surgery was scrubbing for surgery. I told him he had to stop scrubbing and come see the patient. (What chutzpah!) With great annoyance and some reluctance he agreed, and we went to the patient's room. Again, I asked the patient to stand at the side of the bed, which she did. With this, the doctor mumbled, "Oh my God, oh my God." In effect, he was confirming my diagnosis: Tetanus, a potentially fatal disease also known as "lockjaw." There followed an extensive and intensive period of keeping the patient in a dark room, avoiding all noise, thereby minimizing the seizures that accompanied her condition. My responsibility was to carefully monitor and record her course. She also was given various muscle-relaxing medications. Cultures of the sea sponges were positive for the organism responsible for tetanus. There were ten crucial days during which the patient hovered near death. But she prevailed. After six weeks, the patient left the hospital without the repair of her umbilical hernia, but with a reconstructed vaginal vault and no grasp of the seriousness of her illness.

III.

PSYCHIATRY RESIDENCY

Introduction

Sheppard Pratt Hospital in Towson, Maryland, was an early pioneer in the institutional care and treatment of the mentally ill. It is here, beginning in July 1950, that my career started to take shape; here the influences are no longer subtle: Dr. Harry Murdock, Dr. Lewis Hill, as well as others. Here begins a veritable pastiche of new experiences.

Most of all, my teachers were the patients, and it is through their stories that I learned about the nuances and scope of medicine, and especially the mental torment that can befall any of us. Learning to be sensitive to the full range of human feelings: pain, poignancy, joy, sadness, and yes, even humor.

My time at Sheppard Pratt was preparation for what was to come next; the time when I was to meet the conjoined mental and physical pain that is the lot of those afflicted with cancer and other life-threatening illnesses.

Psychiatry Residency:
The Beginnings and Dr. Harry Murdock

Sheppard Pratt Hospital rested in a pastoral setting; a fitting ambience for those burdened by mental illness. I say rested, because since my time there as a psychiatry resident, much land has been sold. In my days, the vegetables were home-grown, milk came from cows on the property, and gardeners did magic with plants and flowers. The dining room was tended by waiters, had white tablecloths and food cooked to order for the staff. What luxury!

The hospital was founded by Quakers and was recognized as one of the country's early psychiatric hospitals with a prestigious and progressive reputation that continues to this day. Dr. Harry Murdock was the Director during my years at Sheppard Pratt. I have had the good fortune to work with talented executives, but none could match Dr. Murdock's laid-back skill.

The rationale for the hospital was patient care. There were two services, acute and chronic, each with its own chief. This was prior to the current use of psychotropic drugs. Hydrotherapy, sheet packs, electroshock therapy, sleep, and insulin therapy were in use at the time. The thrust of therapy was a psychoanalytic orientation. There was a head dietician and a head of housekeeping. All of these services were as one expected—busy but not in a noisy way. Every day, Dr. Murdock would wander the entire hospital grounds, going to all the wards unaccompanied by a doctor or a nurse.

There was also a supervisor of nurses and a doctor on emergency call at night. The latter had the responsibility of making two rounds during the night and would write a report, as would the night nurse supervisor. These were placed in the Associate Director's office. When members of the staff would arrive in the morning, they could read the report and know what had transpired, if anything, with their particular patient. Staff members also could talk to the individual on call the night before if they wanted more details. Some time after 9:30 a.m., Dr. Murdock would read the reports and then go about his solitary rounds. During conferences, he would sit in the back of the room in an unobtrusive way and, if he were called upon to say something, he would. He was well-trained and a highly respected, nationally known psychiatrist, and an active teaching and practicing therapist prior to assuming the Directorship of Sheppard Pratt. He also was an avid collector of Wedgwood china, as well as a leader among greenhouse orchid growers, and a highly regarded bird watcher. His office was a marvel of un-clutter. The large, eighteenth-century office was sparse, with two plants, three chairs and a desk decorated with a single, small copper ashtray.

Now, as to how his leadership pertains to me. I applied for a residency that was ostensibly a two-year residency, although it turned out that Sheppard Pratt had approval for three years. During my internship at USPHSH I applied for residency at Sheppard Pratt, was interviewed by several people, including Dr. Murdock, and was accepted. Some months later, I received a call from Dr. Murdock asking if I would come and meet with him prior to beginning my residency. Of course, I did. He wanted to discuss a fellow intern of mine who also had applied for a residency. Dr. Murdock wanted to know about my relationship with the other doctor. I told him that the relationship was good, and that Bud and I got along very well, and that I didn't understand what this was all about. He explained to me that he wanted the staff to be compatible with each other, and wanted to make sure before accepting the other doctor if it was okay with me. Dr. Murdock also made it very clear that had he hired the *other* doctor first, he would have asked *him* whether he felt he could get along with me.

During the early days of my residency, I was taking night call for the local medical society from midnight until five o'clock for the extra money. Somehow (and I still don't know how) Dr. Murdock learned about this and called me into his office. He said it must be difficult for me to take on those extra, late-night hours. (In retrospect, taking call was a useful learning experience). I told him I was doing it for financial reasons, and he suggested that I not work so hard. My salary at that time was $1,000 a year and he increased it to $2,000 for the year. In addition, he obtained a job for me at a Health Department venereal disease clinic, working two evenings a week, eight to ten o'clock.

Yet another interaction with Dr. Murdock occurred during my third year of residency. First-year residents saw family members on Wednesday and Saturday afternoons. This continued through the second year. If a resident remained for the third year, however, he or she would see family members on Wednesday afternoon and be off Saturday afternoon.

Dr. Murdock had the freedom to approve two second-year residents from the group of residents to continue as third-year residents. Fortunately, I was one of the two selected. The reason that he would only certify two years, was that most of the third-year experience would have to be outside the hospital and was expensive. Child psychiatry and outpatient psychiatry experience were obtained at University of Maryland Hospital in the Department of Psychiatry. Neurology was taught at Spring Grove State Hospital. What this amounted to was, that being a third-year resident, one was at Sheppard Pratt only two days a week. One day, Dr. Murdock called me in and said he had noticed I was seeing families on Saturday afternoons. He asked if that was necessary. I said I was away so much of the time that I was not always meeting families on Wednesday afternoons. Dr. Murdock said firmly that third-year and advanced staff members were supposed to be off on Saturday afternoons. Since I was in my third year it was my *responsibility* to take off on Saturday afternoons. How kind, how sensitive he was.

The necessary ingredients for a top executive: being knowledgeable about his or her position, taking responsibility, being relaxed and not having the appearance of being too busy, being perceptive, and having awareness without being intrusive, earning respect and not demanding it, and having comfortable willingness to delegate to others. But most importantly, a top executive must have the capacity to combine all of these characteristics, all of these elements with warmth and caring. Indeed, the measure of the true executive is the individual's ability to practice the art of making other people feel important.

To Thine Own Self Be True. I was only trying to be the very best psychotherapist, or at least a better one. It was already six months into my psychiatric residency and I was still struggling with imploring patients to express their feelings. Most did, but only a very few rewarded me by "expressing" with appropriate emotions rather than intellectually.

Before I show you what it took to point me in the direction of my goal, a little background. A significant player in my career was Dr. Lewis Hill, a famous, pioneering psychiatrist and psychoanalyst who had retired from active practice and was, at the time, serving as Psychiatrist-in-Chief at the hospital. And it was fortunate for the residents-in-training that he was a kind, helpful, accepting teacher. When a resident would arrive at a therapeutic impasse with the patient, Dr. Hill would be available for a three-way interview with the patient, and the resident. I availed myself of this service at every opportunity.

The format of the interview was constant: Dr. Hill would be relaxed, head bent back, smoking a cigarette, smoke drifting in lazy swirls of cloud-like figures floating toward the ceiling. The patient sat opposite, hands clasped, eyes fixed on the smoke. The resident slumped in a corner chair praying for invisibility while mesmerized by the smoke. Dr. Hill would quietly chat with the patient in a non-threatening way. Within five minutes, the patient would begin tearfully recounting childhood traumas—something we residents could not accomplish in six months or, for that matter, a year.

One day, after one of the three-way sessions with Dr. Hill, I was interviewing a seriously mentally ill patient in my hospital office. I lit a cigarette, and after a time lapse, I tilted my head back, let a puff of cigarette smoke waft lazily upward while posing a question to her. It wasn't plagiarism, honest, I was simply emulating a mentor whom I admired and respected.

Suddenly, I was startled to hear the patient shout, "Who the hell do you think you are? Dr. Hill?!"

It was a not infrequent case of the patient teaching the doctor, and not so gently putting him in his place at that.

All That Glitters Might Not Be Gold. During my first year of residency in psychiatry I had the good fortune to work with a lovely young artist, Rachel, who was admitted to the hospital because of her paranoia. She was a bright little thing with dark hair, flashing eyes and a smile that was a good deal like the Mona Lisa's—very enigmatic. The history that brought her to the hospital was that she was in Rome during a Holy Year studying media techniques from a very famous artist, de Chirico. She had already been established as a well-known artist, designing very intricate and abstract paintings that were then converted into prints for cloth fashions.

Upon her arrival at the hospital she was assigned to me. We discussed in some detail what had happened in Rome. A Catholic, Rachel said she had been overwhelmed by the fact it was a Holy Year. There she began to feel herself being taken over by the religious fervor. Soon, her behavior alternated between being an angel, giving away her clothes and money on the street corners, and being a disciple of the devil, shouting and carrying on in abusive, loud verbal insults at people.

At that time, Sheppard Pratt's "closed wards" were for the seriously disturbed and those who were a danger to themselves or others. As the patient established greater contact with reality he or she would move from the closed wards to the intermediate wards, which were locked only in the evenings; then to the open wards; and finally were discharged. Upon her admission, Rachel informed me in a rather authoritative tone that she was going to check into a hotel downtown and come to the hospital only for her therapeutic sessions. She said she would look for a studio and spend her days painting. Being a first-year resident and not being very knowledgeable, I impulsively told her she would remain in the hospital. During her stay in the hospital and until we both agreed to it, she was not to do any artwork whatsoever. (To this day I do not know what my rationale was for this decision. Intuition? Nonetheless, Dr. Hill just smiled and agreed when I discussed this with him at the next week's visit. He had a particular fondness for patients who bore the diagnosis of schizophrenia.)

Eventually, with therapy and time, Rachel improved considerably. After many months, she was on an open ward. She was then encouraged to do artwork if she so desired. The hospital had a very active art and occupational therapy group but she refused, as she felt that it was unnecessary. Significantly, at this time, she talked much about how she experienced colors. The color gold was very important to her as it represented ecstasy and joy, red represented blood, and white represented semen. At one point during a session she drew three consecutive circles and indicated that one was red, which was the blood of Christ; and one was white, which was the semen that brought Jesus into this world; and gold was the color of golden urine. As time went on, white no longer represented semen, but became the wafer used at communion.

Near the end of her stay in the hospital she said she could tell the difference between a delusion and reality, meaning she could experience something and determine whether it was a delusion. For example, she would, from time to time, have a sensation during the night that members of the staff were coming in to rape her, one at a time. She would smile to herself and know this was delusional.

At last to the point of this story. Eventually, Rachel was in a private room on an elegant, open ward on the first floor. She said she would hear dew falling during the night and it was golden, like urine. She was not disturbed about this, but concerned, was this reality or was this delusional? For several days she greeted me with this story, telling me she felt there was a light rain at night while she was in bed. She would hear the rain falling and yet there was something about it that reflected gold. She was becoming increasingly convinced that this experience was not a delusion and there was something else going on.

One day I arrived at the hospital and Rachel came running toward me, very excited, saying, "I knew it, I knew it, I knew it!" She said she again heard the "rain" falling ever so quietly during the night, but now she was convinced it was urine and not gold. She ran to the night supervisor and together they went to the second floor where a group of senile ladies resided. They discovered that one particular patient, Mrs. A, was urinating in a waste can and then pouring it out her window where it would trickle past Rachel's window. (This was quite a feat on Mrs. A's part because the waste cans had silver-dollar-size holes near the bottom so patients could not fill the can with water and use it in a suicide attempt.) We examined the drapes in Rachel's room, which, of course, smelled of urine.

A poignant post script. When the time came for our parting, Rachel said warm good-byes to Dr. Hill and me, and said she would do a work of art for each of us. Months went by, a year went by, and we would get a little note on a Christmas card from her, but the work of art never arrived. After two or three years I talked with Dr. Hill about it. He laughed and said he did not expect a painting, and he would have been surprised if one had come. He said Rachel would feel that she could never do a painting worthy enough for a gift. There are times when I am reminded of Rachel and I wonder where she is, how she is, and hope she is well.

The Gift. She was a brilliant attorney. She had won cases before the Supreme Court—only this time she was not trying a case. She sat silently in court with a pistol bulging in her purse. Her plan to use it was aborted by an alert guard. In time, this woman in her early forties became my patient. This was in my early days as a resident at Sheppard Pratt.

The woman never had any hobbies, she was not athletic, nor did she know anything about cooking or sewing. To keep her busy in the hospital, occupational therapy taught her how to knit.

It was routine that residents rotated on night call, which meant we had to do rounds in the evening, sleep in the hospital, and be on call for emergencies. One resident who had lost a leg in an unfortunate accident wore a prosthesis and walked with a cane. He would spend unusually long times with patients during his evening rounds, and although we were not permitted to solicit or accept gifts from the patients, somehow he received gifts of various types, whether it was a carton of cigarettes or some piece of jewelry.

While visiting with the patient, I noticed she was reluctantly knitting triangles for argyle socks. There were diamonds of dark blue, light blue, and white. I commented on how well she was doing, and she grunted a "Thank you." One day during our session she said this doctor had asked her to knit a pair of socks for him since she knitted so well. Eventually, she gave him a gift. He opened the box and complained, "It's only one sock." She replied, "Of course! You only have one foot!"

The hospital rule regarding patients' rights was strict. A patient's request for a lawyer or clergy member must be honored promptly. After many months of hospitalization, she asked for a lawyer of some prominence who was known to her. He appeared, talked with her and apologized to me. Apologized, because he was aware of how ill she was, how poor her contact with reality was, but she wanted to be "heard" in court.

In short order, the patient, myself with her chart, hospital administrators, her lawyer and the hospital counsels, and, of course, the judge, all met in court. The atmosphere was solemn, emphasizing my personal feelings—a mixture of uncertainty and expectancy.

The patient's lawyer began the proceedings by putting her on the stand and asking her to tell her "story." She did, calmly relating information about her privileged background, her family, her education, her travels, her awards, and her professional recognition.

Then she said, "I have practiced the law for 25 years. I came to the hospital after a fainting spell at the Supreme Court. Here, I have had my liberty compromised. I relate well to the staff, the doctors, the nurses—I even have friends among the housekeeping people. I read the paper every day and I participate in discussions with the doctors, as well as with patients.

"I am sorely needed by my law firm and by my clients. And I desperately need to get away from Mr. Franklin Delano Roosevelt. I don't know why he has to come into my room every night to screw me. I don't enjoy it, but he keeps coming back night after night. And, I could very well be pregnant."

The judge quietly ordered her back to the hospital, where, after another two years of therapy, she left with the staff's best wishes.

A Weather/Traffic Report. It had snowed heavily during the night. When I came to work the campus streets had been plowed and were left wet, with one exception—the road connecting the basement corridor of the psychiatric hospital with the neighboring Chapman building. Fortunately, a truck had been through there and had left two parallel tracks in the snow.

I had just finished rounds on the disturbed ward, which, incidentally, overlooked the connecting path to the street. Because of the weather I chose to take the shortcut to the Chapman building via this path. As I trod gingerly in one of the truck tracks, one step at a time, one foot in front of the other, a manic female patient called to me in a quiet and protective tone from the ward window above. "Be careful, Dr. Schnaper. That's it. Now watch it, it's slippery there." And much more of the same. As I was about to jump from the track to the plowed road, came her ear-piercing yell, "Look out! You dumb son-of-a-bitch! I hope you fall on your goddamn ass!"

Fortunately, my leap was successful. I did not fall on my ass.

IV.

THE WORLD OF PSYCHIATRY: PSYCHOTHERAPY

Introduction

Now, here is where *listening* changes from a verb to a noun: discipline. As when a psychotherapist is listening to what is verbally said by the patient, listening to the patient's body language, to the affect that coats the words "like white on rice." Whatever is being said is grist for the mill. No idea, no disclaimer by the patient that what is being said is insignificant, "not that important" when measured against those of others who have "real problems," e.g., cancer.

How does one *listen*? By not listening too intently. By not paying too much attention. How can this be? Is this not a contradiction? No. When one focuses on a specific aspect of the patient's presentation, the listener will not recall whatever else is offered. The listener must relax, not concentrating on particularly appealing topics: parents, sex, politics, money issues. This requires discipline on the part of the therapist. But in time, the discipline develops into the *art* of listening. The therapist and the patient are both surprised when the former recalls what the patient talked about a year or more ago. Ironically, the therapist is pleasantly, even somewhat smugly surprised, while the patient might wish that his or her spoken words had disappeared into never-never land—the words were uncomfortable the first time. But it's okay; it's all part of the process toward eventual emotional comfort. Everything is grist for the mill.

The Source

It is 8 a.m. What will the weather bring today? What life stories will the patients bring with them today? Not knowing brings uncertain answers. Will they be happy or sad? Good or bad? Exciting or dull? Sometimes one, sometimes the other, but never dull. That the therapist's anticipation never ends is what makes this work worthwhile. Every given day is not the same given day, but rather an opportunity to look forward to sharing a new experience.

It is 8 a.m. It is a new day. We know now that the weather is clear and, here comes the patient with a new story. As the door opens, the patient tenders the usual greeting to which I offer my usual response, "How am I? More important, how are *you*?"

Listening

Guiding a Patient Through Listening. Tom, a thirty-two-year-old man, was seen regularly once or twice a week for a year after being diagnosed with amyotrophic lateral sclerosis, Lou Gehrig's disease. He never asked about his diagnosis directly, although he seemed close to asking on many occasions. Once, in the third month, he asked if what he had was chronic or if it could get better. He was told his condition could get worse or stay the same. And, although there was some doubt that it could get better, there was hope that it would. On another occasion, he reported a friend had told him he had Lou Gehrig's disease, but he asked no questions about it.

As the months went by, our guidance was aimed toward getting him to grudgingly accept his physical limitations (using a cane, not driving a car, etc.) each at the appropriate time, and to accept help from his wife. His case came to the attention of the National Institutes of Health and his presence was requested for study. He was told this in the seventh month and replied, "I'll go, but not now. As long as I can move around I'm okay. As soon as I get stuck in bed I'll let you know." He was bedridden in the twelfth month, was studied at the NIH for a month or so, and then died.

So guidance is through true, short, simple statements addressed to what the patient is saying or asking. (As with parental discussions with children regarding sex or death.) Whatever is really being asked requires an answer and it must be direct. If the doctor (or listener) is comfortable with the subject, the explicit and implicit demands of a patient can be heard, differentiated, and acknowledged.

Listen, Polly. During my early years of psychiatric residency at Sheppard Pratt there was a famous and powerful lady psychiatrist, Dr. Esther Richards, at Johns Hopkins. She was the "right-hand man" of Dr. Adolph Meyer, then the Dean of American Psychiatry at Hopkins. She was affectionately dubbed a "battle-ax" and was exceedingly stern in the way she did therapy. Today, there is a building at Spring Grove State Hospital in Maryland named after

Esther Loring Richards. Dr. Richards had admitted a patient to Sheppard Pratt who was in her forties, a spinster from the Deep South who was a very frightened kind of lady. When I had a session with her, she would ignore me and instead pay attention to the clicker system, the public address system of that day. Sound clickers would beat out a certain number of clicks to represent each doctor's page. One day I asked the patient, "Polly, were you listening to the clicker system?" and she said, "Yes, I was." I asked who was talking to her through the system. She said, "Dr. Richards."

Subsequently, Dr. Richards came out to visit Polly. She spoke with me first. There I was, this young kid very much in awe of the great, tough-acting Dr. Richards. I told her the clicker story and she smiled pleasantly. Then we went around the ward to see Polly. Dr. Richards chatted very quietly and very pleasantly with Polly. Finally, she raised her voice and said, "Polly, I want you to understand something! If I want to communicate with you, I will do it through Dr. Schnaper and not the clicker system. Now, do you understand that, Polly? Your thinking is way out in left field." Polly nodded and said, "Yes, Dr. Richards, yes, Dr. Richards."

After this visit, whenever the clicker system would go off to page one of the doctors, I would wait for Polly to show some indication that she was listening to the clicker system. On about the fifth day I saw some eye movement toward the sound of the clicker system. I inquired, "Polly, are you listening to the clicker system?" She said, "Yes, I am." I asked her whether Dr. Richards was communicating with her and she said, "Oh no, no, Dr. Richards doesn't communicate with me anymore through the clicker system. Now it's Bishop West."

New Business

Building a psychiatric practice requires referrals. Some are routine, some less so. To cite a few:

Referral One: Assertive. A man in his forties referred his wife, who was in her late thirties, to me as a patient. She told me her husband had encouraged, nearly demanded, that she go into therapy. He felt she was too guilty in her relationships; she never stood up to her mother and never disagreed with him. Her husband did not like this behavior, which was unusual. Some two and a half years later the husband called me and said, "I appreciate the job that you are doing. Actually, you're doing too good of a job. I'm delighted that now she doesn't take any crap from her mother. But she's got a mouth toward me. Anytime I start to say something, she shoots me down!" However, he was laughing the entire time that he was telling me this.

Referral Two: Thanks. When I was at the University of Maryland, early in my career in psychiatry, I spent half of my time on Surgery. The Chief of Surgery was Dr. C. Reid Edwards, who was a very scholarly, white-haired gentleman. He wore a vest with a chain across it. On the chain dangled an honor key, and a gold watch hovered in his pocket. He was of the old school, very dignified, and I was just a youngster in the Department of Psychiatry. Of course, I respectfully referred to him as Dr. Edwards, as did his entire faculty, even the senior surgeons.

One morning, as I was rushing through the hospital, I noticed in the crowd waiting at the elevators, was Dr. Edwards. There he stood, all five feet four inches of him. I greeted him and he rewarded me with a sober and dignified nod. In an authoritative tone he addressed me, "Doctor, can I tell you about a patient?" Naturally, I said, "Certainly," although I was hurrying to give a lecture. I bent my head down to hear him.

He told me about this particular patient who had a neuroma. The elevator door opened and the two of us walked in. I didn't know where either the topic or the elevator was going. He continued telling me about the patient as the elevator rose to the tenth floor. He was still discussing the patient as we left the elevator, headed directly to the patient's room. When we entered the room, the patient was in bed. He turned to the patient and said in a formal manner, "Mrs. So-and-so, this is Dr. Schnaper. He will now be your doctor and he will now write all your orders. Thank you." Dr. Edwards then turned on his heel and left the room. I looked at the patient, and the patient looked at me. She broke into tears and I must confess, I felt like crying myself. But I patted her on the shoulder and pleaded, "Mrs. So-and-so I have a class to teach, but I promise you I'll be back in an hour and we'll talk all about this." I did return and met with her for two or three days. Shortly thereafter, I wrote her discharge orders.

Referral Three: No Thanks. From time to time I would get referrals from rabbis, ministers, priests. I would respectfully respond by letter or phone to any referring source, just as I would to a physician. One Rabbi, an internationally known, brilliant person—and a dear friend of mine as well— referred patients to me. On one occasion, a fifty-five-year-old gentleman came to see me. He said he had been a widower for ten years and was currently seeing a woman who had been a widow for three years. He'd been courting her for a year. He talked about the relationship, and how fond he was of her, but mostly he talked about his business, his friends, and his late wife. He seemed okay to me and appeared to be accepting the situation and was beyond the period of mourning for his wife, as was his lady friend. So I called the Rabbi to thank him for the referral, but asked about what he saw as the man's problem. The Rabbi seemed consternated, shouting, "What do you mean?!" He asked if I knew that this man was a widower, and I said defensively, "Yes, I knew he was." The Rabbi said the man had come to him to say that he was going to Florida for ten days, and asked if it would be alright to take his lady friend with him. "I then said, 'Of course not. You can't take her. You are not married. If you really wanted to take her, you wouldn't have come to ask me. I would suggest that you take this woman out to a very nice dinner and tell her that the Rabbi got you off the hook.' So I told him he needed professional help, and that's why I sent him to you."

Pity the members of the clergy. Members of their congregation call them at any hour, day or night. They spend pastoral hours on end counseling, with or without prayer—and no compensation. On the other hand, psychotherapists demand hours only by appointment, and insist they be paid for their time. So it goes.

How To Be a "Real" Psychiatrist

A "Shaky" Start. As a young faculty member of the Department of Psychiatry, I was assigned to spend half my time with the surgeons: early morning rounds, attending conferences, etc. At six o'clock one morning, I was awakened by the phone. It was a senior surgeon asking me to do an urgent consultation on an eight-year-old neighbor. We met at the hospital an hour and a half later: The surgeon was followed by a beautiful, green-eyed, blond little girl and her parents. He said the child had been in the hospital two weeks ago with complaints of abdominal pains. She had been diagnosed with "hysteria" and discharged after three days. Earlier this morning, at breakfast, she had thrown a fork at her father and therefore was, according to the referring surgeon, "probably schizophrenic."

I led the child into my office. She immediately jerked her right hand to her head as if to smooth her hair. This action was followed by similar motions with her left hand, as she simultaneously crossed her legs in one direction, then reverse. This lasted perhaps only a minute and without conversation. I excused myself saying, "I'll be back in a moment." It was now eight o'clock as I charged into the next-door office of the Chief of Neurology. In a panicky voice I implored him to come with me. He demurred, saying he was already late for his lecture to the students. I insisted, almost dragging him into my office. As I was introducing him to the patient, he put out his hand; she did the same, but jerked it away, again repeating her movements. He frowned and sharply said, "Take her to pediatrics, admit her to isolation and I will see her in an hour."

The child was not schizophrenic. She had rheumatic fever. Her jerking motions were medically known as Sydenham's Chorea, better known as "St. Vitus Dance." The neurologist pointed out that abdominal pain, a result of lymph gland involvement, was a frequent early sign of rheumatic fever, which is caused by a streptococcal infection. Fortunately, this childhood disease with its cardiac complications is rare today, thanks to antibiotics.

The following week, I had a referral from another surgical colleague, "a paranoid old farmer." The patient's wife brought him to my office. He was about sixty years old, unshaven, and somewhat disheveled. I indicated a chair. He sat and promptly began to contort, flailing his arms and legs in all directions and twisting his body. At the same time, he told me his neighbors and the FBI were sending him threatening messages through the radio and talking profanities about him outside his door.

I gasped as I witnessed this, but did not say a word. I sought out his wife, asking her "How long?" and whether any other family members were similarly afflicted. "Yes," and "he became paranoid about fifteen years ago," about the same time his "jerking" began.

Once again, I ran into the neurologist's office shouting, "You *won't believe* this! Come quickly!" He did, took one look at the patient, turned to me with a smile, and said, "That's it."

The diagnosis was Huntington's Chorea, a genetic neurological disease that in time is fatal. The affliction is passed on to the children, who are affected with onset usually in middle age. The disease is progressive. To date, there is no known treatment.

For years after the farmer's diagnosis, neurologists would have this same patient come with his wife to demonstrate the neurological problem to their students.

What an auspicious beginning for the practice of psychiatry—two seizure patients in two weeks!

Dependency:
A Way of Life, a Quality of Life:
Margaret and George

Margaret's Career. Margaret was twenty-two years old, admitted to the hospital for heart valve replacement surgery. She was a pale but attractive, bright, cheerful young woman despite her chronic illness. She had had years of parental sheltering. Prior to surgery, she talked about what she would do if surgery went well and she was cured. She said she would go to medical school so that she might help others who were ill. Her surgery was successful and she was seen ten months later for a follow-up visit. Again, she was cheerful, and this time quite active. But she had made a career decision: In gratitude to God for her "cure," she planned to enter a cloistered convent and become a nun. I conjecture that by virtue of this decision, she could continue her sheltered life by avoiding the conflicts of coping with the "outside world." In short, she was continuing the lifestyle she had utilized for most of her life.

George's Career. As with Margaret's coping, George's case demonstrates what a prolonged period of dependency can do to one's motivation. George was involved in a compensation case, and a lengthy lawsuit contributed to his motivational deterioration.

Physicians often are slow to intervene actively in a compensation case because of the potential legal ramifications. Many people, doctors and insurance officials included, think the patient's lack of motivation is really a mercenary issue because there is monetary compensation for the disability. But this is not true, and, as a matter of fact, the same deterioration of motivation occurs with nonpatients; for example, men and women who retire without any preparation for what to do during their retirement. Stay-at-home mothers can be affected as well, by the empty nest after the last child goes off. Some plan ahead by beginning part-time jobs or volunteer work when the

79

youngest child turns twelve.

So, here's George, a forty-four-year-old man I examined for a psychiatric consultation because of his inability to return to work. He was a chemist. A little more than two years prior to the consultation he had inhaled a noxious substance that affected his lungs. He brought suit against his employers at the time. When I met him, the doctors had determined his disability at less than 5 percent. His legal case, however, was still pending. During the more than two years his suit was pending, he had been receiving only $39 a week compensation, although his original salary was $275 a week. By the end of the first year after the injury, during which time he had been confined to home, he was doing the household chores and his wife had gone to work to compensate for the loss of his income. Eighteen months after the injury, his employers offered him a "light duty" job at $175 a week. He tried this, but only for two weeks, before he quit, saying, "I couldn't, even for the money. I'd have chest pains even sitting down." Dependency had now superseded the advantages of financial compensation; his potential for rehabilitation was rapidly approaching zero.

This scenario can happen with any unplanned retirement. The first six months are crucial in determining whether any rehabilitation can be accomplished. If two years have passed without resumption of activity by the worker or the retiree, zero potential has been met. All self-confidence has dissipated and fear of any new effort has risen in its place. Depression with its black thoughts, poor sleep, loss of libido, and lack of appetite has now become a way of life. If you don't use it, you lose it.

Psychotherapy:
A Duo, (at Times Therapist and Patient)
With One Trying to Convince the Other

I'm Having a Baby. There are times when one is highly motivated and intensely desires to have a baby. The first case is that of a bright, business-like woman physician in her thirties who was unmarried and wanted to have a baby. She did not want to adopt, as she wanted the experience of carrying the baby. She had male friends, some heterosexual, some homosexual. She approached several. Most were unwilling, but a few were eager to help. But there was a catch—each one of the men who was willing also wanted to be a part of the parenting process. They wanted to know the child and they wanted to be part of raising the child. They did not want to be married or on an intimate basis with the mother other than fathering the baby and helping to raise it. She refused this proposal.

As fate would have it, she met a man with whom she fell in love. They tried to have a baby, but ironically she was unable to become pregnant. The couple fretted over this and time was running out. Finally, they decided to adopt, but their age was against them. The solution for them was a foreign country. With a great deal of difficulty, time, and money, they at last adopted a little girl. Now with her hope realized, our hope is that they will all live happily ever after.

The second case was a young gay man in his thirties, who was always good about caring for his nieces and nephews: He could discipline; he could love. He never bribed the children, in effect, he was very capable as a potential parent, which was something he aspired to do. He found, by serendipity, a young woman, a lesbian, who had been married for a short time who had no children but wanted one. The two talked about this many times, discussing how they would deal with children. So they experimented. They had what constituted a rehearsal by going away for a long weekend with many of his nieces and nephews. The weekend worked out comfortably and well

81

for both. She is a rather strong character just as he is. Both have very definite tastes, but they plan to know each other at least for another year or more before they will make the final decision about having a child.

One possibility they considered is to marry, but have separate lifestyles. They would, for all intents, be roommates. He either will inseminate her directly or artificially using his sperm. They still need to work out relationships in terms of the families on both sides. They also will seek premarital counseling. How this story ends I'm not sure, but we'll know one day.

An Adoption Gone Astray. A woman called, urgently asking for an appointment. She wanted to come in with her husband to discuss their fourteen-year-old runaway daughter. Both parents were well-spoken, in the higher echelons of the socioeconomic strata. The woman said her daughter, who was adopted when she was six months old, was "talking back." She said the daughter had run away before. They were very disturbed about it, as much as they "loved her."

When they met with me, the daughter was still missing. The father had very little to say, the mother continued talking in angry tones about her daughter and her efforts to get the child to "behave." She said she had recently admonished the girl, "If you don't stop it I'm going to send you back to the where you came from!"

I remarked to the woman, "I can understand that sometimes we get so angry we say things out of anger that we simply do not mean. Then we feel guilty about it."

The woman became indignant and retorted, "Of course I meant it! Of course I still mean it! I've said it to her many times—not just once—many times, but it has no effect on her!" Finally, still taken aback, I said I wanted to see the child when she returned.

About a month later they brought the child in to see me. She had long black hair, was pretty and rather angelic-looking with pale, transparent skin. The girl told me privately she had never felt a sense of belonging; that she loved her adoptive parents in her own way, but she wasn't sure that they loved her. She said she was severely depressed, and knew if she were home that she would not be able to work out anything with them. I then brought the parents into the room so the four of us could discuss achieving accommodation from both sides. There was to be no accommodation. The girl cried the entire time while the mother continued to be angry with her. The father at no time made any comments, not in the prior visit, nor in this visit. They left saying that they probably would not see me again.

The mother called me a month later, however, saying that the daughter was very depressed and wanted to see me. I talked with the girl, and indeed she was suicidal. She was admitted to a psychiatric hospital from which she escaped two months later. For two years I heard nothing until the mother called to tell me the daughter was in a commune somewhere in the Midwest living with a man some twenty-five or thirty years her senior. And, they loved and missed her.

Sad, very sad.

Read My Lips. It is neither uncommon nor unusual for hearing impaired individuals to be skillful at lipreading. This ability can serve as a protective device as well as for communication.

Jerry, a twenty-two-year-old, was a remarkably brilliant computer expert who sought psychotherapy for relief from his overwhelming anxiety. He became deaf after a severe illness when he was three. He was not mute; he could speak, and to me it sounded as if he spoke with a Swedish accent. He was adept at signing and lipreading. Since I could not sign, our sessions depended on his reading my lips. Communication went very well until the second year of our work together. From time to time it became necessary for me to point out some painful things to him. His automatic response was to put his head down and close his eyes. I then would cross the room, and lift up his chin. He would open his eyes, and I would scold him, telling him that he was here on his own initiative and I needed his attention. In time, he relinquished and would not close his eyes when I said something he did not like. Instead, he would sign the word "shit" with one hand. Eventually this stopped, replaced by the hand sign for "I love you." I now can sign both.

Over the Edge. Lu Lu ("Don't call me Lu Lu, call me Lulah") was a tiny, bird-like lady who was quite personable and a delight to talk with. She was in her late 80s and had been referred to me by her executor guardian because of concern that she was moving into senility. Lulah had been functioning very well and had lived with her son, the head of a prominent university. He was a bachelor, and he and his mother were very close, traveling together throughout the world. She became dependent on him for everything. He did not let her want for anything, or even let her write checks.

Her way of life ended suddenly with an airplane crash. Her son was a brilliant linguist who spoke eight languages, an author, and an artist who had received his doctorate at age twenty-four. He was on his way to Europe to give a lecture when his plane crashed upon takeoff. This ended Lulah's world. At eighty-four, she had been mentally competent up until the crash. She did not want to talk about her son, only that she felt he was, "My joy, my love." She cried as she resisted talking about him, "Please, I'm putting it out of my mind, I don't want to talk about it." Then Lulah found that to cope with the shock of her son's death was to edge into "not remembering." In order to "not remember" the pain of her trauma, she unwittingly was "not remembering" names, places, etc.

It is an empiric observation that elderly people who are alert and oriented often become confused after a serious illness or major surgery. This disorientation can persist. Lulah's loss involved her very life's blood. I have continued to see her every week or so, and she remains a delight, a lovely sense of humor. However, when she is "sad," she does not talk about her son, rather she talks about how difficult and hard her father's life was, a displacement from the painfully unbearable loss of her son to the bearable hurt of the loss of her father.

Sex

In the Eye of the Beholder. Some years ago a depressed woman in her forties talked at some length during her therapy of her "boyfriend." She and her lover were both married, but this affair had been going on for more than a year. She justified the affair by saying that her husband was, among other things, a poor lover. The patient eventually divorced her husband and married, not her lover, but another man. That ended her relationship with her lover, and her therapy ended shortly thereafter.

A few years later, mischievous fate would deliver me another female patient, somewhere in her early fifties. After a period of time she talked about the man she had been having a relationship with for some five or six years. She said he had been married while she was having an affair with him, and he now was divorced. She described how much she loved him and said he was "a fantastic, creative lover." They were considering marriage. One day, during a session, she mentioned his business and his first name. Another day, she mentioned his last name. And there it was; the first patient had described her husband as being "a lousy lover," and that's one of the reasons why she was having an affair. The second patient was describing her boyfriend, the former patient's husband, as "the greatest lover in the world." The point in all this is that like beauty, politics, religion, and sex are all in the eye of the beholder.

May I? There are those people who need "permission" to enjoy sex. Sometimes it is possible only if they feel they are not emotionally involved in the act, then they are "just having sex," which is therefore permissible. Others may need to feel they are "in love," thus they are in a sense "making love." These are some of the more obvious and comfortable ways of giving one's self permission to enjoy sex in many of its forms. Also, well-known, are those who need alcohol or other drugs to be able to release inhibitions.

Some patients had unusual personal techniques that demonstrate extraordinary means of obtaining "permission." One young lady suffered from phobias. When she would feel arousal for sex while with her husband, she would nonetheless wait for him to initiate sex. On that level she was relinquishing responsibility as well as getting permission since, "It's not my idea, I'm not doing it. He's making me do it." Another patient, during the time she was having sex with her husband, would fantasize about her mother having sex. Therefore, "If Mother is doing it, then it's okay for me to do it." This patient's mother had demeaned sex and threatened her with excommunication for considering premarital sex.

Another patient was able, on the surface, to forgo getting permission to enjoy the sexual act. But what she would do during the entire experience was to pray for forgiveness. This is somewhat difficult to understand; how could she possibly enjoy what she was doing when at the same time she was praying? But to her, the quality of her prayer was giving herself over to Christ's forgiveness and having an overwhelming feeling of ecstasy.

Sex in the Office? Many times a patient has a positive emotional transference to the therapist. One patient talked very amorously about what she would like in her sexual relationship with me. One day, she came over and sat on the floor with her head on my knee. At that time I was not quite the novice, though not too far from it. But I, without thinking, said, "I don't think that we can work like this, Ms. So-and-so." At which point she simply stood and went over and sat in her chair. My saying the right thing even surprised me.

Another patient went further than sitting beside my knee—she sat on my lap. She was a seriously sick schizophrenic young woman whose contact with reality was meager. Again, I was at a loss as to what to say, but luck was with me. A pharmaceutical detail man came into my waiting room, opened the door, and walked into my consulting room. The patient looked at him and got off my lap. We learned later that in this patient's confused mind, she was a little girl. Not an adult, but a child sitting on Daddy's lap and wanting Daddy to stroke her hair, hold her, and be very caring, loving, and supporting. This precluded any adult sexual activity.

And then there was the patient who came up with a "great idea." She would rent an apartment and we could have a "very warm, intimate relationship" and could meet daily in her apartment even though she was married. I asked what would we do about the sessions for therapy. She said we would meet in my office and have those as well. I pointed out to her that people having sexual relationships do have fantasies, sometimes they tell the partner and sometimes they don't, and this would perhaps make treatment difficult. She reluctantly relinquished the "great idea."

Then there was the "tell it as it is" patient who at one point when I stood, indicating that our time was up, started for the door, turned around, and exclaimed, "When are you going to stop blank blanking around and blank me?" Still not too far from being a novice as a psychotherapist, in my discomfort, I blurted out, "Perhaps we need to talk more about this next time." She laughed and at the next session talked of my discomfort, not hers. It is an ill wind that does not blow some good, however. After considerably more psychotherapy, she came to understand this incident, that she was denigrating males, manipulating them, much as her mother had done to her father.

Although the previous examples are females, males share similar sexual propensities: sado-masochistic fantasies, sexual promiscuity, inhibitions, successes and failures of partnerships, sexual interest and lack of same, misdirected sexual activities—some immature, some sick—none are gender limited.

There are those who begin a "relationship" with sex at the first encounter. That's okay, but they need to understand they are having a *sexual* relationship. Should they want a meaningful relationship, they must be willing to spend a period of time "getting to know each other." The time period might be weeks, months, or whatever it takes for them to comfortably share feelings leading to intimacy.

And there is the not-so-subtle difference between "making love" and "making sex"—euphemistically speaking, avoiding the street vernacular. It's all in the meaningful relationship, and, like the devil, it's all in the details.

Sex, Love, and Trompe L'oeil. It had been two years since his divorce. The breakup was not acrimonious, but it was not that comfortable, either. She was convinced she no longer loved him. Oh yes, he was a nice guy, maybe too nice. Sometimes women go for men who are more controlling, maybe even abusive. But that was no longer a problem for him, she was into her career, he was into his, as a successful architect. Fortunately, their ten-year marriage had produced no children.

Now here was George at forty-five. He had done some dating and hated it. Nonetheless, the shallower the transient relationship, the more attractive it was, usually, followed by a period of depression. Encouraged by his friends, he sought out a shrink. His therapy was insightful and educational. George recounted memories of how his mother was so needy that she had had little time for him. There were periods when she was away for a few days at a time. As he grew older, he began to suspect she was having an affair or affairs. His father had time for him—ball games, fast-food places together when Mother was away. Father seemed, to George, to either accept the situation or condone his mother's behavior. Sadly, he had no siblings to share this past with him, no reality check.

True, George had gained some insight, but it was all intellectualization, not emotional—it was in his head, not his gut. So, the intermittent superficial contacts continued. Sex? Yes, for what it was worth. It was perfunctory screwing, not a sharing of lovemaking. Then it happened. "It" was a wake-up call for him emotionally.

As part of his compulsion for superficiality, he occasionally would seek out the topless bars in Baltimore's titillating sex district, "The Block." There he would buy one of the lap dancers the overpriced, much-diluted alcoholic drink. If he did not, she would move on to sit and wiggle her derrière on the lap of another customer; her job depended on it. He knew the routine; paying for the exorbitant drink was his ticket to be a player in this game.

"It" was meeting and becoming attracted to one of the girls. She was knockdown beautiful. Her long hair and large round eyes were like black lacquer. Her skin was pale, translucent, matching the color of her small, pointed breasts. They seemed to hint of a future like that promised by the developing breasts of a nubile adolescent. He was beside himself in the glow of her charm. When her eyes and lips smiled, he forgot the world. He knew that any description of her to any of his confidantes could only suffer by being painted in clichés.

He bought her the mandated drinks, but did not have her dance on his lap; rather he just bought her the watered-down drinks and languished in the generosity of her conversation. This they did, once or twice a week until the wee hours for several weeks. As long as he lavished her with the profusion of expensive drinks, her boss felt no compulsion to intervene in their meeting. He told her everything about himself, even confessing he was in psychotherapy. She admitted that she, too, was in therapy, that she was from the Midwest, had been an attorney, but felt constrained and unfulfilled as a person. She had come East to find herself, and twinkled, "I'm getting there."

He did not want this to be just another of his casual relationships. Days were spent obsessing about her, but this time it would be different, a meaningful relationship, more "getting to know each other first." So despite mounting sexual tension, they spent their meetings with cautious handholding, no lap dancing. Occasionally, they would steal a kiss, aware that it was against the bar rules. Also against the rules was meeting customers outside the bar. Yet they yearned to be together, free to play with abandon.

Finally, giving in to their impatience, they broke the rules, and set a time to meet in her apartment. It was after work, three thirty that morning when he picked her up. Since this could not happen anywhere near the bar, they met several streets away from The Block. In her apartment at last! The joy! They hugged, sharing long, passionate kisses. She tore off her blouse as he was caressing her breasts, kissing them with the intensity that he had fantasized he would. Next, off came her skirt, and—and then her panties fell to the floor.

Time froze, his heart and breathing stopped. His eyes popped out in disbelief, drawn as if by some magnetic force to the unbelievable. Was this really what he was seeing—a *penis*?! Yes, there it was, she had a penis—really.

How could this have happened? To him? To "her"? He explained he was in the preparatory process leading to transsexual surgery. He already had taken massive doses of feminizing hormones, had undergone electrolysis and now was working as a female until his scheduled surgery. He told George that he, as well as many other sex-change patients, usually spent their transition time working as bar girls in The Block.

He reminded George that he had informed him that he had come East to have his life fulfilled and had said, happily, "I'm getting there." And, indeed, he was well on his way. And George? What happened to him, to them, to their warm and tender relationship after George recovered from the numbing shock of the revelation?

That's a story in itself. Ask George.

The Extramarital Affair: A Caveat

Anticipating the very idea of an affair can embellish an actual or fantasized relationship. That it would be clandestine titillates and excites. There are even rare times when, put into practice, an affair can offer a singular, somewhat questionable, solution to a sterile marriage. In the typical sterile marriage, the participants are polite to each other: he helps her on with her coat, opens doors for her; she rewards him with a polite smile; they correspond via "Yes, dear," "No, dear." They never argue, choosing to defer to each other, there is never overt anger. Sex (not "making love") is the Saturday night routine, neither wanting it, but each feeling it's what the other expects. A tasteless, sterile marriage has no resemblance to a working marriage, only dustings of sugar and occasional salt and pepper.

It is in this bland marriage that one or the other, or both, may surreptitiously seek an emotionally gratifying extramarital relationship. This singular approach can go on for many years; never at any time is there any thought of dissolving their marriage. I am not recommending it as a therapeutic correction for a sterile marriage, but believe me, it does happen.

For those who are in, or contemplating, an extramarital affair (or extra-committed partnership), be aware of the complications and whether one is willing to accept them. (Although I am not encouraging the experience, nor am I being moralistic, I feel it my responsibility to point out the hazards of the same.) As the relationship begins, there are mutual expectations, e.g., meeting at a certain time at an agreed place. *But*, she is in the emergency room with a sick child and is unable to contact her lover, who of course gets angry. He cannot get away from his family holidays, no shared birthday celebrations, she feels left out.

And, there is *the* problem: guilt seeks (demands) recognition. There are many ways that the wanderer can unconsciously telegraph the covert activity to the spouse. A sudden blossoming into concern for appearance, both personal and clothing. New perfume, the ubiquitous lipstick smear, the odd

90

telephone bill, the plane or theater tickets left in clothing, and more.

The pressure to lie one's way out of being found out can be intense, and worse, it requires quick and facile verbal inventions and indignant denials. The woman who attributes her repeated nightly lateness to "flat tires" and "car trouble," which he willingly chooses to believe. The man who comes home from a business trip, gives his wife a peck on her cheek, deposits his suitcase next to the washing machine, as per routine, and settles down with a drink. She unpacks his suitcase, as per routine, then calls up to him, "Which is your clean and which is your used underwear?" (He usually just tosses the used underwear in his case.) His wife continues, "They're all folded." (His lover packed for him.) "The suitcase was crowded, so I folded the underwear to make it easier to pack." Which she chooses to believe, as does the wife who finds women's underwear in her husband's case, for which he explains, "You know I always throw my dirty clothes in a drawer, and I guess some female guest left her stuff in the drawer and I just grabbed what was in the drawer and packed. I was in a hurry to get out and get home."

Lady Macbeth had it easy. She knew what her sin was as she tried her damnedest to try to "out" it. Not so with Henry. His "sin," while not yet in his awareness, was nonetheless traveling a complicated and tortuous journey to expression. Henry was a pleasant, seemingly happily married man, a devoted father. A hard-working businessman whose business necessitated a monthly visit to New York City.

He would depart his home promptly at six o'clock on a Monday morning and in four hours would enter his familiar hotel and immediately contact his vendors. He would work Monday and Tuesday, leaving for home early Wednesday morning—his usual and customary pattern. Arriving at his home city about noon on Wednesday, he would check into his regular hotel where his lover would be waiting for him with drink in hand and lunch on the table. The next day, at noon, Thursday, he would return to his office.

But Henry's wife had a very different understanding of his schedule. She had been under the misconception that he always returned from New York on *Thursday* afternoon, going directly to his office.

Now we come to that special, fateful Wednesday—the Wednesday when Henry could well have understood Lady Macbeth's anguish. Leaving New York, he was anticipating his tryst as he has these many Wednesdays for the past several years, the same eagerness, confident the same fantasies will soon be realized. Shortly after noon Henry enters his usual pre-registered hotel room, is greeted warmly by his lover, his drink in hand, lunch on the table.

Helped by his lover, Henry vigorously addresses his arduous task.

About six p.m., relaxed, savoring another drink and tidbits, Henry, the ever-dutiful husband, calls his wife, as he does every evening. After an exchange of greetings and inquiring as to the health of the children, Henry shakes his glass so that his wife might hear the clink of the ice and says, "I'm having a drink now, watching the news on the TV as I dress, then I'm meeting the guys for dinner." Before he could add to the conversation, his wife interrupts to exclaim, "I didn't know that Josh Trumpel broadcast the news in New York!" Waving furiously to his lover to turn down the volume on the TV, and at the same time, his voice strident, saying to his wife, "I know, I know. I've thought the same thing. Every time I watch the news while I'm in New York I think this guy sounds just like Josh Trumpel." (But here's the secret—Josh Trumpel happens to be the most popular television news anchor in Henry's hometown.) Fortunately for Henry, his wife could not see his face pale and beads of sweat collect on his brow.

Women's *radar* is usually more sensitive than men's in picking up subtle nuances that suggest that something is not quite kosher. They suppress the signals, however, rather than rock their emotional boat.

There is a sure-fire way to halt a happy, fun-loving extramarital ride. The inherent complications have been few and easily traversed. Things are great, that is until one partner decides to be even more simpatico. Until now, much of their conversations, when they did talk, encompassed one partner's complaint about a non-understanding spouse; not only non-understanding but nasty, and, at times, even verbally abusive. The listening lover nods understandingly, but says nothing. Nothing, until heeding some dumb impulse, agrees out loud, repeating the criticism of the spouse. First, the partner feels pleased, but soon, discomfort sets in. The internal script is, "My lover is not only knocking my spouse, but also is criticizing my judgment in picking my spouse in the first place. I don't like this—or my lover." The same dynamic prevails when parents disagree with their teenager's choice of friends. It is felt as a criticism of the teen's judgment and mandates an angry, at times, rebellious, defense of the choice.

Oh, the lovers do make beautiful music together, until one sings off key and the tune goes flat, that is. One in the dyad is married, the other is not. Time goes on, frustration builds within the partner who is single. The other was going to get a divorce—right? But when? The pressure mounts, fueled by arguments leading to the death of the affair or to capitulation, i.e., the promised divorce. If they marry under these circumstances, their marriage is doomed. A few years pass, they argue about the usual, normal, everyday things married couples argue about. These soon crescendo into accusations: "You're having an affair! I know it! You cut out on your spouse with me, so why not now?" or "You're no different than my spouse. You forced me to get a divorce. I should have stayed in my marriage," etc., etc., etc.—and, divorce.

And, when morning comes and the party is over? There is a vast range of responses available to the aggrieved partner—from acceptance, with or without forgiveness, through reconciliation and/or divorce, to revenge by way of physical or non-physical techniques. They provide many stories that are played out in newspapers, movies, television—and, indelibly in the lives of their children.

So it goes.

Prizes

"My life is like a trashy novel, a B-minus movie—and my husband put me there!" cried out Nora sardonically.

Extramarital affairs are just that, adulterous liaisons, and it is hoped they will die a quiet, natural death, never to be heard from again. Unfortunately, and cruelly, they can make themselves heard, even from the grave. (This narrative is a composite representation of the separate individuals involved.)

Hundreds came to his funeral; it was standing room only. So many dignitaries. So many cars in the cortege. Police directing traffic. And, the eulogies! The spell-binding orators! Each speaker was more laudatory than the last. Each bore testimony for their hero's contributions to his church and the community, his courage, his generosity, his financial genius, and above all, his dedication and warmth to his caring wife and children. His family listens, trying through their tears to hear, trying to make the words soften the pain of their loss. The words were not new; those same accolades were in his obituaries, printed in prestigious newspapers across the country and abroad. They yearned for solace, seeking to find it in their pride in his many achievements. They were so proud they had been so fortunate to have shared him as a husband and father.

Lying there, he does not hear, he cannot read, nor can he speak. True, at his funeral he did not speak, but in the days to come he will speak—he will shout out his past. His widow will be flooded with a cascading rush of raw feelings: the pain of loss and betrayal, anger—intense anger—wounded disbelief, desolate self-doubt, wishing she were deaf. The confusion, "Who was this man? This was not my husband. All these years with him, always telling me how much he loved and adored me, and I believed him. I don't recognize him. I never knew this man!"

Discovering his infidelity required little effort on the widow's part. After the funeral and after consoling friends and relatives had returned to their busy lives, she finds she is now very alone. The house is quiet, the nights are

94

particularly lonely, the bed empty. The days are filled with reminders: the scent of his clothes, his comings and goings, big things, little things, his chair, his way of arranging things around the house. She misses him so much. Her insides are in a knot that won't go away. It's quiet and now to get busy, there is work to be done. Do something with his clothes, his collections of odds and ends—decisions, decisions. Now she must gather up his papers, meet with lawyers, work out the estate. Check his notes, his correspondence.

This is where *it* happens. She finds incriminating letters. Evidence of a twenty-year relationship, assignations locally and in other cities, even other countries. Trysts with her girlfriends! This man's behavior could not be that of her husband, it is inconceivable. But, could it be him? The frustration is so terribly overwhelming. She cannot confront him so that he could convince her that her painful discoveries were not true and thereby reassure her, or grant her an opportunity to vent her fury verbally, perhaps to punish him physically. "How could he do this to me? Why did he do this to me?! How could he find the time? Why is he not here? I want answers. I want him to know what he's done to me. Why?! Why?!"

Why? It is too facile to label him a sex addict. True, he was very busy with his sexual promiscuity, but there was something else going on. Follow me as we try to understand, but not condone, this guy's behavior.

First and above all, he was an overachiever. He had a tremendous ego, and was very successful, charming his business and social contacts, gender irrelevant. He was collecting *prizes* in every sphere of his relationships: financial, political, academic, religious, the community—*and women*. Women held the same prize value for him, no more and no less than his other prizes, his trophies. His charm was given freely to both men and women. His charm enveloped his wife, making her feel special—he told her frequently that she was. The intensity of his verbal and physical adoration of her was reflected in her devout conviction that he loved her and only her. In his mind he also believed his devotion, with a slight twist. He loved all women equally, only his wife, to him, was more equal.

How did he find the time? Remember the old adage? If you need to get a job done, give it to someone who is busy. (Witness the alleged sexual proclivities of some of our past enchanting, overachieving presidents.)

At some earlier time, he must have experienced personal rejection within his family or his social environment. As a result, for him, each task, whether materialistic or emotionally charged, must be met head-on, controlled and overpowered. It matters not if it's a scholastic grade, a business or political position, another million dollars, a male friend (employer or employee) or a woman. It's all the same. He is forever on the merry-go-round, reaching for the brass ring, the prize. The technique is brain power, money or charm, whatever it takes to win the award.

He is needy. He needs affirmation that he is accepted and loved, by individuals and by groups. But, unfortunately for him, the affirmation is short-lived. He must seek it again and again, and do more, because he sorely needs reaffirmation. He is driven to continue to collect the ever evanescent prizes, a Herculean task. Love, acceptance, equate with the prize.

His wife loves him, and (in his own way) he loves her. Sure, he gets affirmation from her, but why does it not suffice? She loves him unconditionally, but she *has to*, she is his wife. Hence, he has to extract the affirmation from the other women he meets, women who don't adore him, but do after he turns on the charm. Again, the affirmation is transient, and, like the butterfly, he moves on to the next award, the next woman, the next prize.

He was smart, so how come he did not destroy the evidence? Perhaps he died suddenly, perhaps he thought himself immortal and he would do it eventually. Facetiously, I could conjecture that leaving the evidence behind is posthumous bragging in the service of his inflated ego. On a serious note, I would propose that unconscious guilt was playing a role, prodding him to confess—so cruel, so thoughtless. Not unlike the unconscious need for those in extramarital relationships to "telegraph" their activity to their respective spouses.

Not so facetiously, it is an ill wind that does not blow some good. Her husband dies, thrusting her into this turbulent situation wherein she is in abject mourning, sad, feeling painfully sorry for herself. Then, the revelation and she discovers that she does not know this guy she was married to, and anger engulfs her. No longer is she feeling the misery of depression. Now her only feeling is fury; which is not a good feeling; it's a terrible feeling. But it is more *bearable* than the torture of mourning. In time, the anger will dissipate, sadness will return and time may heal.

There is irony here. During his lifetime she, his family, could bask in his successes, in the reflected glory of his prizes—animate and inanimate. Must she now practice acceptance of his other prizes, now colored feminine?

V.

THE WORLD OF CANCER:
THE PATIENTS

Introduction

This chapter represents forty-some years of psychiatric-oncologic practice. Half a lifetime of sometimes laughing, sometimes near crying. It has, and continues to be, an emotionally moving experience. For many of the forty years, it has not been a ride on a carousel, rather like a ride on a roller coaster. Would I have spent these forty-odd years on this path had I known what it was going to be like? I cannot answer for sure, but on reflection I don't think I would have it any other way. I did take the ride, and I'm glad.

You will discover that, through my work, I have met many and varied people in terms of their outlook, intellect, socioeconomic status—different in so many ways, but alike in their battles with illness, coping, fighting to live. In meeting and sharing with them I have been graced.

So you, too, will meet and share vicariously their lives through their stories. Also, they will tell you about their trials and tribulations through philosophical essays as filtered through me.

We have no control over the hand we are dealt. *How* we play the hand is what is paramount. As you will see. Read on.

Cancer! The word still evokes terrible thoughts—a death sentence, emaciation, pain, mutilation. To many, the diagnosis precipitates shock, followed by a feeling of futility, with no prospects of resolving the problem. As recently as thirty-five years ago, the word "cancer" trumpeted an ominous sound, and it even suggested a believable stigma. Rather than whisper the awesome "word," euphemisms were utilized: "He died of a long illness." There were some families who even preferred "tuberculosis" as the cause of their relative's death. Death by cancer shared the glare of shame with suicide: "He died suddenly."

Terminal? Not so. Today, the approach to cancer has been revolutionary, the progress measured exponentially. Stigma, for the most part, is no longer attached to the diagnosis. Diagnostic procedures are well honed and available for early employment. New treatments are being developed daily: new drugs, cloning techniques, definitive surgeries, pin-point radiation surgery, microwave and hyperthermia therapies, bone marrow and stem-cell transplants, blood vessel generation and inhibition, and more. Thirty-five, even twenty-five years ago, survival was measured in months. Today, survival is measured in years.

Tomorrow? Research is ongoing. Computer technology is enhancing gene therapy. The collaboration between the patients and researchers does not stop, not for a moment. We do not know what will be coming around the corner, so we can feel hopeful about the future. It has been said that the last thing that dies is hope. Yes, there *is* light ahead in the tunnel. What comes next bears moving testimony to this conviction.

Philosophy
(The Work in Oncology)

Death and Dying. There are those who welcome death because life is emotionally burdensome. There are those who find death a surcease to a physically painful life. There are those who believe there is a time to live and a time to die, and now it is their "time." And, there are those who fear death. Some express this fear by hypochondriasis, some by a free-floating anxiety. Both share an ever-present unshakable anticipation of death, a constant, intrusive, nagging thorn in their side, a preoccupation that demands immediate reassurance from physicians, clergy, family, and friends. There are moments, even hours, of enjoyment of people, places, or things, but only fleetingly so. They resent their compulsion to fear death.

The fear of death is the fear of *life*. Life is viewed as temporary, to be enjoyed for the moment, only to be cut short by death. The obsessive concern for what will be "missed": relationships, birthdays, anniversaries, and longed-for and worked-for successes. To enjoy life is to lose life. The future is tomorrow, which becomes today, which is viewed as yesterday. Life is anticipated in reverse—the past is depressingly *now*. Risk is never to be taken; life is already too "maybe." Nothing ventured, nothing lost. Be careful: to love is to lose love and be bereft. To care too much is to hurt too much. This is the constant dilemma that plagues those who fear death, a fear over which they have no control.

The poet John Donne (1573-1631), approached death by challenging its powerfulness, almost in a patronizing way. Note the famous opening sentence of his poem, "Death": "Death be not proud, though some have called thee/Mighty and dreadful, for thou are not so...." And his defiant last sentence: "And Death shall be no more; Death, thou shalt die!"

Many, weighted down by life-threatening illnesses share the fear of death like the others, but of necessity. The patient with cancer, however, begins a yearned-for remission with welcome joy. This joy soon turns into anxiety

101

that life is only temporary, that relapse is imminent. The axe will fall. Unfortunately, when relapse does occur, the patient experiences a peculiar sense of relief—he or she no longer has "to sweat it out." And so it goes.

If one lives long enough, everything good or bad will have happened. The challenge is in addressing the next "thing"—good or bad.

Technique:
Working with the Patient
Coping with Cancer

My approach to the patient who has cancer can sometimes be viewed as unsympathetic. This is obviously not true, but is based on the fact that I regard the patient as sick, not dead. So, frequently I will tell a patient, "Yes, you are feeling sorry for yourself and that's okay. But if you want to feel sorry for yourself all day, it is counterproductive to your getting well. It's in your best interest to limit feeling sorry for yourself to one hour a day. So perhaps you could get off your butt and walk around the room and find that you *can* accomplish something." This approach applies even to the patient who is near the end stage of his or her disease. It is in the patient's best interest to judge what contributes to their own quality of life. At least get out of bed, try to move from bed to chair, get out of bedclothes, perhaps watch television, or, if the weather is good, sit outside. The patient alone must decide what particular activity is chosen because every individual has to determine for himself or herself what defines their quality of life.

Patients' willingness to submit to the most painful and humiliating experiences has always evoked amazement and admiration from me. I feel the same emotions when patients convey their suffering as their quality of life ebbs away. How do they tolerate these onslaughts? Clearly, they draw from within on their "bank accounts" of collected past experiences of mobilizing inner strength. Each in his or her own way must now search their inner resources. Yes, support from family, friends, religion, and medical and non-medical caretakers does help. But inner strengths, such as self-discipline, can only be accomplished by the self.

There are times when a patient will, with great anguish, tell me that he or she can no longer continue treatment either because of the therapeutic complications (such as nausea, vomiting, pain, and weakness) or because it is time to escape this poor quality of life. Enough is enough. It is then that I counsel that they must make a *decision*, and it must be made one day at a time. Not like Alcoholic Anonymous' "one day at a time" commitment to achieve sobriety each day. No. Patients afflicted with cancer must decide each day, and make a choice, not a commitment. Their autonomy dictates that "*I'll* try to continue for today. Tomorrow, *I'll decide* whether it is worth going on, or whether to stop." They retain control over their bodies. They are equal partners in designing the therapy. The emphasis is on *choice*, as painful as it is.

And, more often than not, the patient decides, "I'll wait one more day." Those who decide to continue therapy, do so, and live to be thankful for it. Those whose quality of life is—to them—unbearable and have considered an end-of-life decision, usually decide to "wait one more day," then quietly die in the manner demanded by the disease.

When the person is indeed imminently terminal, however, my approach can be openly more sympathetic. While the person is fighting for their health and a "cure" from cancer, I join them in a denial that equates with hope. This gives us the opportunity of working together to better the patient's quality of life. When that person is terminal, I will do house calls, whether it's to the hospice or to home or to another hospital and visit with the patient as a non-chargeable social visit.

One day, my technique caught up with me. Tom was in the cancer center, bedridden and dying, but at the moment still alert. I visited with him, which was not unusual. Later I said, "So long, Tom," and I bent down and kissed him on the forehead. As I got to the door, he called me back, saying, "Dr. Schnaper, I'm dying, aren't I?" I turned back into the room and said, "Yes, Tom, you are." He replied, "This is the first time in two years that you have been nice to me. That's how I knew." I said, "I'm sorry," and he responded, "That's okay, I want to thank you for the past two years." Again, moved emotionally, I bent down and kissed him, and left the room. Several days later he drifted into a coma and a week later he was dead. Peace.

Yet another motivation for choosing a career in oncology: We meet good people who are also memorable. It helps the oncologist, in an ironic way, that the "turnover" rate is what it is. Though the previous patient is well remembered, mourning is short in that a "replacement" soon enters the oncologist's life.

Some of my colleagues had another reading of my therapeutic approach to the patient. Dr. Chuck Adams described it ever so succinctly. But, first I have to build you a clock before I can tell you the time. Here goes. In the 1970s, the early days of the Baltimore Cancer Research Center, sign-out rounds were full-staff, two-hour sessions. The goal was to alert the Fellow on night call about potential patient problems and dangers. It could be a simple matter of reporting one-on-one to the designated Fellow, but not so with the BCRC. Each patient was discussed in lengthy and meticulous detail: diagnosis, a change in therapy, prognosis, non-compliant behavior, ethical and psychosocial problems—everything was grist for the mill. The brainstorming of therapeutic ideas clashed with appropriate noisy thunder, egos slammed—with a brief nod to respectful deference—and the outcome was always education, clarification, and the patient's benefit.

Now, I can tell you the time. One evening, the group was laboring over a patient compliance problem. The patient was presented as emotionally vacillating between self-absorbed, high-handed demands and silent withdrawal. It seemed that he was somewhat entitled to challenge the staff, as he was a bright doctor with some oncology experience, although known to pontificate as to how and when his therapy should be meted out. As usual, everyone had ideas on how to deal with this patient. He was new to me, so I just sat back and listened to the loud debate: firmness, veiled threats, reasoning, perhaps even shared responsibility, and more were offered as solutions.

Suddenly, a Texas-accented voice pierced the hubbub. It belonged to Dr. Adams. "Ah think this patient needs Doctuh Snappuh's leathuh finguh up thuh ass treatment." The referrals asking me to administer the "leathuh finguh" continued for some years.

Coping

The Rocket Scientist. "It's the Rabbi," groaned the nurse as she handed the phone to Dr. Joseph Fontana, the on-call doctor that Sunday in the Cancer Center. "What's the problem, Rabbi?" asked Joe. "Your temperature is what? 101.6? Come on in. I am sure you're right, erythromycin can reduce your fever. No, I won't call your pharmacy. Maybe your doctor, Meyer, will do it if he's done it before. No, you have to come in for cultures and examination. You know better, Rabbi. Come on, I'll be waiting for you."

Joe hung up the phone, while complaining to the nurse, "He sure is stubborn." The nurse looked at Joe, shrugged her shoulders and said in a patronizing tone, "Well, you know our patients are not rocket scientists." Joe laughed, "True, but this patient happens to *be* a rocket scientist."

Rabbi Norman had leukemia, a disease about which he knew everything there was to know and beyond: the diagnostic factors, the natural history of the disease, its treatment, its prognosis, its "normal" and unusual complications, who was doing what research-wise. You see, the Rabbi had doctorates in mathematics and physics, was an ordained orthodox rabbi, well-read and educated in areas unrelated to his occupation as an inventor and designer of rocket projectiles. He was sought out as an authority on computer "acrobatics" and quantum mechanics. Truly a brilliant and accomplished man. But ill with leukemia nonetheless.

You've seen him many times, blending in with a group of orthodox Jewish *Lubavitchers*; their uniform, their badges manifested by the black clothes, the black felt fedora with the wide brim, the beard, facing front avoiding the possibility of eye contact with a female, usually in heated discussions— religious or business—with one or more companions. If you've seen one *Lubavitcher*, you've seen them all.

Not so fast. Not this one. Not Rabbi Norman. The thin face under the black hat was intense, his sharp nose, red-rimmed deep eyes that challenged, demanding, "What can I learn from you?" And his beard. What a beard! Like his eyebrows, it was salt and pepper in color. But the hair was like straight wires, untrimmed, reaching out in all directions, emanating from the central core of his nose and mouth. Each hair rigid and pointed outward as if emulating so many of the missiles he fathered.

Where he worked and what exactly he did with rockets is none of our business. Go ask the government. His leukemia was and is our business. He was knowledgeable about his disease and that knowing was part of his technique for coping with it. And he coped very well, using his tremendous knowledge to retain some autonomy and personal control. (It also helped that he had some control over the doctors.) His deeply religious conviction was a great source of strength for him as well.

There was a mystical aura about his approach to the tenets of his belief. As an inpatient, he prayed in his room three times a day, morning, afternoon and evening, always wrapped in his striped prayer shawl, standing eyes closed, rocking gently back and forth. The doctors' and nurses' respect for him mandated that they mold their procedures and other contacts around his prayers. When he was confined to the hospital over the weekend, a small refrigerator would be brought in, but he would eat only Cheerios in rice milk. The Sabbath would be consumed by prayer and rest. It was fascinating to observe other patients, whether sharing a room with him or not, and regardless of their own religion, fall prey to his quiet charm and religious devotion.

It was a personal source of amusement for me to witness his visits to the outpatient area. The female clerks and other staff members would grab his hand fondly, shake it, smile, "Hi Rabbi!" He would smile back graciously, move on, and I would have an inside chuckle. Orthodox Jews are not to look at women or to touch one—an anathema. Yet he carried it off just like the trooper he was.

During one of his hospital stays he shared his room with a man named Bud. Bud was born Jewish, but was never interested in the practice of any religion. It was enough that he accepted the fact that he was Jewish. In short order they became fast friends, interacting with each other's families. The Rabbi did not proselytize, and Bud did not become an observant Jew. The relationship continued for some time, admittedly not long enough for either Bud or the Rabbi. Bud died shortly before the Rabbi. At that moment, the Rabbi was on portable oxygen. Yet Rabbi Norman, short of breath, had to climb stairs to console Bud's widow. He could not do otherwise.

Now it was Rabbi Norman's time. He brought his valuables with him whenever he was admitted to the Cancer Center. Included were his prayer books, his prayer shawl, and a large photograph of his beloved *Lubavitcher* leader, *Reb* Schneerson. Although the *Rebbe* was ailing after a stroke, he was, according to the Rabbi, still vigorous, and communication between them was full and frequent. The *Rebbe* was a sage, the worldwide leader of the *Lubavitcher* sect. His faithful adored him, many even worshipped him.

It was winter and Rabbi Norman was failing and, of course, he knew it. Did he slow down? Certainly not. As usual, he actively continued in his research. He celebrated his daughter's wedding according to serious orthodox ritual. This meant a considerable significant portion of ceremony was outside under the stars at twelve degrees. He did it. Not too long after the wedding, he was spending more and more time in the hospital, digging deeper into his therapy and into his relationship with his God. He asked his friend and doctor, Meyer, a non-observant Jew, to join in the morning devotions with him. His doctor complied.

I would visit him daily, having answered his questioning eyes, "What can I learn from you?" He knew everything about me, past, present, and future. And it wasn't just me, he had searched out most of the staff. And we never found him prying or intrusive, it was his charm. He knew that I was a *Kohain*, a priestly descendant of Aaron, the brother of Moses. A *Kohain* is privileged to give the priestly threefold benediction during important Jewish holidays.

So it came to pass one day that I visited. He was in a chair, wrapped in a blanket, weak, eyelids drooping. He opened his eyes and beseeched me, voice wavering, "Bless me as a *Kohain*." Stunned and uncomfortable, I protested, "I cannot, I am not observant. I do not even say the usual prayers." "No matter," he said. "Regardless, it is still your responsibility as a *Kohain* and I know that you know how to do it in Hebrew." He handed me a skull cap, and I offered the blessings in Hebrew:

"May the Lord bless you and keep you.

"May the Lord lift up His countenance and be gracious unto you." At this juncture he opened his eyes and interrupted, "No, that's the third blessing." "No," I smiled, "the next is the third." He was still trying hard to retain some personal control.

"May the Lord turn His face to you and grant you peace." We both said, "Amen." Feeling humble and inwardly shaky, I bent down and kissed his forehead, and left.

On a Friday shortly thereafter, his nurse came rushing down the hall toward me. She was one of the very few nurses from whom the Rabbi accepted ministrations. "The Rabbi is dying," she blurted out. "I know, but not yet," I said, attempting assurance. "No, I know he's dying. This is the first time he has asked me to bathe him for the Sabbath. He has always insisted that he do it himself, so I would not touch him."

His death was imminent. So was *Reb* Schneerson's. It was the next weekend and we had heard that the *Rebbe* was living moment to moment, but we were admonished not to tell Rabbi Norman. The phone rang in the semi-comatose Rabbi's room. It was a recorded message for all the *Lubavitchers* to hear. The venerable *Rebbe* had gone to join his forefathers. The Rabbi in his haze picked up the phone, heard the news, his eyes flung wide, his senses came fully alert and remained so for the next day. Then, at last, Rabbi Norman quietly left to be with his most beloved *Rebbe*.

Did the *Rebbe's* spirit go to Rabbi Norman and grant him another day? Some do believe, and who am I to say otherwise?

Blessings of Cancer. The patient, a middle-aged woman, had metastatic breast cancer. As a young girl she had been a child prodigy with the violin, playing for Franklin Delano Roosevelt's birthday. When she was in her late teens, she became a novice nun. Eventually, she was promoted to mother superior and functioned very responsibly in that position. In time, however, she had a disagreement with the church and resigned. She did not marry, but instead obtained her doctorate in music, wrote books having to do with music, and taught in a southern university.

She felt as if she were gaining strength through her cancer and dying; that out of adversity comes strength, "the blessings of cancer." She returned home to die on a little farm she owned. She dug her own grave and boarded it up with old wood saying, "This is an old body and I'm not going to waste new wood on it." And, in time, she did die. A next-door neighbor saw to her final care, as well as to her burial. She was a very courageous person indeed. (Despite the woman's feeling that she was getting strength from her cancer, she was actually using the defense of denial, looking at "reality" as a way of coping. This was consistent with her life-long personality development.)

Yuck. It is common knowledge and understandable that patients become conditioned to their chemotherapy and its concomitant nausea and vomiting. Some patients get so conditioned that the reaction has its own label "anticipatory nausea and vomiting." Sometimes it can be very severe. It can be associated with the clinic or even a chemotherapy nurse—seeing the chemotherapy nurse can evoke waves of nausea. Some will experience it on the way to the hospital. (I recall a special case years ago, where the patient's anticipatory nausea was so severe that he would vomit at curbside at the hospital. It was solved by giving him his chemotherapy in a nearby building.) This problem, many times, can be dealt with by using tranquilizers, hypnosis, or both.

The case of Allan is a little different as this young man did not become nauseated or vomit because he anticipated his chemotherapy. He found that certain foods served during his hospitalization would bother him even when outside of the hospital, because of his association to the *hospital* smell of it. He would get slight nausea or a feeling that he could not chew the food, or put it in his mouth, or swallow it—he just felt such revulsion. As an example, he frequently got a turkey sandwich in the hospital during the time he was getting his chemotherapy, so from that stay on, he could not eat turkey sandwiches even outside the hospital. He decided that when he went to the hospital, he would make sure the foods he loved would not be served to him, thus rendering them abhorrent. For example, he loved pizza, so he didn't want pizza of any kind to be brought into his room by a friend, relative, or by dietary. Therefore, pizza would not become part of the chemotherapy quilt. He was so sensitive that he would ask what food was being brought in for someone in the next bed. Besides that quirk, Allan was a well-adjusted and pleasant young man and very compliant to his therapy.

A Doctor Copes. The most powerful defense we utilize in coping is that of denial. There was this bright cardiologist whose wife had pancreatic cancer. Over a period of eight months she had begun to deteriorate physically. Both were in their late eighties. She refused aggressive therapy after having surgery and learning her diagnosis. She wanted some quality of life. She had had a rather good quality of life, horseback riding, tennis, music that she loved, and friends and parties. This had been her lifestyle, a free spirit. The husband did not prescribe for his wife, but he treated her as if he was the nurse, always analyzing and "figuring out." In his words, "understanding the physiology of the process." He sought counsel from the physician caretakers, and would call her doctor for approval when he wanted to change her medication. Each day, he would offer the physician in charge a meticulous case presentation, much like what a good resident or Fellow would do, explaining signs, symptoms, and the beloved "physiology."

Nothing in this account is pejorative, and it's certainly not a value judgement. This was his way of coping, which did not interfere with her lifestyle, nor take over her medical treatment. This, I am sure, was a most difficult process for him, because he was always a serious figure in cardiology, and his personality and style were consistent with his role as a physician. As used by others, this coping technique was an intellectual denial about the possibility of her death, which, of course, was imminent.

Sleepytime. Another technique for coping with a serious illness such as cancer is the use of sleep. Dear Jane's diagnosis was leukemia. She was an attractive woman from the hills of Tennessee who had had a rough life up to that point, including a couple of broken marriages. Once she became familiar with the prescribed therapy and its IVs, she would go to sleep when she came in for her chemotherapy. Routinely, she would return to the hospital for more chemotherapy, at times receiving IV antibiotic therapy for her infections. She visited off and on for a number of years, each time falling asleep as soon as therapy started. Jane would eat very little, as a matter of fact, most of the time she would be fed intravenously.

As new Fellows came on for a year or two of training, they would become disturbed by Jane's uninterrupted sleeping and ask for a psychiatric consult. Their interpretation was that this patient was indeed very depressed. The Fellows would be reassured, and in time would learn that this was the way Jane dealt with her therapy. When her therapy or intravenous antibiotics were finished, I would rouse her by yelling, shaking her, and asking whether she was ready to go home. She would say "Yes," and I would tell her, "You must start eating, and if you are eating you can go home." She would eat, and within thirty-six hours she would be on her way home.

Lost? Not Really. Bob, a bright, middle-aged, retired attorney, was working hard at overcoming a cancer of his brain. He had had intense and difficult meetings with radiation and chemotherapy. And here he was, again submitting to chemotherapy in an effort to reverse a relapse. Chemotherapy was not the only thing in his coping armamentarium. Bob also utilized his hail-fellow-well-met personality. He walked about in casual dress, smiled easily, offering cheer and helpfulness to other patients and staff. In short, his denial was working well for him.

That was until the day he went for coffee in the ward kitchen. A nurse, Margaret, called to tell me that Bob was in his room sobbing uncontrollably. Indeed, there he was, dressed as usual, IV pole beside him supporting the bags of chemicals that were being transported to his veins via his catheter leash, overwhelmed by tears. "I was lost! Lost!"

With much anguish he related what had happened in between sobs. He had gone for his coffee, as was his custom. When he came out of the kitchen dragging his IV pole, he recognized the ward, but had no idea where his room was. He wandered in a panic until he came upon a nurse he knew, Margaret. "I'm lost, I don't know where my room is!" Margaret gently guided him back to his room, then called me.

Margaret and I talked reassuringly to Bob. Yes, it could be a "brain thing," but his periods of confusion were much less frequent than in the past. It could have been the chemotherapy, or whatever. "What is important, Bob, is that you were *not lost*," I said. "You simply did not know *where* you were. This happens to all of us. If we are out in the ocean, desert or forest and no one is around, we are indeed lost, but hopeful about being found. But where there are people, landmarks, maps, etc., we can find out where we are. We are not lost."

I told Bob that as long as we are willing to ask for directions we are not lost. We can ask people or even go into a gas station and ask for directions. "This is what you did with Margaret, you asked for directions. *You were not lost, you simply didn't know where you were*. Bob gave us a half smile. Within a short time his denial was back on track, and he was coping just fine, with smiles for everybody.

Lost? Not really, it only feels that way.

Only Nice People Get Cancer
(And Why Doctors Prefer Them): An Essay

It was September 14, 1982. This overcast day introduced two new patients to the University of Maryland Cancer Center. In a surprising and uncanny coincidence, both were male and in their early fifties, had the same diagnosis, had been married once, had three children, and were scheduled for the same surgery and chemotherapy. They died within a week of each other: One enjoyed an honored eulogy and testimonials to his philanthropy and independence, the other received subtle barbs that the disease shortened his prison sentence for murder. One "nice," one not so "nice"?

Because, however, one is of a particular socioeconomic group or has attained a highly respected status, or is aging, or has a life-threatening illness, or is dying, does not suddenly make that person holy or good. Once a bastard, always a bastard. He will age or die in the manner in which he has lived. Nonetheless, both are entitled to the professional's therapeutic and compassionate care. This is the concern of this essay, the need to view diseases and their etiologies via implied value judgments.

Frederick B. Levenson. (Stein and Day, 1985). Mr. Levenson, a lay analyst, invokes "unresolved conflicts," "irritations." He accepts the role carcinogens play, but theorizes that if there are no internal irritations, the carcinogens will be rendered impotent. He continues that love, for the most part unconditional, bonds the internal irritation and the cancer—*any* cancer—is therefore preventable. (Ignoring the fact that a "cure" for "cancer" is difficult because there are so *many different* cell types, solid and hematogenous cancers.) Mr. Levenson misuses psychoanalytic theory to develop and buttress his thesis, leaning heavily on the many possibilities and ramifications of traumatic separation.

His book, and other writings with a similar thrust, offer no contribution to the state-of-the-art in cancer therapy. His theories of self-healing are near faddish, assumed neuropsychoimmune, mind-over-matter and harmful. The painful burden of cancer is compounded by exhortations to those suffering to "control" the progress of their disease by "visualization," "positive thinking," "relaxation," "stress reduction," etc. What a cruel and terrible indictment to dump on an already distressed person! When that individual relapses, he or she can only feel guilt. The now relapsed patient, in my office, bathed in tears, says, "I failed, I did not try hard enough to cure myself." These techniques are useful only in the direction of a better quality of life, not survival.

Given that there are many types of cancers and many types of personalities, there are no organic or physiological factors, or theories at this date that can cause, treat or prevent *all* cancers. How an individual has coped in the past predicts how he will cope with cancer or any other critical illness. ("What's past is prologue," as William Shakespeare says in *The Tempest*.) The mind-set of these "psychological thanatologists" inadvertently encourages understandably desperate patients to seek unorthodox, unproven therapies, such as coffee enemas, megavitamins, laetrile, metallic compounds, etc. More than fifty percent of patients with cancer take this path.

The American Cancer Society Board of Directors approved a position statement on May 24, 1984, including this portion: "At the present time available evidence does not support the theory that the use of techniques for reducing stress can change the risk of developing cancer and the duration of survival in humans. The use of psychological interventions which claim to alter tumor growth or progress cannot be recommended."

And there is more. When the time comes for the patient or his or her surrogate or family to make decisions about taking extraordinary measures or withholding or withdrawing therapy, then the professionals' beliefs determine their own particular mind-set. (The controversial ethical issues require a separate essay.) When an alert patient refuses further treatment, which is his or her prerogative, and the patient's professionals agree, then there is no issue. If there is disagreement, however, there are some professionals who will seek psychiatric consultations to prove their patient incompetent. To these professionals, the compliant (i.e., "nice") patient, be he psychotic or retarded, is always competent.

Those who have cancer, who are experiencing losing and loss, need ordinary calm, non-angry, hopeful, human contact, not the psychological-sociological-philosophical intellectualizations of pseudoscientific thanatologists.

Patients Are People, Too

Getting to Know You. It is worthwhile to consider that there are patient-patient interactions that can contribute to emotional problems for a patient. These interactions go on in the inpatient areas as well as the outpatient waiting room. There are patients who feel threatened by the remission of another patient. Others are threatened by another's relapse. There are patients who form close relationships, and others who keep their own company. All are human reactions: The resentment that another is "getting well while I am not," or frightened that another is relapsing, "Am I next?" Closeness with other patients sharing a common experience, or getting too close to those who may soon die, "and it hurts." Obviously, interactions of such intensity as these are more apt to be played out more often in a cancer unit than in the office of a general physician.

A poignant example of patient interaction concerned two lovely young women diagnosed with melanoma. Neither was married, both were in their early 20s. They formed a close relationship due to the timing of their diagnosis and chemotherapy. They insisted that whenever they came to the hospital for inpatient treatment that they share a two-bed room. When one would relapse, the other would feel terribly anxious, and in a short time also would relapse. When one went into remission the other would anticipate remission; and this, too, would happen. Unfortunately, finally, fate intervened and one of the women had a relapse and died shortly thereafter. The other young lady went into a severe depression, which lasted about two months. She came out of the depression, but a month later relapsed. A month after that, she too, sadly, was dead.

No Thanks, Doctor. There also are those who find it necessary to be help-rejecting patients. They come in several varieties. There are those who seem to be compliant, but somehow misuse their medications. They take it at the wrong times, or they "forget" when they are supposed to take the medication, etc. And there are those who simply will say, "I don't want this medication," or "This is the wrong kind of medication." There are those who feel they need to be intensely in control, to the detriment of their treatment. To cite an example, a rather brilliant doctor had to frequently correct his doctors that this or that symptom was an indication of such and such diagnosis and that he needed a different, more appropriate medication. Also, that if he had a pain in a local area or in a certain bone, he was sure that this was metastatic and needed to be radiated with a specific number of rads, etc., regardless of the lack of confirming evidence. The need to control is understandable. It is an effort to deny the helplessness, a way of coping. Again, nonetheless, these patients are entitled to our professional compassion and concern.

Pets

Then there are the patients who are "pets" of the staff. These patients generally have a sense of humor, even if it is sometimes used defensively. As a rule, they are the more attractive male or female, and the younger patients. The patients who, with their families, are very appreciative and express their gratitude at all times to the staff are often considered as pets. These feelings are reciprocated by the staff. Then there are patients who may share the same age group as the specific nurse or doctor who is responsible for the patient's care and who soon may identify with the patient. The staff person involved will sometimes treat the person as a VIP. This has its drawbacks, however, as VIPs do not always get the best treatment. This is so because the patient, with their doctor's tacit approval, sometimes will try to run his or her own therapy, which is usually detrimental. Also, the caretakers can be so emotionally involved with the patient that their judgment in treating the patient is impaired to the point that the treatment is counterproductive. Being a VIP is surely not in the best interest of the patient.

The Porn Star Who Loved Cats and Dogs. "The business of sex is sex. And, the business of cancer is cancer." Simple, yet profound, a metaphor for Leslie's character—all business. That was how she addressed her insight to the oncology staff. Yes, Leslie had colon cancer, but having been dealt this hand over which she had no control, she would now take control over how she would play this hand, true to *her* style.

When Leslie presented, newly diagnosed, at our hospital, she was 34, beautiful in an exotic way (as an erotic lap dancer, pornography star should look). She had long, jet-black hair, a heart-shaped face, a smooth, dark complexion with iridescent skin, almond-shaped eyes suggesting an oriental quality. Her lips were full, half-smiling, half-pouting. She was tall; her body not too thin, not too voluptuous, but sufficiently well-proportioned to convey sexiness. (Of course, as befits a porn star.)

Leslie spent her adolescent years as a fashion model. It was only a short step into becoming a model for *Playboy* and *Penthouse* magazines, gracing the *Penthouse* pages numerous times. In February 1992, she was honored as the *Penthouse* "Pet of the Month." In time she became a celebrated porn star, performing in popular *Penthouse* videos. Always comfortable with her body, always utilizing a business-like approach to the business of eroticism. Prostitution—should you ask—was never a consideration.

In 1995, Leslie founded a non-profit cat and dog rescue operation called Pets4Pets, with shelters in Maryland and Virginia. Funding to support her endeavor was through rallies and charming friends and colleagues. One very successful fundraiser was her eighteen month Pet of the Month Calendar. Each month featured a different pet; dogs, cats, a lion cub, parrot and even a goldfish, each accompanied by their own human "playmate." The latter were all Leslie's colleagues, who happily contributed their services *pro bono* for the cause.

Leslie confessed to "forever" loving and collecting stray cats and dogs. It was not unusual for Leslie to have her pets pose with her for her magazine "shoots."

Leslie's cancer begged her attention when she noticed rectal bleeding. At first, and only briefly, she tried blaming hemorrhoids. She sought out her physician, had a colonoscopy and received the diagnosis: colon cancer. Surgery, chemotherapy. Leslie hit the Internet, quickly becoming sophisticated about the disease, the therapy and who was doing research or whatever and where—here and abroad. Collaborating with her doctors, hungry for information, she constantly picked their brains. A journal, always in her hand, registering accounts of her treatments, emotional and physical progress or lack thereof. Her appointment book was crowded with medical and performing schedules, including national radio and television appearances to discuss the disease—always business-like.

There were the inevitable setbacks. From time to time the irrepressible cancer would surface, necessitating further surgeries, and radioactive treatments to halt the spread, usually, in her liver. Her approach was always, "Okay, let's do it." A clever example of one of her many coping mechanisms is reflected in her determination to work regardless of the demands of therapy. She needed an in-dwelling intravenous access line to accommodate the infusion of her current chemotherapy. Leslie asked that the access line not be placed in an area of her body where it could be visible. She chose to have it placed in her upper arm, between her elbow and shoulder. Now, she could hide it under a fancy garter belt, and off she went to Las Vegas to perform.

No matter what part of the hospital she visited for her various medical procedures, the doctors, nurses and clerks were there to welcome her with hugs and kisses. The fact that she was a porn star did not get in the way of their feelings for her. Leslie was Leslie; "what you see is what you get." She was perceived by the staff as pretty, bright, warm and "gutsy." They loved her.

The end came quickly, like when a silk stocking gets a run in it and it dissolves. Surrounded by friends, Leslie faded into coma and died quietly. She was 36. There were laudatory obituaries in the newspapers. Notably, *Penthouse* magazine in its *In Memoriam* column eulogized, "Leslie who was truly extraordinarily beautiful both inside and out..." (November, 2000).

That was Leslie, who looked at life through her business prism: the erotic business, the sick and abused, homeless cats and dogs business, and finally, the cancer business.

Those who knew her—friend, colleague, or medical professional will always remember business-like Leslie with a warm smile.

More Coping

My Friend, God. "Finally, today, we are friends again." This was Jack's greeting from his wheelchair at the beginning of our weekly session. Eighty-year-old Jack is now old. He was young until six months ago when he began chemotherapy and radiation treatment for lung cancer. He had been happily retired for thirty years, active in his Florida community, playing his beloved golf daily. When we first met, immediately after he received his diagnosis, he was angry—no, *furious*. Why did he deserve this disease? He had been a caring husband, father and brother. Forever independent, now he had to "impose" on his daughter and son-in-law. "I do not think I'm going to take treatment. I should go home and die. What does God want of me? To go home and die? I'm furious."

Nonetheless, Jack decided to go along with the therapy program. Our weekly sessions produced repeated threats that he would discontinue the chemotherapy and radiation. He wrapped his words around himself in an angry mantle. (With a good deal of justification, as the side-effects of his treatment were plenty and severe).

But today, he is no longer angry. Why not? Because today is (possibly, hopefully) his last treatment. "God has brought me to this day. The weather is beautiful. I can now take showers again. How long can anyone stay angry? Anger is not like me, it's not my style. I am glad to be friends again with my God."

The Wig Party. Thirty-year-old Susan, a fourth-grade school teacher, had been treated for breast cancer. She was bright, alert, perky, sort of "smart-alecky" with what she had to say, but her sense of humor made it sound pleasant and non-offensive. Her mother had died of breast cancer at age thirty-two, as had her maternal grandmother. Despite all this, Susan's sense of humor helped her cope and kept her going. As a side-effect of her chemotherapy she had lost her hair and now flaunted a wig. She shared the humor of her wig with her fourth-grade pupils. She sometimes let the children feel it, try it on, and at other times would wear it askew. On one occasion, Susan reported that she and the children had been outside for recess and the wind blew the wig off. The pupils and Susan were much amused, laughing, shouting, and clapping.

In time, her hair did return. For a while, with her short hair, she looked like a pixie. One day, she decided to get rid of the wig. She assembled her children outside and they had a wig-burning party. Susan had ice cream and cake and little favors. She dropped the wig in the fire can, and the children danced around the fire, which was happily chewing up the wig. It was quite a party, lots of fun.

Within a year after the party, unfortunately, Susan's metastatic disease progressed, and by the end of six months she was dead at thirty-two, sharing the same age-survival as her mother and grandmother. Dear, brave Susan.

The Mack Truck. Many times patients struggling to cope with cancer receive superficial, uninvited, and useless assurance from well-meaning friends and relatives. Venturing into the marketplace of philosophy, they tell the patient, "Well, that's the way life is, because who knows, I could walk out into the street and be hit by a Mack truck and my life would be over." When I hear friends or relatives, no matter how well-intentioned, telling this to the patient, I feel quite perturbed—no, annoyed. While it is true that any of us could walk across the street, encounter an accident, and be dead immediately, the difference is, since we don't have cancer, the Mack truck will take us completely by surprise. The patient with cancer, however, knows only too well that around the corner is a Mack truck just *waiting* for him or her to step off the curb and into the street, and that would be the end. Some patients will listen resignedly to this counsel and assurance from friends and relatives, grimace, and say nothing. Others may get angry about it but rarely lash out— it takes too much effort.

The Dr. Jekyll and Mr. Hyde Medicine

Happy Steroids. Steroids can be the best and the worst medicine in the world. It is the best medicine in that it can "cure" asthma, Crohn's disease, and lupus, and it does many good things, including reducing brain swelling when there has been surgery or trauma to the head. It does all kinds of wonderful things for allergies, it even can be taken orally for poison ivy. On the down side, however, it can make the individual fat, can make one happy, sad or psychotic. It can give the patient arthritis, gastrointestinal ulcers, and can make the skin slough. It can do many good things, but also can have potentially very unpleasant, unhealthy side effects. Steroids, the medical chameleon. An unpredictable Dr. Jekyll and Mr. Hyde.

In the early days of the Baltimore Cancer Research Center, financial support was the responsibility of the National Cancer Institute. This meant we had easy access to use of hotels, so we could bring in patients from as far away as Europe and beyond. Their families would come and stay as well. Everything was paid for the inpatients, there was no need for insurance or grants. (This was long before the existence of our current Hope Lodge, a low-priced residential facility for patients and their families.) On a particular protocol, their families could stay in the hotel free as the patients had free care, free everything. Even the use of the telephone was included. (Halcyon days!)

One recipient of this largess was a young man in his early twenties who had leukemia. He had come from somewhere in Appalachia. He was poor and arrived wearing farmer overalls, with no socks, his shoes dilapidated and torn. Obviously, he had no money, but nonetheless he soon began to play the stock market on the telephone, even though he had not completed high school. Dr. Peter Wiernick, the director, told me about this young man's calls to stock markets in New York, London, Berlin, and Switzerland. I had several meetings with the patient. He told me he was interested in building a cancer center, and had informed Dr. Wiernick that the doctor was to be the head of it with a salary of five million dollars a year. I listened to more of this, then went to Dr. Wiernick, saying, "Peter, this young man is heavy into steroids and the only way to get him to come off making all these expensive foreign calls is to cut back on his steroids." He was gradually tapered off of steroids and went back to being as poor a young man as when he first came to the hospital. This result was without joy or a sense of accomplishment for me, or the staff.

When I go to cancer-related meetings and cross paths with Dr. Wiernick, he introduces me to whomever he is with as the "shrink bastard who talked a patient out of giving me five million dollars."

More Happy Steroids. Another patient, a married lawyer in his early sixties, was being treated for lymphoma. As part of his chemotherapy he was receiving steroids. He was somewhat hypomanic, relating in a very joyful, happy way how very appreciative he was for what the staff was doing for him. He expressed his gratitude by giving wristwatches to the nurses.

Talking with the man's wife, she said he had worked for many years as a lawyer for the government and was now semi-retired, doing some free legal work. Before his illness, he was pleasant, but quiet, shy in fact. She said he was not given to passing out gifts, and was not generally the life of the party. Nor was he eager to pick up the check when they went out with friends for dinner. I asked the wife if he could afford to give the nurses the watches, and she said he only spent about $8 for each watch, which were copies of well-known more expensive watches. She said there was no way he was going broke. I pointed out to her that if he was spending beyond his means, for example, if he was buying a yacht, or investing most of his life savings in the stock market, or spending money unrealistically, I would be very concerned about it. She said he was not doing that, but he was somehow different. I said as long as he stayed within his financial bounds, I was not concerned. Patients who are on steroids can be happy or sad or whatever, and he happens to be happy.

From time to time, I saw the two of them together. They came to my office one June while the patient was being tapered off the steroids. He admitted that he was being less enthusiastic, less gay, but still was quite happy. In this particular session with me, he said he had been to New York with his wife. He had seen a ring and wanted to give it to her for their forty-ninth wedding anniversary in November. She said that while they could afford it, the ring was too expensive, and he said, "No, it was only $10,000." She admitted that she loved the ring. I asked, "Why not take it?" She replied, "Well it's kind of too expensive, kind of spending money foolishly, but I guess I *would* like to have it." I looked at him, then I looked at her, asking, "Do you *really* want it?" She softly said, "Yes." I said, "Take it *now*, because in November when he's off steroids, I'm not sure you'll get the ring." I don't know for sure, but I hope she got the ring.

More Special People

The Right Answer. On rounds one day, I stopped to chat with a young man. He was in his late twenties and laboring under the heavy diagnosis of leukemia. It is not unusual for me to follow the doctor's rounds, asking patients, "What do they have planned for you?" With this question, I am hoping to learn what the doctors have planned for the patient in terms of radiation, more chemotherapy, or whatever. Most times I knew what was planned, but the question would be a way of determining whether the patient understood correctly what he or she had been told. When I asked this particular patient what was planned for him, however, his sober response was, "To make me an old man." I chuckled and said, "I think that's great, and I'm all for that, but what else are they planning for you in terms of therapy?" He smiled and responded, "Well I am going to have a bone marrow transplant. But whatever they do to me will make me an old man—I hope."

The Good Deed. Harold, a young man in his early twenties, had been diagnosed several years earlier with cancer. He now was waiting out his time; he knew that he could be dead within the year, if not within months. Harold had a good friend, Jon, who was living with an illegal immigrant from South America. The latter was a sensitive, dedicated, hard-working young lady also in her twenties. Harold thought very highly of her—I suspect he had feelings beyond compassion and warmth for her. Nonetheless, as time went on, the three, Harold, Jon, and "Mary" would spend a considerable amount of social time together. Harold frequently would have to go to the hospital for dehydration or infection and Jon and Mary would be attentive and supportive.

Dark clouds began to form on their personal horizon. Although Harold's friends seemed to be in love with each other, neither was willing to make the emotional commitment to the other. But the need for a green card became rather urgent for Mary, as there were rumblings of a crackdown on illegal immigrants. Mary, despite the help of Harold and Jon, had been unsuccessful in getting legal help. Harold then made a very substantial offer: He would marry Mary, not only for her sake, but also for his friend's sake. Harold was fully aware that his time was limited, and that his relationship with Mary would be a "business relationship." This way, Jon would continue his relationship with Mary. The plan was, that should Harold live for two years he would give Mary a divorce, and by that time Mary and Jon would be certain whether to marry or not. Regrettably, all the planning was for naught; because three months after the marriage, Harold had cardiac arrest and died.

What happened after that to Jon and Mary, I know not. I do know, however, that Harold left a little bit of money, which was all he had, to Mary. And, as well as wishing to give her the gift of her green card, he gave her the gift of love—unrequited, unconditional love.

The Gift of Self. Sam was in the hospital having recently suffered a relapse. Chatting with him, it was clear that he was angry and frustrated, complaining that his life was being interrupted. He had an older sister by four years who was pregnant when her husband walked out on her; so she moved in temporarily with Sam, who was living alone. She brought her four-year-old daughter and eventually gave birth to a son. This was twenty-odd years ago, and his sister still was living with him. Sam never married nor did his sister remarry, although she had had several relationships.

At the time of Sam's relapse, the oldest child was in college, and the second child was finishing high school, ready to go off to college. He has raised the children, who call him "Dad," or "Uncle Sam," taken them to their various athletic and club activities, and participated in the PTA. His current anger and frustration is related to the fact that he "has to see" these children finish college and get settled in their lives. Then he would be ready "to bow out." He had always been religious. He prayed to God to give him "the gift" of survival, at least until the children were well and comfortably established. Meanwhile, he said he would dedicate himself to fight, to get well so that he could be around to further his role as a parent to these children. He became tearful as he talked of his love for them. He said he was not doing anything unusual by raising these children; it was "the expected thing to do." I pointed out to him that he was indeed giving of himself to the children, which is quite different than just giving them shelter, a place to live. More realistically, what he was giving was the precious gift of himself. Unfortunately, God had other plans for him.

Have Gun, Won't Travel. Willie, a middle-aged farmer and native of deep Appalachia, came to the hospital for cancer treatment. At first, he was abrupt and gruff whenever he spoke—which was infrequent. He was a very private person, Willie.

One day, a nurse informed me that Willie had a gun in his locker. I approached him and asked, "How come the gun? Is it for yourself or the doctors?" His reply was succinct. "If I don't like what the docs say, then it's for them. If I don't do good, then it's for me."

I told him that I was confiscating the pistol and giving it to security, and he would get it back at the time of his discharge. I added, "If you want to blow out your brains, don't do it here. Wait until you get home and make a mess there rather than here." He smiled.

In time, Willie was to become a favorite of the nurses, "a character." He had a dry sense of humor that was a delight. He died several years later, and his widow has corresponded with some of us on the staff to this day with birthday and holiday cards. It was a pleasure to have known Willie. He is missed.

I Told You So. Leonard, a forty-seven-year-old man hosting lymphoma, was a pleasant kind of guy, helpful around the ward, and quite a favorite of the staff, particularly the nurses. Leonard had many visitors with one exception, his son-in-law Frank. Frank was certain that lymphoma was contagious and therefore refused to visit. He felt strongly that if he visited and did not become ill directly from his father-in-law, then it could happen indirectly from the various patients on the floor. Frank called Leonard on the telephone instead to offer his concern.

Leonard did rather well, and went back to work. We heard good things about him until five years later when Leonard's daughter Linda was brought to the hospital, also diagnosed with lymphoma. Linda happened to be Frank's wife. Her illness convinced Frank that he was right, he "knew it all along." Frank was then convinced he would "catch" lymphoma from Linda, and in short order, the marriage was dissolved. Good riddance.

Unfortunately, there still are people who have the misconception that cancer is contagious. It is hoped this notion will, in time, fade completely.

Secrets. There are patients, who, for their own reasons, refuse to let anyone know they are bearing the burden of cancer. Some have always functioned as private people. For the most part, they are VIPs who do not want the information disseminated through the public media. There are those who choose not to let anyone know that they have cancer because they feel cancer carries a stigma. Unfortunately, there remain a few who still share this conviction.

Consider two examples reflecting personal reasons:

The first is Marvin, who had a prognostically poor sarcoma. He had surgery followed by chemotherapy. Marvin was an entrepreneur, and a rather successful one at that. He did not want anyone other than his wife to know he was in the hospital for sarcoma. In discussions with him, he said he did not feel that cancer was a "sin" or a stigma. His need for secrecy was for serious business reasons. Since he worked with high finance, he occasionally went to banks to make loans for millions. To him, it would make sense if he kept his illness a secret. If the banks should discover his illness, then "Why would they want to lend me money if I might die before the loan could be repaid?" I suggested in a rather naive way that if the banks gave him a loan, certainly they would expect some kind of collateral. He laughed and replied, "The way I do business, it's on a very personal basis, usually with a handshake and no solid collateral."

Consider the case of Robert, who had melanoma, and was doing rather well, but did not want family members—except his wife—to know. He implored the nurses to erase his name off the board and replace it with an alias; this they did with a chuckle. He chose to stay in his room and not walk about the ward. His secret was somewhat like Marvin's in that it was for "business reasons." He had a successful marketing business. When he was having chemotherapy, his partners believed he was taking time off for mini-vacations. He thought if his clients found out about the cancer they "would feel" that he was too ill and cancel their business as he could die at any time. In further discussions, Robert began to talk about how the stigma that goes with cancer was underlying his reluctance to have anyone know his diagnosis. After more discussions, he became aware of what was realistic about his illness and treatment, and he began to call close friends. He revealed to them why he had not attended various functions. Just in time. Some people were beginning to wonder, after seeing his wife attend functions without him. A rumor had begun to circulate that he and his wife were splitting. This gave him incentive to let people know that he had cancer. A further incentive: He knew there was another patient on the ward who could recognize him. When the other patient died, he relaxed his vigilance and began to walk about the floor.

The conscious or unconscious bottom line in both examples relates to fears of inevitable death. Displacement of the fear of death to the fear of others "finding out" tempers the anxiety, only slightly. Concern that others might view them as "dying" is a projection of their own conviction.

And there are patients who live in the opposite camp, who let people know with a great deal of glee that they have cancer—even to the extent of calling up everyone they know and crowing loudly, "You'd never believe what's happened to me! I have *cancer!*" The patients who relish telling the world their diagnosis, are in a sense defining the meaning of, "It is an ill wind that does not blow some good." Many people wish to let the world know they have something that might gain for them a moment of concern, of caring, of attention. This is not pejorative; there's no value judgment. These are the people who choose to share their good and bad fortune with those around them. There are times we see this concept fulfilled in children who have a critical illness, be it rheumatic fever or leukemia, etc. The families then relinquish control, encouraging the child to manipulate the family and his or her environment. The parents lean over backward to do anything to indulge their child, either out of guilt, or out of trying to make the child happy, or both. This is not in the best interests of the child as it guarantees the child's infantilism.

A note. On the other hand, for those who need to have "secrets" about their illness, I would suggest that the only one who is convinced that the secret is indeed a secret is the one who believes it's a secret. Those in the patient's environment quickly sense that something is awry.

Relationships, and Thereby a Positive Contribution to Quality of Life: Linda, Susan, and Barbara

The Problem. "Will it hurt if I hold you?" he said softly to his wife, Linda. "That would be wonderful, just be careful of my left hip," she answered with a warm smile of appreciation.

A serious illness can bring partners together or precipitate a separation. It can enrich a relationship or diminish it. For the most part, the illness solicits tenderness—at times, may even repair a rift in a relationship.

I have had the good fortune to share vicariously the closeness and empathy of others during their illnesses. An elderly couple—she, the patient, in bed, asleep, and he asleep in the adjacent chair. Their hands held comfortably together. Another couple, this one in their twenties. He, the patient, asleep in bed, on his back. She, on her side, cuddled next to him, her nose snuggled in his neck, her left knee over his legs, both breathing in unison. I took pleasure in teasing both couples about "sleeping together," and threatening to secretly take their pictures for the purpose of extortion. There are, and have been, many such opportunities for me to bear privileged witness—some married, not married, homosexual, and those of many religions, colors, and creeds.

To observe the dedication, the tenderness and the way the gay and lesbian community showers its caring love on a friend or lover afflicted with AIDS is to experience poignancy. This is not to deny the intensity, the warmth and caring of individuals in other relationships—partner, parent, child, relative, or friend. Both individuals and groups are immersed in the relentless, demanding, and inexorable path to some sort of resolution. But the homosexual experience in the ambiance of AIDS differs only in that it is usually *group*, rather than one-to-one sharing. Although illnesses are not God-given, they nonetheless leave little room or tolerance for value judgments, be that of the individual or the relationship.

Cuddling. "Doctor? You have a moment?" she asked, her face reflecting her uncertainty. "Sure, Susan, but not here in the hall. Come into my office." We entered; she sat opposite me, embarrassed, crossing one leg over the other, then repeating the opposite action. Now in her forties, her combat with chemotherapy was, for the moment, victorious—her face still bright and beautiful, her short hair heralding its return, giving her the look of a pixie.

"Yes, Susan?"

She hesitated, a shadow hovering over her face, still crossing and recrossing her legs. "I feel stupid. It's so insignificant a thing."

"Susan, don't editorialize. I'm ready when you are."

"Well, doctor, you know I lost my right breast two years ago."

"Yes."

"And you know John and I have been married for twelve years and I love him very much, and he loves me—I think."

I said nothing.

"It is so wonderful to cuddle at night, particularly after making love, and to wake up with him beside me in the morning. And, when we do cuddle, we're both on our sides, he faces my back."

I nodded. Susan and I each waited for the other in silence. After several moments, she took a deep breath.

"The problem...the problem is..." she paused. "I feel silly," as she squirmed uncomfortably.

"I'll decide that," I interjected.

"Well, we're both in bed on our right sides and we fall asleep cuddling and his left arm is over me and his hand would hold my right breast. But not anymore. I have no breast, and I miss him holding my breast more than my breast." Her tears fell unrestrained.

I held her hand, and after a reflective silence on my part, I asked if she had discussed this with John. She had not. And, why not?

"John has seen my scar and doesn't seem to be upset about it. I used to sleep in one of his shirts, but I don't do that anymore. We still cuddle, but he keeps his arm at his side. I don't know why. He's a proud person who doesn't talk about feelings."

I asked Susan if she could discuss with John the possibility of sleeping on their left sides. This way we might discover what objections, if any, that he might have.

A few days later Susan bubbled into my office.

"We talked! He was afraid that if he put his hand on my scar I would feel

131

uncomfortable physically or otherwise. And last night we made love, slept on our left sides, and we fell asleep with John holding my left breast. It was wonderful! Thanks!" She gave me a quick hug and was gone.

Forbidden Love. Cancer claimed Barbara's left breast when she was twenty-one. Now at twenty-four she was receiving radiotherapy to her cancerous lower spine in an effort to stay the progressing paralysis of her legs.

Fate had not been kind to Barbara. Her life had been a cascade of unfortunate events: She was an illegitimate child, was brought up in a foster home, worked a low-level job providing only the bare necessities, had endured a rejecting relationship, and now she was suffering the recurrence and spread of her cancer, just as her current relationship of two years was moving toward a hopeful outcome.

Barbara shared a small two-bed, semi-private room in the hospital with an elderly lady who spoke only Spanish. Communication was limited to nods and smiles, and restricted by the curtain between them. One day on rounds, I asked Barbara how the radiation and physical therapy were going. "OK, I guess," she said with a wan smile. "Tom visited last night, but only for an hour."

"Only an hour?" I puzzled.

"He's a mechanic down near Washington and he works ten or twelve hours. And, it takes him more than an hour to get here and he's so tired. He wants to stay, but he has to get some sleep and it's another hour or more to get home."

We chatted for a while. I asked Barbara if it would help if Tom could sleep over and share her bed. "But keep in mind, your counts are down, and making love could mean you end up getting an infection." Her face lit up. "We'll just have a longer visit and he'll have a chance to rest." I told her I would alert the doctors and nurses on the ward that Tom would be visiting overnight.

The next morning I entered her room, forced by the scene to stop abruptly. The tableau did not require translation. There was Barbara, standing between the beds on her weak legs, her Spanish roommate braiding Barbara's hair. Barbara's face was flushed, radiant, and for the first time—beautiful.

"Barbara, I told you not to!" I frowned with mock sternness.

"I know, but it was so good to be held, so wonderful, so happy. Can he stay tonight?" she begged, using a lifted eyebrow and wrinkled nose.

"Okay" I mumbled, feigning reluctance.

132

However, sadly, the visit did not come to pass. Tom could not come that night, but would come the following weekend. He did not make that visit either, as that weekend Barbara's fate chose to end her life of travail. But like the clichéd candle, her life burned bright before it went out.

Caring

I feel. Once upon a time, there was a young couple living happily together. No big deal. Peggy and Fred had a very warm relationship. She had leukemia. The staff felt warm toward the two of them, seeing how they cared so much for each other. Inevitably, Peggy became weak from her chemotherapy. She had lost her hair and was feeling debilitated. Whenever she came to the hospital, however, inpatient or outpatient, Fred was close by her side.

On one occasion when she was an outpatient, Peggy wanted to tell me something privately that deeply concerned her. She said she felt guilty because she could not participate in any sexual activity. When I asked if Fred was pressing her, she said, "No, not at all." He was not doing anything except cuddling with her, but she felt guilty that she ought to be doing something, anything, to satisfy him sexually. I reassured her that she need not feel guilty, and walked down the hall. As I passed Fred, he waved me over to talk with him in the corner. He wanted to tell me that he felt guilty about cuddling with Peggy. Fred was concerned that he was cuddling for his own benefit, and perhaps he was hurting her because she seemed to be aching most of the time. I reassured him that he didn't have to feel guilty. I told him I didn't think Peggy was really concerned about sex, if that's what he was thinking. He said he was not pressing her for sex, and if he got "horny," he could go into the bathroom and masturbate.

It's interesting how both partners, from their own perspectives, were feeling their own guilt and unaware of the other's. Kind of like an O. Henry story, huh?

Peggy did very well with treatment. The pair married and a group of us from the hospital attended the wedding.

Caring—But Too Much. This was the dilemma for Margaret, who was ill with leukemia. When she became ill, her boyfriend of five years became very attentive. Then to her consternation, a "concerned" friend told her he occasionally was having one-night stands with various women.

Subsequently, it became clear that his feelings toward Margaret reflected how much he did care and that guilt over his affairs was not the motivating factor. The encounters were unconscious efforts to dilute his emotional attachment to her. They had been talking about marriage before she became ill, and now he was "too scared" that she might die. He had recently lost a close relative, also to cancer. Even though she understood his behavior intellectually, she had difficulty understanding it emotionally. Margaret and her boyfriend broke up, yet they have remained good friends, and he continues to be supportive.

The difficulty in expressing caring and feeling too much is not limited to males. It has been my empiric observation that this situation actually prevails more among females feeling threatened by the possible demise of their male partner, but it is manifested differently.

For example, there was a woman in her early sixties, who was married to a very macho man who had never been sick a day in his life. He was diagnosed with lung cancer and was becoming increasing ill. One Thanksgiving, she and her husband went shopping for the grandchildren in a toy store where he broke down and cried. She told me she felt guilty because she wanted to leave him because he had cried, and she had never seen him cry before. I pointed out he probably was feeling that this might be his last Christmas. (It was.) She accepted this explanation but said, "I just don't want to be around when he dies."

She was, after all, with him when he died. While some women do actually leave, others do not. The latter, as with this wife, feel the guilt for *wanting* to leave, but don't abandon their spouses.

Another example involves two healthy young women in their late twenties. Both were married to patients, one in his late fifties, the other in his mid-thirties. They would travel to the clinic together, as a foursome. They were good friends as they shared the same small-town neighborhood. One day, however, the woman who was married to the man in the thirties appeared at the clinic with the older man. She had left her husband and now was living with the older man. Soon, it became evident that the older man had a statistically better prognosis.

A familiar scenario plays out among many wives—they not only don't want to be around when their partner dies, but they also don't want to see this "tower of strength" deteriorate. Further, the more dependent the female, the more threatened she is by the possible loss of her husband. Men can, for the most part, be busy with their job during the day, therefore not be overwhelmed by witnessing the daily ravages of the disease as it progresses with their female partner. (I have known men, however, who have taken a leave of absence for months just to be with their partners.)

On the other hand, there are women who do not work outside the home, who devote themselves to their partner and the hospital, never taking time for themselves. The net result is that they become overwhelmed, want to escape, and feel guilty about their wish to flee. For this reason, we often encourage partners to "Pace yourself," "Have a friend take you out to lunch, go to a movie." Don't "hang out" at the hospital, and don't "hang out" at home with the patient. There will come a time when the person loses their relative, and, in essence, at the same time loses their *"job."* It's very much like a forced retirement and then the patient's partner is at sixes and sevens, not knowing what to do.

I Hear You. Dan, thirty-six, was a critically ill leukemia patient intubated and on a ventilator. He was temporarily deaf, a complication resulting from his treatment. He would meet attempts at communication with him were met with closed eyes and a solemn turning away of his head. The nurses knew he could read lips, and would hold his head still to get him to "listen." It took much reassurance on the part of the staff, nurses particularly, to get him to cooperate. The change came about when he felt he could trust the staff, and the staff acknowledged his feelings of isolation. Further enhancement of communication came about when he was moved to a large, bright room where his family could visit, reinforcing trust. It was a subtle way to support the patient's coping.

Every Cloud Has a Silver Lining:
Some Thoughts and Kind Words for Families

It is an Ill Wind that Does Not Blow Some Good. The business of dying from cancer can sometimes be a quiet, peaceful demise; sometimes it can be heart-rending for the patient and family. Nonetheless, as painful as the thought of death and the process of dying can be, one can still have some perspective about the business of dying from cancer. When one has a sudden heart attack and dies quickly, many people think, well, this is a great way to die, "I hope that it happens to me this way." But one can draw on the perspective and realize that everything is relative. The families of the patients who die suddenly, for example, on the street of a heart attack or trauma, have not had the opportunity to say their good-byes. In the case of the patient who is dying from cancer, however, there is time to work out family relationships, the opportunity to say, "I love you," or to have reconciliation for all the angry arguments in the past. Support for the patient from an ex-spouse or a divorcing partner is not uncommon. When the person does finally die, perhaps the family can feel less guilt because of the reconciliation.

The Sick Child. There is a singular family encounter that tugs at my heart and clouds my brain—the *dying child.* Of course, it is axiomatic that when a child dies, he or she cannot be replaced; the parents, if they wish, can have *another* child. Parents, spouses, relatives and friends can be replaced, not so a child. Mourning for a lost child is endless—an aching sorrow. The parents die, the children can be labeled "orphans." A spouse dies, the partner is called a "widow" or "widower." A child dies, what is the parent called? Nothing. But what clutches at, and shakes my clinical detachment, is sharing the parents' and the dying child's reactions until death declares a truce, if not an end to the commanding power of parental guilt.

Many years ago when rheumatic fever in children was prevalent, and antibiotics were not, the kids were sick. The threat of heart complications hovered over the families. The young ones, sensing parental apprehension, soon learned the art of controlling their environment, even involving the extended family. Toys, gifts of great value (perhaps even a car to console the ill adolescent), no discipline, the child yelling orders—all giving the child the uncomfortable burden of being in charge. And this could ensue for years.

Not so for leukemic children in those early doctor days of mine. Fortunately, survival today is in years; then it was measured in months. Nonetheless, the parental guilt is just as powerful today as it was then. A composite portrayal of the family interrelationship resembles the following: The child, overtly or covertly, blames mother or father or both for the disease's onset or relapse. The parents tearfully plead (or whine) that they are not to blame; that they wish it was them instead. The child now has completed chemotherapy, is at home watching television, and orders mother to bring a glass of water; mother cannot say, "Get up, dear, and get it—the exercise will do you good." No, the child might fall and mother will feel even guiltier. And the same thing happens many times over. Each tear, each mournful sigh, each painful grimace ignites the compassion that fuels the flames of parental guilt.

And the parents, yes, the poor, dear parents. They can verbalize that, yes, they are capitulating authority to their child, but this is said without any real conviction. But the guilt is so overwhelming that they cannot see they are emotionally infantilizing their child. Are they bad people? Of course not. This is *their* child, their baby. They cannot help themselves, oh, if only they could suffer the illness and spare the child. Caught in this web of turmoil, who would not fall victim to this pervasive guilt?

All the while, a storm rages inside their heads. Am I indeed guilty? Genetically responsible? Maybe it's not me; it's his (her) genes. Most of the time, these accusatory thoughts are out of their awareness, manifested only by surfacing feelings of uncertain, free-flowing unease bonded to guilt. There are infrequent times, however, when parents actually do blame each other. I have seen couples who have come closer together and others who have become bitter, angry with each other, secretly pledging separation and divorce when the ordeal is over. Alas, the child dies, they want to divorce, but they are too emotionally and financially exhausted to do it.

There is no room here to criticize the parents—they have no choice but to try to stay afloat as they fight the waves of guilt. Even a gentle effort of insight offered to them is of no avail. To softly suggest that relinquishing control to the ever-demanding child might engender resentment toward the child, therefore, it would be kind and in the child's best interest to say "no." The suggestion is met with a deep sigh, "I know."

And, there is no criticism, no fault, to be levied at the child. The child is sick, unhappy; other children are free, doing things. "I have this terrible thing—why not use it for me?" Secondary gain? No, that's pejorative. It's kind of like the child is trying to make a silk purse out of a sow's ear. That's right: *It's an ill wind that does not blow some good.*

There is Also Another Guilt. There are times when a family holds a death vigil that goes on inexorably day after day, after day. The children come from different localities, traveling some great distance. They have been at the bedside for a couple of weeks, and they are tempted to go home because mother hasn't died yet, but they feel too guilty about leaving. As time goes on, they fear they will feel even guiltier if they leave. If they stay, however, and time goes on, they will begin to resent the fact that the vigil continues endlessly; they have work to do and would like to go home to their own nuclear families. So they have to weigh the difference between feeling a horrible guilt for being angry with mother for keeping them there, and being angry at themselves for allowing the guilt to hold them there. Or they must confront and bear the less horrible then, but now terrible, guilt that they would feel had they gone home to do their thing without anger and mother dies, despite the fact that good-byes have already been said.

Further, there are families who move in and overwhelm the patient and the staff as a way to preclude later guilt. They do everything possible for the patient, their loved one. This strategy does not work, however, because when the patient dies, the guilt and the concomitant grief is still there, including unrealistic guilt, which is ubiquitous in survivors.

For example, one patient, Ned, was near terminal with prostate cancer. His daughter worked in the hospital, and was rather knowledgeable about pharmacology and nutrition. Needless to say, she had many suggestions for her father's treatment. She was nearly overwhelmed the staff, the doctors, and the social workers with her ideas, some of them quite appropriate. Of course, she was caring and well-intentioned. It is almost the rule for family members who are professionals, they are understandably trying to overcome their sense of helplessness.

But there is the other side of this coin. We have seen family members who abandon the patient once the diagnosis is made because they consider the patient is already dead. There have been times when we have called families to insist that they come to visit. On occasions when the excuse is not having the wherewithal to come from a neighboring city, we have provided them with the money. Because the patient is already dead in their eyes, they anticipate that mourning will be minimal or not at all. But neither overwhelming nor abandoning the patient can spare us the painful mourning process.

There are times when the patient is acknowledged as terminal, and the family members slowly, ever so slowly, approach acceptance and resignation to "the worst." Then, suddenly, the patient seems to recover. But, alas, just as suddenly, the patient relapses, only to recover again. The family begins to feel as if they are a "yo-yo." Subtly, quietly, seeds of resentment are being planted, which in time will be reaped as guilt. This phenomenon, known as the "Lazarus Syndrome," can and does occur in children as well. It is a repetitive pattern of a cruel and fickle fate.

In the Middle. Grace was in the intensive care unit, on the verge of death. Grace's husband is Jewish, but her family is not. This was only a small irritant, the real problem was possessiveness. Grace's parents and two sisters came from Chicago to spend time with her. Soon the husband and the parents were at odds with each other about who was doing the most visiting and who was getting the most time with Grace. Then, one sister decided to side with the husband, complicating matters.

Be all that as it may, the arguments back and forth, the "bad looks," and the snide comments were beginning to distract the nurses. Even though they wanted to take care of Grace, they were reluctant to do so because the family had arguments in the room while the patient was believed to be unconscious. I was aware of all this, but decided not to get into the middle. The charge nurse, however, requested that I meet with the husband and the parents as a group, which I did.

I listened to them for two hours while they complained about each other and finally told them I wanted to speak to them as if I was Grace. I said, "You are punishing me by the way you behave. You are my husband and you can't talk to my parents, you are my parents and you can't talk to my husband. What are you doing to me?" Then, I said I wanted to speak as Grace's advocate, "Here at the Cancer Center we allow visitation twenty-four hours a day. At other intensive care units it's five minutes every four hours. I would appreciate your cooperation with each other, Grace, and the Cancer Center."

They met separately and remained at odds with each other. I met with them and helped to set up a visiting schedule. They agreed to half-hour visits, morning, afternoon, and evening with all of them except the sister who sided with the husband. She sent a message through one of the clerks that I should "Go fly a kite." Then Grace began to improve, regaining consciousness. They rearmed, and started the battle again. The husband would be visiting, for example, and would say to Grace, "I don't want to go." Grace would tell the nurse, "I want my husband to stay all day." Then the parents would come in and the father would say, "I want to stay," and Grace would say, "I want you to stay." This went back and forth. Finally, the parents claimed the husband was permitting them to spend only about an hour a day with Grace and this made no sense to them. This motivated them and the one sister to return to Chicago.

Grace was then transferred to another floor where her husband and sister could visit whenever they wanted. The combatants gone, the war is over for the moment, peace Grace.

It Could Have Been Me. Jim was every bit of nineteen years of age when his physician diagnosed a brain tumor. The physician was concerned about informing Jim and the parents whom he felt were highly "nervous" people. The doctor shopped the family and finally picked Jim's sister, Helen, whom he felt was the most stable relative and told her the truth about Jim's tumor. Subsequently, Jim went to surgery and a week later, died.

A year after Jim's death, Helen fainted at a cocktail party. She was not hurt by the fall and was alert within seconds of reaching the floor. Nonetheless, she was taken by ambulance to the emergency room. A careful medical examination and studies by her own physician provided no evidence of a medical problem. He informed Helen of his lack of findings and attributed the incident to the August heat and alcohol on an empty stomach. Aware of the fears Helen and her family had over cancer, he reassured her that cancer was not an issue, or even a concern in this case. With this, Helen frowned, tears poured out, and she said, her voice rising to a shout, "No, no cancer?! But you didn't tell Jim either."

Custody. There was a young man I'll call Bill who had Hodgkin's disease, and, significantly, a plastic bag in his pocket. When I first met him, he was in the late stages of his chemotherapy. At that time he was a patient at the Public Health Service Hospital before the Cancer Center moved to the University of Maryland Hospital. I saw him in my private office outside the hospital. During the first session, he suddenly began to heave and pulled the plastic bag from his pocket, and threw up in it. That was that. From time to time, this would happen when he came to my office for a session. One day, he pulled out a plastic bag and vomited into it. By now I was taking this behavior for granted, seduced into feeling that everything was routine and okay. But then he started to heave again. I blurted out, "Bill, don't you have a bag?" And he said, "I only brought one." In panic, I ran out of the office into the bathroom, pulled out about twenty paper towels and put them in his lap just as he was vomiting. Needless to say, that night I stopped at the market and bought a can of Lysol and a box of plastic bags.

But there is more to this story. As airline passengers nearing our destination, we hear first, "The Captain has begun our descent into the airport. Please fasten your seat belts." Shortly thereafter comes the next familiar announcement, "We are now making our *final* approach. Please have your seat belts securely fastened, tray tables put away and seatbacks in the full upright position. Thank you." Well, Bill had completed his descent, and was now in his "final approach"—he was terminal, now limited to a wheelchair and bed.

At that time, his son was four years old. His wife came to see me one day, privately, to tell me she was going to leave him. She didn't want the little boy around his dying father. I suggested she should give this plan considerable thought before acting. Time passed, and with it his disease progressed. Then came the day I learned his wife had left Bill and they were already divorced. She was now seeking full custody to keep the little boy from having any visits whatsoever with his now rapidly deteriorating father. Meanwhile, Bill's father had retired and he and his wife were taking care of their grandchild and Bill when the child would visit.

Then—the custody case. One of the oncologists testified that Bill was indeed terminal. When I took the stand, I asked the judge if Bill and his ex-wife might leave the courtroom and not hear my testimony, as it might be viewed with despair. Her lawyer refused, but Bill's lawyer wheeled him out of the room.

Her lawyer calmly inquired if I had ever been to the patient's house. I had not. Her lawyer's tone changed immediately as he began to interrogate me, asking me had I ever met his wife. I said I had. He then asked if I had ever been to the house and observed her with the child. I said I hadn't. The lawyer persisted, "Didn't you think that she was a good mother?"

"Yes, I thought she was a good mother."

He said, "But doctor, you have not been to the house, so how can you say she's a good mother?"

I said, "I met her. She had come to me; we talked. I assume she's a good mother."

His tone became increasingly badgering as he said the ex-wife did not feel it was necessary to have the little boy spend time with a father who could not get out of bed. He asked, why should the child spend time in the patient's bed or with the patient's parents when she alone could do a better job? I said nothing up to that point. Her lawyer, his voice rising, challenged, "Well, do you have any comments about the fact that you've never been to the house to see what kind of mother she is with her little boy?"

I was annoyed. I turned to the judge and said, "Your Honor, I'm feeling quite vehement about this, and I hope you will indulge me in what I'm about to say."

The judge said, "Go on doctor."

I pled, "Frankly I do care very much for the patient and I care very much for the patient's wife. I think they are good people, but at this moment I don't give a damn about their interests. My interests and concerns are for this little boy who needs his father even though his father is dying. He needs to have some finality with his father. This is something that he would feel very guilty about in later years, if his father died and he had not been around during the terminal period. Thank you, your Honor."

Then her lawyer turned to me again, and said loudly, "Now doctor, let's get back to whether or not you had observed Mrs. Smith caring for the child."

The judge interrupted, "Counselor, sit down. Will the court social worker please come forward to the bench." She approached, and he said, "I'm giving full custody to the patient, he can determine all his visits and the length of the visits. And, I want you as the court social worker to supervise this and ensure that my order is carried out. That's it." He stood up and left.

Three weeks later Bill died.

Family Holidays. In the early '70s at the University of Maryland Cancer Center, on holidays such as Thanksgiving and Christmas, the patients would have their meals (either by mouth or by vein) in their rooms. Families, spouses, children, parents, and grandparents would come visit and then go home for their big meal. We decided that we, at the Cancer Center, would serve a community meal so families could share the meal with their relatives who were patients. With staff helping, we set out tables and converted the waiting room on Thanksgiving and Christmas. We would have the big meal, with turkey, ham and all the fixings. Patients who were able or not in isolation would come into the waiting room, pushing their IV poles. We would serve soft drinks to the children and I would provide vodka for those adults who wanted it. We would make screwdrivers or bloody Marys. And Dr. Janice Dutcher would entertain with her viola. There was a feeling of ease and family—kids spilling soda, laughter, tears. Some family or staff members would volunteer to perform. The talent was uneven, but it always was great fun and the tradition continues to this day. However, we no longer serve vodka.

Religion at its Best. Sometimes, incidents relevant to the church take place in the Cancer Center. Jerry, the patient, and his wife had both used drugs, but were now clean. Despite his former drug abuse, Jerry was approved for the use of marijuana for his nausea and vomiting. Jerry was obviously dying when I came to visit that day. His wife was in tears, and without my asking her, she said she and Jerry were both Catholics and that he wanted to take Communion. I was mildly surprised to hear there was a problem because there was a Catholic Chaplain, I think a Palatine, on the staff. Jerry said he had asked the Chaplain and received a "no" because they both had divorced and had not gotten an annulment.

I went back to my office and called one of my friends, a priest who had been at St. John's, but was now at a Catholic college in Baltimore teaching theology. I told him the problem. He grunted that this man does not "know anything about being a pastor, and moreover, doesn't know a blankety-blank thing about the Church." He said he was leaving town in about half an hour, but would have someone come to see the patient. Sure enough, within three hours there arrived a young Catholic priest who not only gave Jerry Communion, but gave it to his wife as well. He visited every day for more than a week until Jerry died. To me, this is religion at its most merciful and meaningful.

Allison and Bill, More Caring. Twenty-five-year-old Allison was a very attractive young lady, her face an ivory cameo. She had had a sarcoma in her abdomen that had been resected about eight years ago. She had done well despite an occasional crisis, another surgical procedure, and another need for an experimental antibiotic. During all this time, Allison and her boyfriend, Bill, were together, sometimes traveling, and sometimes just hanging out. Whenever Allison had a crisis, Bill would interrupt whatever he was doing and return to her side. On one occasion, some three years previously, Allison's disease came crashing back after Bill had left to do a year's work in Spain. He had been away a month when he heard that there was a crisis with

144

Allison. He gave up his trip and returned to help with nursing Allison. This was normal for Bill; he did not object to it. When Allison was confined to the hospital, he would interrupt his work to stay in nearby Hope Lodge so he could be nearby.

Then, another crisis hit. Allison was to have serious surgery to have rods placed in her back. Bill was about to do some archaeological research, but again gave that up to be with Allison. Allison's mother and father were divorced; the father and brother lived together. Her mother was remarried and living some distance away. According to Bill, Allison's mother had never been easily available to her. Interestingly enough, Allison never offered any complaint against her mother.

The nurses were upset because Allison told them, and me, that her mother was not going to come down prior to this serious surgery. Apparently, her mother felt Allison would be in and out of anesthesia and it would take a week or so before they could talk. Allison said she thought that "was a good idea," but a few of the nurses did not agree and were personally annoyed. When it was time for the surgery, the surgeon had his nurse repeatedly call for Allison to come to surgery, that he was ready for her. But Allison's nurse refused, telling the surgeon's nurse, "Not until somebody comes to say good-bye to Allison," in case she died during surgery. Bill was en route to the hospital from Spain, and subsequently, her father and brother came in, breathless, and only then did the nurse release Allison to the surgeon.

Time went by, Allison began to deteriorate rather rapidly. The question was whether to continue another experimental therapy in the hospital or go home. Allison decided she would not continue therapy, but go with Bill, who lived in Pittsburgh. One of Bill's three sisters was an oncology nurse, and the three sisters would take care of Allison during the day and Bill would care for her at night. Meanwhile, he had gotten work at an investment house in Pittsburgh. Allison's nurses were happy that she was going to stay with Bill's sisters. Allison believed that she would get her strength back so she could join her mother. For two months, Bill and his sisters took care of Allison and nursed her. Although she was bed-ridden, they would move her outside to sit in the sun.

Allison died two weeks later. Bill awakened at 4:30 in the morning, changed her diaper, as he did most nights, kissed her goodnight, and laid down on a cot in their room. At six o'clock his sister came in the room, woke him up, and whispered that Allison was dead. Bill was quietly upset and tearful, but then the sister said to Bill, "I have something to tell you. I went to the doctor yesterday and he told me I was pregnant." The sister and her husband had tried desperately for eight years, even trying *in vitro*-fertilization, and they had been unable to get pregnant. One of the nurses suggested "a transfer of souls." Who knows?

Allison left some money in her will so Bill could deliver her ashes to Big Sur.

Sadly, two years later, Bill, having lost his "job" of caring for Allison, was still floundering, not an uncommon event for people who dedicate all their time and energy to the patient without interruption for years. The death precipitates a great force of unpreparedness, leaving the caregiver lost, empty, and without ideas or motivation as to what to do.

Marriages are Made in Heaven? Not All. "Do I really give the bride away? How do I do it?" The perplexed young doctor fearfully asked the group. Well, here's the explanation for the doctor's apprehension. But first some background.

It is not rare that there are patients who, aware they are terminal, decide to marry their long-term partners. So it was with Gregory, a feisty, sixty-year-old machinist. His lifestyle fit his rugged, no nonsense, commanding personality. Calli and Gregory had known each other for twenty-five years, living together for twenty. They had never talked about marriage; Gregory made sure of that.

Now he was in the ICU, and knew he was dying, getting weaker, losing weight, and impatiently awaiting relief by death. "I want to marry Calli," he said, abruptly interrupting our usual dialogue one day. "I'm not a minister," I said in a smart-alecky tone, thinking I was responding in kind. "No, I'm serious," he said. "By us getting married she gets my pension and Social Security." I agreed that the idea sounded good. Soon, the nurses and staff were involved, eager and excited. There were cakes to be baked, punch and decorations to be made, and other details to see to.

After discussions with Greg and Calli, it was decided that I would seek the services of a minister friend of mine. I would have the honor of being the best man, and Calli wanted the young doctor attending Greg to be at her side.

Soon it was the wedding day, adrenaline flowing everywhere, patients, staff, and visitors, but, unfortunately, no known relatives. The waiting area was decorated as if for the Mardi Gras, people stumbling over each other. Calli was prettier than ever, wearing everyday clothes, a veil fashioned by the nurses and in her pocket the marriage license.

146

But, as it inevitably happens at the last minute at weddings, a problem arose. The young doctor did not own a jacket. (Most researchers disdain semi-formal attire. They wear jeans and short-sleeve shirts while in their laboratories.) But it was no big deal, he could wear one of Greg's. The doctor was slightly built, weighing about 115 pounds; Greg, once weighed 270. The doctor seemed to be hidden in Greg's jacket; sleeves hovering over his knees.

The minister was poised, ready to officiate. Greg insisted on standing, with me at his side, holding him by the back of his belt while he leaned against another doctor braced at his back. He was beaming, his beard glistening, his eyes now surprisingly bright, his posture proud.

The minister was moving right along, having been informed of Greg's physical limitations. When he asked, "Who gives this woman to this man?" The young doctor panicked, "Do I really give the bride away? How do I do it?" A hurried conference was in order, you see, the young doctor was a Muslim, born in the Middle East. "Giving away the bride" obviously had serious connotations to him. He was reassured, "Just put her hand in Greg's." He did. The marriage done, Greg and Calli lived happily ever after. For a blessed, short, time.

Quality of Life:
Always a Personal Decision

At Death's Door. It is difficult, if not impossible to have *emotional* awareness that one is indeed in a terminal phase and soon will be dead. Some dying patients can verbalize they are dying, but this is an intellectual process, a defense in the service of denial.

What does it *feel* like to be dying? To be, *literally*, at death's door? There are and have been many moving personal accounts of dying that have been written and are on film. If one listens carefully, however, it soon becomes evident that the verbalizations are clearly intellectualizations.

The state of death is impossible to conceptualize, and the thought of dying terrifies. Since "being dead" cannot even be imagined, a void evolves only to be filled with superstitions, fantasies, and poetic creations. In 1915, Sigmund Freud wrote of our need to deny the possibility of our own death. Although we insist that death is a necessary outcome of life, that we all must die, it usually is thought of in terms of others dying. (Our own state of death is indeed unimaginable, and whenever we make the attempt to imagine it, we find that we really survive as observing spectators.)

Death, as a general topic, had surfaced several times spontaneously in my talks with Tony. I asked Tony if we could talk specifically about the feelings of dying. He agreed.

A thirty-year-old man, Tony was imminently dying of myelocytic leukemia. At this point, he had refused further chemotherapy treatment, including supportive transfusions. His only request was that his infections and his pain be treated in an effort to sustain his physical comfort. At the very end, in his wife's presence, he could barely talk in a whisper as he had severe mucositis in his mouth and throat. Whenever he did speak, it was with shortness of breath, hoarseness, and great difficulty, all of which was obvious to the listener.

I asked what it *felt* like to be dying and he had difficulty expressing himself.

I asked if he accepted the fact that he had just a short time to go. He answered, "Yes, I have. We've been considering my options—whether to receive more treatments. There is a happier, easier way for me to go. I'll be over with this damn disease, and the way things are going, I wouldn't have been happy anyway. They wouldn't have been able to help me again. I'm not afraid to die. Everybody dies—everybody gets born. It's not that bad—so everybody dies so it can't be that bad either." Tony talked about how he had hoped to see his little boy at least through the next several months prior to Christmas. But he felt his quality of life was really over and that wish "will have to go by the board." He was convinced that no medicines could help him, and with a great deal of "soul searching, I know I'm going to die."

He did not want to take narcotics to end it. With his background as a respiratory therapist, he knew that he would probably die from the lack of platelets, bleed, and that it probably would be quick. Besides, he wouldn't take drugs because the narcotics made him hallucinate, and he wanted to be alert. His wife, a licensed practical nurse, was in agreement with Tony's decision. She shared in this; they both felt that the illness had brought them closer together. She appreciated that the staff had been especially supportive.

I asked Tony when he thought he would die. He said that he would probably die over the weekend, which would be over the next four days. I asked him rather firmly, "But what do you *feel*? Do you *feel* like you are dying, Tony?"

Tony's reply: "I feel that I'm ready."

I then said, "That you're ready? It just seems to me Tony, that one has a great deal of difficulty putting into words, defining what one *feels* that one is dying."

His answer had to do with his lack of quality of life as he dealt with "all these IV's, chemotherapy, sepsis, and wishing to die quickly or that a remission would be able to come!" I also asked about what he felt about life after death, to which he responded, "I am reserving judgment for that until the time comes." Then, with an apology from me for pressing him to describe what it was feeling like to be dying, he said, "All I know is that I have leukemia and I'm going die."

Tony did not make it through the next four days. His body, as he had wished, without platelets, precipitated a gastrointestinal hemorrhage, and he died, very quickly. His wife, Susan, was with him.

I am not passing judgment on the fact that Tony had difficulty conveying what it feels like to die. None of us are capable of doing so. We all practice intellectualizations even when we protest that we are "expressing feelings!" Psychologically, this inability spares us the torment of the unknown. Some sidestep any concern with the unknown by anticipating a continuation of life through transmigration of the soul or belief in a hereafter in the kingdom of God. Use of denial as a defense can equate with hope for those with life-threatening illnesses. This defense permits individuals to subject themselves helplessly to humiliating, but necessary, therapeutic procedures.

La Rochefoucauld stated the problem succinctly, "Neither the sun nor death can be looked at steadily."

Life: Five Patients
"Profiles in Courage"

It happens to all of us. Our quality of life waxes and wanes. So it goes. Fortunate are those of us who can tell when it is no longer waxing, but rather that it is inexorably waning. Enough.

A Final Decision. The first patient was a brilliant scientist who knew all aspects of his disease, "my cancer." He knew what to do about it and what his prognosis was. With his physician he discussed how he might end his life should "that time come that I can not move to go to the bathroom, that I have to be turned. At that time I choose to be dead." As a scientist, he knew what medications he would need to end his life. When he was indeed terminal, he discussed his plan with his wife. As he grew even more dependent and finally totally bedridden and in severe pain, his wife said to him, "You know what to do. It's your decision." To which he replied, "I'll wait another day." That night he died peacefully.

Not Me. The second patient was a prominent businessman who was paralyzed from the waist down as a result of a rare neurological disease. He was able to have a very productive life running his business from his wheelchair. He, too, was very bright and knew what to do to end his life when it became unbearable. He discussed this with his doctor, his wife, and his children. He felt the quality of his life decrease day by day. Finally, he shared a warm and tender "good night" with his family, and the next morning he was dead, and peacefully so. He was not going "to let anybody but me decide when I'm going to die and how I'm going to die."

Requiem. The third story is about a bright author. As his disease advanced, he became increasingly bedridden. He told his doctors and his wife that he was considering overdosing with a sedative. I was one of the doctors he told.

151

I simply listened. One day, his oncologist called me to say the wife knew her husband was talking suicide, and while she was very sympathetic to his feeling, she did not want to be a part of it in any way.

I visited the author several times at his home. On one occasion, he commented that he might soon undertake the task of dying since he was now totally confined to bed. He said he must do it before he lost all of his strength. At that point, I suggested to him that if he was losing all of his strength, he might be passing into coma, and he might wait a few days to see what would happen.

The next day, however, I received a call from a state trooper who informed me that the patient had committed suicide. I asked how he knew that. He replied, "The wife had called 911." When the paramedics came, they could not resuscitate her husband. There had been a bottle of 100 pills and now there was only about forty. I told the trooper that, yes, the patient had discussed suicide with me, but the patient was aware that suicide could sometimes leave skeletons in other people's closets. Therefore, the patient had told me he did not want his family to consider his death a suicide, but rather that he had died of natural causes. I suggested that the state trooper talk to the patient's oncologist.

This man was bedridden, indeed would have died momentarily. Perhaps his overdosing, if he did overdose, was unintentional. Perhaps he had taken several of the sedatives to sleep and then groggily taken more and more. That this is not an unusual way of "accidentally" committing suicide.

Requiem.

Mission Accomplished? "Dottie, why?" I asked, sounding more pleading than demanding, knowing full well "why" while trying to deny what I knew. She had a loving husband, two twin beautiful daughters, carbon copies of their mother. Dottie, barely in her fifties, had a prestigious position with the government. So why, with those incentives to live, had she swallowed seventy narcotic pain pills in an effort to end her life? Now here she was, Dottie, the lovely red-head, her stark white face now pallor, lying there, her face blending with the white sheets, projecting an image of some kind of saintly icon.

"You know why!" She shouted, that pale face contorted with rage. I cringed, feeling guilty and deserving the bitterness of her tone.

"What kind of quality of life is this?! I've got a belly full of cancer. Treatment is of no help. I'm a burden to my family, most of all to me. I can't do anything right! I took the whole bottle, seventy pain pills, and all I accomplished was to sleep for two days, and I still hurt. Tell me, why didn't it work? Why?!"

Should I tell her? I struggled for an answer. Would it help her to know? Would it help her to succeed next time? Dottie and I had shared an honest, up-front relationship for two years, and I wasn't about to change now. Anyway, I assured myself that she was at the stage of her illness, close to succumbing to the ending demanded by her disease; making moot, irrelevant, any answer I might give her.

"Dottie, you were taking forty pain pills a day, a very large dose, but that was and is, necessary and appropriate. But you have been taking them for so long that your body has built up a tolerance to the drugs. So, taking thirty more only put you to sleep for two days."

She stared at me without blinking as I offered the answer to her question. Her silence caused me to wonder whether she was absorbing any of what I had said, or what planet she might be visiting. Two weeks later, Dottie brought an end to my wondering.

Somehow, she had managed to obtain pain-killers not related chemically to what she had been taking. This time, Dottie's determination to end her suffering in a manner of her own time and choice, was successful.

Peace

(This story reflects a composite of patients who, lacking medical sophistication, have tried unsuccessfully to put an end to their suffering. Many are motivated by their need to retain control of their bodies, their identities and their destinies—no matter what.)

Color Me Red. Red socks and I go back for many years. I wear red socks all the time. So what's the big deal about red socks? I'll tell you.

Louise, in her late fifties, had relapsed after eight years of being on semi-equal terms with breast cancer. After a period of investigative chemotherapy covering the past two years, she asked, through her husband, to have a "serious talk" with me.

Louise had been a bright, energetic, outgoing person who was not one to look around bleak corners with rose-colored glasses. We met at her house, she lying on one bed, her husband on a chair adjacent, and me opposite her sitting on the edge of the other bed, facing her. "I've had it with this crap and

I want out."

"Louise, we've been here before," I reminded her. "We discussed your decision possibilities two years ago."

"I know, but the new drug came out, and I wanted to give it a shot. But it's now two years and look at me. No hair, my belly is swollen out to there. I'm in torture. I get no relief from pain. I'm bedridden, a pain in the ass to everyone, and, and—*why the hell are you wearing a pink shirt with red socks?!*"

"Well Louise," I smiled, "there's no problem with your competency."

There was more discussion, a litany on her quality of life rushing down hill. We decided to postpone any further decisions until the next day. I kissed her good night and left her house at six o'clock. Louise died quietly and peacefully at 8:30 that night.

Ashes to Ashes?

"How do I die?" Please tell me how," the patient said, his voice flat as he plopped into a chair. A not unusual query posed by the now resigned patient burdened with cancer. It was not the frequent question about odds for survival, but rather a yearning for a *how* to die. My answer is not a hedge, but a simple, "I've never died, so I don't know how. But perhaps I can help you in the preparation for *after* dying." Easy, yes? For some it is. For others there is a superstitious fear that planning for death will shortly precipitate it.

A plan can be determined via progressive questions like this: Do you have a will? Do you want to be buried, cremated, or donated for organs? If the latter, have a document prepared, and inform your doctor. If you wish to be buried, you will need a burial plot in a cemetery, or other place of your choice. If you do not have a place, get one now as your family will be at a serious economic disadvantage as they seek to carry out your wishes while overwhelmed by emotion. If you desire to be cremated, where do you want your ashes to find their final resting place? In either case—burial or cremation—would you like a religious service? If so, how large, private or public, what prayers would you like, will there be a eulogy, and who will give it? Are there any thoughts, wishes or desires for other activities, a special ceremony, or a party?

Finally, write down your wishes and keep your family informed of any changes. Having done all this, one is *ready* to die. All of this should have been done early on, when one was young and healthy, when one's mind was unencumbered and available to make decisions clearly. A caveat. Do not put your wishes in your will. The will is read after one is finally laid to rest. Heed the unwitting mistake made by the man who noted in his will that he wanted to be cremated. His wife, was aware of his will, but preferred her husband be buried. She made it clear to everyone that the contents of the will would remain sealed until much later, after the burial. It was. Other family members, however, took their protest to the courts. The court decreed that the husband's wish be honored, so his body was exhumed and cremated. Where his ashes eventually ended up, I know not.

The ashes of a loved one are just that—the loved one is still the loved one. There are those who keep the ashes in a special, honored place in the home, not letting go of the love or the reverence for the dead. Others prefer the permanence of a crypt in a mausoleum. The design and style of the container or urn reflects the person's and/or family's emotional investment. Some people bury the ashes in or near their home and plant a tree to be nourished by the ashes so a living entity comes forth. The destiny of the ashes is determined and limited only by the degree of the bond and the creativity of the survivors.

There are times when the emotional force of the survivors' relationship with the loved one can pull the ashes in different directions, at times with great heat and acrimony, and fortunately, at other times with amenable compromise.

Steve and Vicky had married young, too young, too beautiful, too soon for Steve to succumb to the onslaught of his brain cancer. The marriage was hardly beyond their Elysium courtship phase, a phase shattered by the busy demands of the illness and its adversary, chemotherapy, radiotherapy, and the "normal" complications of the latter—hair loss, weight loss, nausea. Nonetheless, they found time to love and communicate with each other. It was in this context, and during a tender moment carefully chosen by Vicky, that she asked Steve what his wishes were.

"Cremated," was Steve's immediate response.

"And, what about your ashes, Steve?"

"Put them in a garbage can! I don't want you spending any money on a damn urn!"

Steve was serious, but Vicky quietly was thinking otherwise. Vicky held the plastic bag of ashes, noting the whitish color and soft feel. "So small an amount for Steve. Steve was big, over six feet tall," pondered Vicky aloud.

What container to use? Steve had been adamant—"No urn!" Anyway, to Vicky an urn would be without warmth, and Steve's ashes deserved something more meaningful, something that could speak to their love. Vicky emptied Steve's teakwood box, her gift to him last Christmas. It was dark in color, strong and smooth to the touch. Steve had used it for his collection of trinkets, cufflinks, and coins. "Lovely," mused Vicky as she poured Steve's ashes into the box. Soon the box was full and overflowing, spreading all over the table and even to the carpet. She gently gathered the overflow, tenderly, with her tears to water them, buried the overflow ashes under the azalea bushes outside their house.

Steve's mother, a traditionalist, wanted his ashes buried in a cemetery near her. Vicky wanted them near her—as close as the azaleas. In her heart, however, she knew that she, and surely Steve, would really want them scattered from the top of "their" waterfall, the one in the campsite where they had shared so many times when their life was blissful and uncomplicated. But Vicky held up her needs against those of her mother-in-law, and decided the latter's were more important and greater. So Steve's mother buried the ashes near her cemetery plot.

Fourteen years later, when Vicky was moving to a new house she was building, Vicky found herself in a quandary. She debated with herself, should she shovel some of the ground from under the azalea bushes and take it to her new home? A repeat of burying Steve's ashes? With tears cascading down her cheeks, she let go of Steve's ashes, but not Steve.

There are those who designate their ashes to rest at a place that recalls a warm, quiet, peaceful time, such as Allison, who wanted her ashes to be spread at Big Sur. Others have chosen places for a past meaningful experience, the Greek Isles, Mt. Washington, or the family farm. And, there are those who have sought to have their ashes buried at a favorite baseball park, and some Damon Runyons even elect the finish line at a cherished racetrack. Some ashes are handed down from generation to generation. Some, unfortunately, end as unremembered, unidentifiable ashes.

That would never happen to Bert's ashes, no way, not so with Trudy, his wife, around. Bert was a dedicated scientist, Trudy a dedicated nurse, and each was devoted to the other. They worked hard at their individual careers, yet found time for each other. They had no children, but they played together as children, romping joyously in the outdoors, traveling, climbing, hiking, skiing, swimming, flying—vigorously embracing life.

In time, they discovered their own little territory, a tiny beach edging its

156

way between two farms, hugging the Chesapeake Bay. Whenever they could, they would steal away to picnic and swim in their own private Shangri-La. Sadly, trouble thundered into their paradise: Cancer struck Bert. As always, they fought his illness together, each treatment, each complication was met and dealt with head-on. As with all their past trips and challenges, which eventually came to an end, mercifully, the cacophony of painful symptoms orchestrated by his disease came to a quiet end. Bert's journey was over.

It was no surprise that Bert wanted his ashes to be spread on the Chesapeake Bay near their secret beach by his beloved Trudy. In time, Trudy took Bert's ashes in a plastic bag, a picnic basket, and her girlfriend, Marge, and went to do Bert's bidding. Arriving early in the morning, they were greeted by a rainbow in the light mist; it had rained during the night. It was an appropriate a send-off for a man who had been a lifetime partner with nature, and who had labored in the science of the stars, the planets, and the heavens.

Trudy and Marge sat and reminisced about Bert, competing with each other to remember another poignant or funny memory of Bert. They laughed, they cried, and then they picnicked. Soon, the sun appeared, inhaling the mist. It was time.

Holding the bag with Bert's ashes, Trudy swam out into the bay, kissed the bag and emptied it into the current. Turning back to the shore, she approached the beach. As she slowly rose out of the water, Marge exclaimed, "Trudy, look at you!" Trudy looked down and there were Bert's ashes lying snugly in her bra and bikini pants. Laughing and crying as she turned to swim back out, to shed her suit and return Bert's ashes to the bay's warmth, his eternal home, said to her friend, "That's Bert. He's not ready to leave, and he knows just where he wants to be."

Princess

Her pale, round face, her so smooth, so shiny, bald head, her closed eyes covered by puffy, reddened lids, ever so still and artfully framed within the white pillow. Lying there, the constellation presented a lifelike picture startlingly reminiscent of Gower's portrait of the virgin queen, Elizabeth I.

Annie couldn't be any sicker; a little more, and she would be dead. Even so she was nearly there—in and out of awareness. Lying there, barely visible, she was swallowed by her bed of pillows—an effort to soften the pain in her every muscle, her every bone; morphine only nibbling at the edge of her pain. Her belly was so swollen it seemed to paint her as wide as she was tall. Her round head showed green and yellow, like a ripe honeydew melon, advertising her blood disease. Lying there, she was so innocent, so still, perhaps she was dreaming of good times past or future, maybe; the present—ever present, cloying and obscene.

It had been almost two years ago to the day since we met. A frightened, petite twenty-two-year-old woman, appearing barely twelve years young. A waif of a girl, a porcelain doll, Raggedy-Ann eyes sunken into a pale white face, her hands and fingers gloved in transparent white skin, weighing almost ninety pounds. It was at the Cancer Center admissions desk; I was hanging out. Annie was being admitted for treatment of her newly diagnosed leukemia. Hovering were her anxious parents, offering reassurances that neither she nor her parents believed.

Trying not to sound cheerful, I attempted conversation. "You're pretty. What happened? Where's home? School?" After a kind of Mona Lisa smile, her answers came in whispers: frequent large bruises, an apartment in a neighboring county, community college, English major, likes to read and loves her ten cats. She happily displayed photo albums of their antics.

Soon, Annie embarked on her two-year career to rid herself of her leukemia, intensive therapy her weapon. There was chemo, along with its "normal" complications. In-patient, outpatient, in the hospital, out of the hospital, in her apartment, in her parents' home when too sick, too weak, brief, giddy sojourns back in her apartment. Welcome, happy remissions, shocking, unwanted relapses. Her mother took leave from her job, and was constantly at Annie's side, achieving a sophisticated ability to master the vast and complicated bedside machinery as well as subtleties of nursing. Bathing, comforting, feeding, slowly administering antibiotics through a syringe into Annie's mouth, even on hands and knees, scrubbing her room—could she be the mother of all mothers? Father, befuddled, was in the background, frightened, awkwardly offering support. Annie had no siblings.

As time went on, Annie and I became fast friends. Now answering to "Princess," she—in the better times—would reward me with a smile of greeting. She was—in the better times—an avid reader. She was going to go to college and one day she would teach, be an English professor.

The axe fell. Annie slipped into her third relapse. But there was no panic. Neither Annie, her parents, nor the staff perceived this as the end, rather as an obstacle. She was a possible candidate for stem cell transplant therapy, and Annie and her parents decided to go for it. Like chemotherapy, stem cell transplant has "normal" complications, not unlike those of chemotherapy, but with a "graft versus host" reaction added. The transplant was successful and Annie was in remission, leukemia-free. After several months, however, her body, the host for her stem cell transplant, began to resent the graft and they battled, not gently, but with intensity. She suffered persistent itching and rashes, her skin turned yellow, her kidneys, preferring to sleep, were now reluctant to manufacture urine, her muscles and bones moved from sore to painful, diarrhea: She was lost in a plastic jungle of IVs. Enough. To continue to describe the scene is personally too painful.

Daily communication between us had become uneven. At times she would give me a faint smile of recognition. At times as I would "wish you better," she might or might not move her head or fingers. As she slept, which was most of the time, she evoked a picture of a tiny child, her full face at peace, the tips of her frail white fingers peering out over her Linus quilt. Daily, I offered her the date, time, morning or afternoon, and hoped she was hearing me.

One day, as I met with Annie's parents outside her room, they, in a tired voice conveying sadness, that this roller coaster ride could end. Mother was concerned that Annie might be "giving up." I demurred. It just seemed that way—what does happen is that a patient, overwhelmed with tiredness, becomes exhausted from the long, painful, humiliating, hard battle, devoid of quality of life, and finally the body cries out, "Enough!"

Treading on the bridge of our relationship, I gently asked if they had any thoughts should a worst-case scenario occur. Mother quickly responded that Annie had stated her wishes very clearly and adamantly at the time of this last relapse. Under no condition was her room at home to become an altar. Every possession was to be distributed to her friends according to their preferences. Nothing was to be kept; not clothing, books, dolls.

Her mother continued. When Annie was a pre-teen, she loved to play in the back yard of their house. It was her own special world, free for her to fantasize pleasant experiences to her heart's content. Annie would often lean against her precious tree to rest and dream. There, too, would rest her ashes.

Most of us are not prepared to die. No will, no decision about burial or cremation, no spoken or written wishes. Annie, the Princess, the little porcelain doll, so unlike the rest of us, was ready to die. And now, suddenly overwhelmed by the abrupt, rapid, and relentless force and fury of the disease and its ramifications, dear little Annie no longer had the strength to battle back. Unlike those of her beloved cats, the nine lives of the Princess finally ran out.

Peace.

VI.

DOCTORS:
R A. COWLEY AND MORE

Introduction

Where there are patients, there must be doctors. A few doctors are greater than other doctors, some are as good as others, and there are few that are not as good as others. No matter their skill level, doctors must cope with their omnipotence in the face of dire threats to same.

Having said this, I take time to single out Dr. R Adams Cowley, the creator of the Shock Trauma concept and its banner, "the golden hour." Dr. Cowley, after much research, was convinced that when an individual suffers multiple body injuries from an accident of any kind, including stabbing and shooting, there exists only a *one-hour* window before fatal shock takes over. The Shock Trauma hospital he designed in Baltimore addressed this emergency, utilizing helicopters and ambulances and a hospital hierarchy of levels of urgency to expedite the saving of lives. Today there are such facilities throughout the world—recognition of *his* omnipotence. More can be found about the concept and Dr. Cowley's struggles to bring his ideas to fruition in the book, *Shock Trauma* (Jon Franklin and Alan Doelp, St. Martin's Press, 1980).

Dr. R Adams Cowley could well be a metaphor for the revered doctor. He manifested the professional skill, the omnipotence, and the clay feet of an ordinary human being. Here, we get only a brief glimpse of R A., the unforgettable person, as well as an opportunity to look at doctors as doctors. To accomplish this, our vehicle includes stories, ideas, reports, and an occasional essay.

R A. Cowley
and
Shock Trauma

R A.: Shock Trauma. R A., Shock Trauma, MIEMSS, Maryland Institute for Emergency Medical Services System; they are synonyms—just different ways of saying R Adams Cowley. (No. The lack of a period after the R is not a mistake. His name was R, just that, R.)

"When are you coming up to Shock Trauma?" nagged R A. just about every Saturday at our shared breakfast in the hospital cafeteria. "I'm a shrink," would be my stock response, "I can't talk with dead or unconscious patients." This was 1969 and Saturdays were psychiatry seminar times for me with the residents. His rationale for bugging me emanated from our contact during my early experience with surgery and surgeons.

One day after the seminar I wandered into the twelve-bed unit for a begrudging two-minute look. Patients unconscious, machines buzzing, lights flashing, gowned and capped doctors and nurses, tension heavy—organized chaos. After several hours in the area, I sought out R A. "I'm hooked. This place is a psychological gold mine, the patients maybe, but for sure, the staff and *you!*"

Yes, the patients were generous in their availability for fascinating, meaningful, and emotional stories, as well as for research. The excitement for me, however, was my relationship with R A., *the most unforgettable character of my life.*

A quote from the book, *Shock Trauma,* is attributed to me, "Cowley is a mold of contradictions. He's a genius, but he's *stupid.* He is very sophisticated, but he's a little boy. He's warm and generous, and he's a bastard. He's a nice guy and he's a pain the ass. And he is a very lonely man."

If the young doctors demeaned or were critical of the nurses, they would suffer his wrath. There were occasions when an emotionally upset Fellow would call me late at night to complain that Dr. Cowley had fired him over the telephone. As I was chief of the Psychosocial Service, staff would turn to me to serve as a buffer in their dealings with R A. I would reassure the doctor and tell him to meet me at Dr. Cowley's office in the morning. In the morning, I would give R A. hell for firing the Fellow over the phone. I would bring in the doctor, and I would instruct R A. to tell him, "Don't do it again or your ass is out of here!" R A. could never remember why he had fired the doctor, only "something about the nurses" justified the dismissal. And, of course, the pattern would repeat. R A. had selective memory.

There were times when he would disagree vehemently with head nurse Liz Scanlon (his right-hand person from the beginning), and me about policy matters. Usually, it was Liz and I on one side of the issue, and he on the other. Frustrated, he would show his anger by sarcastically calling Liz "Ms. Scanlon" and me "*doctor*," instead of Nate. Typically, about 10 p.m. he would suddenly and without a word. leave. Around midnight would come a phone call, "I called Liz, you're both wrong, but I'll do it your way!" Predictable.

When a staff member of any level would experience a loss of any kind, or a disappointment, he would be very tender and sympathetic. Many times, he personally intervened to help that person. Sure, his "ego" was huge. He cringed and was dejected every time he lost a battle with the administration. He was hurt and coped by roundly cursing the offenders. What follows, however, is a personal anecdote that reflects how his "ego" could be contained.

I was planning a trip on a small ship and wanted to borrow a set of surgical operating room "scrubs" to use as pajamas when sleeping on deck. I approached his administrator, Mr. John Murphy, who worked just across the hall from R A. I asked him for a set of scrubs, and in short order they were in my hands. On a lark, I suggested to Mr. Murphy that I would like "*R A. Cowley*" stenciled on the seat of the pants. "I can't do that, Dr. Schnaper!" Mr. Murphy protested. I continued to ask, but to no avail. Finally, I walked across the hall and told R A. that John had obtained scrubs for me, and that I wanted "*R A. Cowley*" stenciled on the seat of the pants. "Okay," R A. said. "But John won't do it," I said. At that, R A. shouted across the hall, "John, stencil my name on the seat of the pants for Dr. Schnaper!" I smiled smugly to Mr. Murphy, who pleaded, "Please, Dr. Schnaper, anything but that. I'll be out on Greene Street selling apples."

Since then, I have asked much of John Murphy, who is still with MIEMSS, and he has never refused me. In January 1999, the new MIEMMS building was designated the "John M. Murphy MIEMMS Building." A sweet and deserving guy.

I spent five active years with Shock Trauma, and have continued less actively through the present. In time, Dr. Cowley died and was buried in Arlington National Cemetery with full military salutes and honors. As the procession made its solemn journey to Arlington Cemetery, it passed under many overpasses and through small towns. At each overpass or town, fire trucks and ambulances with their staffs honored R A. by standing at full attention and saluting. It was my singular privilege and honor to be a pallbearer. I am grateful for the time we spent together, R Adams Cowley was, and still is, the most unforgettable person I have known. I still miss and love him.

A Case of Mistaken Identity: His/Her. Most cats have at least one life, some nine, but longevity is not an issue in this case. This cat suffered non-life-threatening indignity while innocently inflicting embarrassment to a person of some prominence. Here's the story.

Spotty was a cute six-week-old kitten, a product of a chance encounter by his mother in some unnamed alley. He was a gift from my mother-in-law, who opined that the kids "needed a pet." (For the next fourteen years, she complained about the necessity of having an "animal in the house." But that's another story.) Several months later, a visiting friend, a cat authority, informed me that this cat was a male and could "spray," a discomfiting, malodorous event. My friend's counsel was to have Spotty neutered and soon.

Dr. George Yeager was a well-known academic surgeon and a friend. During a chat with him, I mentioned Spotty and our problem. Professor Yeager was, at the time, responsible for the animal experimental operating rooms, where new surgical procedures were tested and honed before they were performed on humans. The operating rooms were sterile, and surgery was performed under the same standards as those in the hospital. The animals were treated humanely; many became pets of the staff after recovery. These procedures continue today and are even more stringent.

Dr. Yeager suggested I take Spotty to the animal operating room and he would alert the technician in charge. Spotty would have a simple five-minute procedure. Sure, the task would take only five minutes, but the technician informed me the animal laboratory rules dictated that Spotty must stay in "recovery" for three days. Fine, okay. Three days later, I returned to take

Spotty home. "No way," said the man, exhibiting considerable discomfort, "Spotty has had major surgery and must stay a full ten days and receive penicillin." He walked me to Spotty's room and there he was, countenance doleful, belly shaved from chest to his bottom, with stitches everywhere. "What happened?" I shouted, not hiding my annoyance. The man, with some hesitation, related that Spotty was in surgery and, "after an hour had passed, I looked in the room, and there was Dr. Cowley and the whole team; surgical assistants, anesthetists and everybody, working on your cat. I called to Dr. Cowley and asked, 'What are you doing to Dr. Schnaper's cat?' Dr. Cowley said, 'We're looking for the ovaries.' I said, 'Oh, my. Dr. Schnaper's cat is not a female.' That's it, and now he has to stay ten more days. Laboratory rules."

The focus of the embarrassment alluded to earlier in this story is Dr. Cowley. At the time of Spotty's surgery, he was perfecting cardiac surgical techniques on dogs. Working with Dr. Cowley during those early years in Shock Trauma, I took mischievous pleasure in reminding him of Spotty as often as I could. His response? A growl.

Is This Child Salvageable? Crisis was the usual and customary ambience in Shock Trauma. Patients arrived by ambulance or helicopter. The ticket of admission was that the individual had been shot, stabbed, in an auto crash, in a common or unusual accident—and had multiple injuries.

Once a patient arrived, it became the responsibility of the staff to vigorously ensure his or her survival. This required knowledgeable, urgent, and intensive activity on the part of the staff members who worked in teams. On this particular day, Jason Sedda was the team captain; and, indeed, a dedicated doctor he was.

It was six o'clock one morning when a 2½-year-old, unconscious, beautiful child landed in the unit. Jason and his team were ready. They surrounded the table bearing this tiny, crumpled, doll-like boy. Tragically, and lamentably, the ground had met his fall from the window with great force. The boy must have been half-asleep, confusing his destination, and had wandered in the wrong direction.

The room was silent except for Jason's quiet commands, "A cut-down now," "Tilt to the left," etc. His orders were few; there was no need to elaborate as the team was experienced. It seemed as if Jason was conducting some talented orchestra. Time was rapidly being exhausted. Dr. Cowley came in, observed the action for a few minutes, looked at me, and asked,

"How long have they been working?" I looked at the clock, "An hour and eighteen minutes." Dr. Cowley leaned over the huddled team and quietly asked, "Is this child salvageable?"

Except for Jason, the team moved away, leaving this soft little bundle, so small in comparison—like a football lost on a football field. The child, the table, and Jason were almost a portrait. He continued, working intensely, head down, oblivious of the world. After several minutes, Dr. Cowley put his hand on Jason's shoulder and asked, "Is this child salvageable?" Jason looked up, saw that he and the child were alone, and put down his instruments. His head down and his shoulders sagging, he went slowly to the waiting area in a futile attempt to console the parents. Returning tearfully to the unit, he bitterly questioned his choice of profession.

The epilogue: This doctor went on to become a most talented, well-known, highly respected, cardiac surgeon—always caring and loved by his patients. Many well-known doctors are products of Shock Trauma training.

It seems that those doctors who are dedicated to mastering death are the ones who really are approaching omnipotence. These are the people, the health care professionals, who choose to go into such specialties as shock trauma, which treats the most desperate near fatalities. Also included in this group of doctors are those who seek a career in a field such as oncology, where life's odds are against them. These are the two medical specialties that are most challenging—the doctors and nurses who are attempting to reverse an ominous outcome. Neurosurgery, of course, is well known to be challenging, as is cardiac surgery and transplant surgery, but as a rule those doctors do not *begin* with a person who is headed for dire consequences.

The Shock Trauma Patient

Going Up? Or Going Down? "I thought I was being sold into white slavery. This is ridiculous, I'm too old." This was the frightened and breathless conviction of a severely physically traumatized forty-year-old widow, Anna. She had been admitted, unconscious, to Shock Trauma via helicopter after she drove over an embankment. She had suffered life-threatening injuries to many body areas and functions.

It is not unusual for patients who have suffered severe multiple injuries and unconsciousness to report similar surprising, near unbelievable experiences. Unconsciousness is a void, an empty space in our waking lives. As nature abhors a vacuum, so do our minds reject a mental void. We dream to fill our sleep time, and so do those who have been unconscious. As with dreams, thoughts, ideas, and pictures fill the void *retrospectively* when patients awaken, usually with considerable embellishment and revision.

Anna, herself a bright nurse, had been working overtime on the fateful day of her accident. Anna was not without exposure to previous clichéd slings and arrows of fate. She had a childless marriage of twelve years when any hope for children was suddenly thrust into oblivion by a faulty airplane part. Her husband was the pilot of his own small plane, which he used to scout land areas for future development. It crashed, and her prospects for parenthood went with him.

Her recall, once she became conscious and after three weeks of rehabilitation, was like a suspense movie with one new revelation after another. With much emotion, she described what went on while she was unconscious. She felt she was paralyzed, and could hear, but not move or speak. She was terribly frustrated, not knowing whether she was alive or dead, but she was reassured when someone touched or talked to her. She tried to urinate, thinking, "If I'm alive I can do this." (She had an indwelling catheter in her bladder.) At one time, she thought she was in some sort of crisis, perhaps bleeding, when she heard a nurse say, "I don't know why we have to do this; she is going to die anyhow." On another occasion, she felt she

169

was being moved; thought she was being sold into white slavery. This caused her "to really panic," thinking that the nurses were "cruel" to hold her prisoner.

Anna's strangest fantasy concerned her concept of death. She believed she was on a stretcher in a hall facing an elevator. "I began to see transparent images of many people of all ages, in all sorts of garb. Regularly, the doors would open and a group would get on the elevator and leave—like it was this day's toll of death." She concluded that, "These people were dying, and I was not put on the elevator because my time had not come."

When asked if there was any significance to the elevator going up or down (heaven or hell?), Anna smiled whimsically and said, "I'm a Catholic." Later, she stated that she did not fear death, but admitted that she had yearned to see her "yet-to-be-born children."

Filling the Void. Joe was in his early thirties, and his experience differs from Anna's only in the personalized recall created by the void in his consciousness. He, too, looked at death, but from the other side. He had been working on the hydraulic system of his dump truck when the chassis fell, crushing his chest. After he was flown to Shock Trauma he was treated aggressively by medical and surgical means. He remained unconscious for more than a month. Several months later, he was transferred to a rehabilitation unit where in time he related how he tried to make sense out of his stay while unconscious in the unit.

Joe said, since he was a truck driver, the word *"accident"* (which he heard after he was about to become alert) filled him with panic. He was convinced he had crashed into a bus full of children with his heavy equipment, or into cars loaded with women and children. (Joe's injury occurred while his truck was parked.) He, too, was convinced his "incarceration" was a result of his "accident."

Then, reluctantly, he revealed his painful "dream." "I dreamt, I dreamt...." With this Joe sobbed uncontrollably. He was sitting in a wheelchair, which he rocked back and forth, banging the table with the arms of the wheelchair. After several moments, stuttering, he continued, "It was in a cemetery. It was like I was looking at a television screen. I could see my wife wearing a black veil and see the faces of my children." Sobbing and speaking haltingly, he said, "They were looking at the tombstone in this cemetery. Then, it was like the camera spun around behind them, facing the headstone. Oh my God! There it was. I can still see it. My name was on it!" Unrestrained sobbing flooded the room. Joe's calm slowly returned. For me, it was like the feeling one gets when the summer storm is thankfully over.

One can readily identify with patients in this position. They are incarcerated in a featureless cubicle, tied down with IVs and catheters, and have no contact with the normal world. There are no windows, no pictures, no flowers—just masked, hated, uniformed wardens who usually inflict pain. If they are conscious, they are deprived of sleep by the twenty-four hour monitoring, the hiss of the respirator, and background noises. Their transfer by helicopter makes its own realistic contribution to the patient's sense of physical disorientation. (Recently, there have been successful efforts to change the ambience of the unit: Renovations have lightened the areas and orientation by staff is frequent. Quiet alternates with sounds, and calendars, clocks and family photographs aid the patient.)

An addendum: Not one of the patients who have shared near-death experiences (indeed, actual near-death) ever described their "journey" as "pleasant."

The Near-Death Experience. "Dear Jesus, I'm Dead!" This is the story of Grace, who had Hodgkin's disease early in life, then went into remission. Twenty-four years later she relapsed. She was a caring person, often helping others in the outpatient area. She was attractive, warm, bright, cheerful, and loving to any and all staff and patients. In time, she began to deteriorate physically and was soon confined to bed. The nurses and the rest of the staff continued to be supportive to her. She had a husband and a son who also were very supportive.

One Saturday morning, the surgeon came to see her, and was greeted by Grace shouting, "Dear Jesus, I'm dead! You must be Jesus Christ, I'm dead!" He reassured her that he was not Jesus. As a matter of fact, he did not even look like Jesus in any way shape or form, as he was short, clean-shaven, and rotund. Nonetheless she persisted. This lasted for 48 hours, during which time she kept insisting that she was "Dead, dead, dead, dead." An interview with her during this period was limited to how "dead" she was. This lasted for another 48 hours, and then she became lucid and could be interviewed. She talked tearfully about her childhood, how her mother would punish her with the "silent treatment," not speaking to Grace for days. She said she felt the experience of being "dead" was a very "painful one in which I felt abandoned, lost and cold. I don't ever want to die, it was so terrible." She also reported that before the episode she had an awareness of some kind, a premonition that she was going to die. Laboratory and other studies revealed no unusual abnormalities during her experience to explain it. Two weeks later she did indeed die.

I propose that the anecdotes about life after death can be explained phenomenologically as altered states of consciousness. There are three primary etiologies: *physiological*, including hypoxia, anoxia, hepatic delirium, uremia, and Meduna's carbon dioxide therapy; *pharmacological*, including "mindbenders," narcotics, steroids, pentylenetetrazol, insulin, barbiturates, and other psychotherapeutic medications; and *psychological*, including dissociative reactions, panic, and psychoses. I conjecture that Grace's near-death experience was brought on by a psychological disassociation, which again, in a way, is a defense against death—to no avail, as always.

Near-death experiences, regardless of etiology, are predicated on the past, and thereby take their theme and color from past experiences, as do dreams. Perception *is* reality.

Merry Christmas and an Unhappy New Year. It was New Year's Eve, the Trauma Center's busiest night of the year. The helicopter gently transported in a young couple, both in their twenties, both strikingly handsome. Both had bullet wounds: He had one in his side, and another had grazed his head; she, sadly, suffered a bullet wound that severed her spinal cord, resulting in complete lower paralysis. They had been working in a liquor store to save money for a ski vacation, which now was not to be. A gunman had come in to rob the liquor store, and had ordered them to lie face down on the floor. Then, in an act of unprovoked evil rage, he randomly shot them. And now, they were being vigorously attended by the Shock Trauma staff, the intensity of their labors momentarily distracting them from the inner smoldering feelings of rage they had toward the brute, competing with the pain in their hearts for this beautiful couple.

They had exchanged Christmas gifts in anticipation of the ski trip. She had given him a ski jacket, and he had helped her try on his gift to her of ski boots.

The Physician's Omnipotence:
Some Random Thoughts

Caring?? The patient was a forty-six-year-old female, an artist by trade, who unfortunately had advanced metastatic lung cancer. She said had been getting experimental chemotherapy. She said she and her oncologist had a most magnificent relationship, very warm and friendly. He was available to her for telephone calls, and all of her many, many questions. But when the patient became bed-ridden, she lost all contact with her oncologist. She could not understand why the doctor no longer called her to ask how she was doing, nor what her needs might be, since they had shared many years of a warm relationship.

This particular oncologist was known for his warmth as well as for his caring for patients throughout the medical community. And this problem, the loss of contact with him, was even more upsetting for her, because the doctor lived near her and did not even "stop by."

I would surmise that this is an example of the threat to the physician's omnipotence. This was a very warm physician who did not give up hope in his therapy with the patient, but finally, when he felt all of his ministrations were failing, he then found it much more difficult to relate to the patient. Again, I am sure, this was totally out of his awareness, but nonetheless, it is an example of omnipotence threatened for one who was quite capable of being compassionate.

While the doctor can be concerned about his or her own death and mortality, and his or her own omnipotence, there is something more. Why does one become an oncologist? Why does one choose to deal with a person who has such a high probability of dying? Why does one get into this kind of business? Whether it is the surgeon or the surgical oncologist, whether it's the medical oncologist, whether it's the psychiatrist who is doing oncology, the radiotherapist, why do they deal with patients who threaten their omnipotence at all times?

There is another perspective on the question, and that is that in some way, those who do deal with the dying patient perhaps are trying to deny death itself. But, further, I would suggest that those of us working with the patients who are potentially and inexorably heading toward death are perhaps trying to remove the mystery in and around our own death. Thereby, in a sense, even if these doctors don't defeat death, at least they subjectively master it. This effort may be defensive, but nonetheless it encourages the oncologist to utilize his or her defenses, keep working, and cope with the inevitable.

I would suggest something else, which is reiterated in so many ways: The goal of medicine is the promotion of life. However, I feel that it can be manifested as prolongation of dying. The physician sees death (his or her own, as well as in others) as an enemy, always to be resisted. To be truly helpful, the doctor must accept the fact that death is inevitable, and that the nature of death is in effect a life event, a process. Put another way, the chief cause of death is life.

So, why are we laboring in this vineyard? I propose that there are two sides to the coin. One side of the coin is the omnipotence that gets us into the kind of business that deals with the critically ill or severely physically traumatized patient, the dying patient, the so-called "hopeless" patient. The other side of the coin is our dealing; those of us who work with the critically ill patient are in some way trying to not only to understand death but again, also, to master it. This is despite the fantasies that death evokes in all of us. Since no one has come back since Lazarus, we have to fill the void, the notion of death with different fantasies: some are poetic, some make it beautiful, like the near-death experience, which is an attempt to soften the threat as well as the experience of death. If we do not have poetic and so-called graceful fantasies about death, we are then preoccupied with the fears of death: Is there a day of judgment? Will our bodies be biodegradable? Will we be eaten by worms? Also, there is the fear of loneliness, that we will be separated from supporting people, the people we love, and the things that we are going to miss by virtue of our death. We fear losing control, that someone will decide what is going to happen to our bodies, will make life and death decisions for us, and we fear being dead. Then there is the fear of regression, that we will have to be dependent and be taken care of, which we resist. Most of all, we fear the fact that we will lose our identity.

We anticipate that during the process of dying we will be emaciated, our body image will change, and that we inevitably will be in pain. (This is not necessarily true). I would add, however, that the connection between life and death can be put in the idiom of existentialism: One has to deal with one's feelings about death, which is to confront one's existence, one's living, one's life.

Burnout

"Burnout" is a phenomenon that particularly occurs with those who are working in intense areas such as ICUs, but also occurs with patients, teachers, parents, secretaries, assembly-line workers—anyone dedicated to his or her work.

The dynamic is stress, which has its basis in the failure of all-powerfulness on the part of the individual. This stress predisposes the individual to feelings of depression, irritability, and withdrawal. It may cause individuals to lose interest, blur creativity and productivity, suffer from insomnia or anorexia, or use drugs and alcohol.. All are manifestations of depression and/or anxiety, which can bring with them somatic symptoms such as increased heart rate and respiration and diarrhea.

Particularly in the ICUs, which are inherently stressful environments, coping requires some degree of defensive detachment. There are the machines, the constant stimuli, and the overload of patients, some of whom are bloody, incontinent, dying. There are other aspects in the intensive care units: the physical—sound, moaning, crying out of the patients; sights—blood, vomit, and death. These experiences further not only anxiety, but also nightmares, anger, loss, helplessness, fear of mistakes, work pressure, lack of staff cooperation, double shifts, and marital strife.

Ironically, the satisfaction of working in intensive care units as well as taking care of patients who do have a life-threatening illness such as cancer, heart or kidney disease, or trauma can evoke the burnout syndrome. This source of satisfaction can provide a feeling at times of elitism similar to one who does dangerous work in the outside world. Despite the fact that this type of work can be a source of satisfaction, they can be the source of this very intense stress. Friends and relatives of staff members who work in this intense environment find it difficult to understand how they can work in these places, particularly Shock Trauma and in the cancer unit with their ever-present threat to the workers' omnipotence as the patients deteriorate. It is difficult, indeed, to explain why one does. Conjectures as to the motivation are: a sense of altruism, an intellectual denial of one's own mortality, an effort to master death by increased knowledge, a need to rework a personal loss, and, possibly, responding to the challenge to and thereby *proving* one's omnipotence. Not to be overlooked is the conviction that one is doing interesting, worthwhile and important work with its potential for a gratifying and nurturing feeling.

Management rather than treatment is an approach to the problem of burnout. Prevention is even better. Some respond to a transient "blue period" and then discover a renewed dedication to their work. Some need a job change, while some use relaxation techniques: joking, teasing, and "one-liners." This is common in the surgical operating room, and it also relieves stress. Workers take vacations or use sexual release, outside activities and interests, rotations between job responsibilities, ventilation sessions, support from colleagues and superiors—anything that gives one a sense of self-worth and pride in one's endeavor. Sometimes moving from clinical work and getting a clinical distance from the patient is accomplished by a period of doing medical research. This shift enables the person to experience partial omnipotence. We cannot, in reality, achieve total omnipotence, but to successfully function with *partial* omnipotence is quite an accomplishment.

To sum up, again, why do people submit themselves to this possibly painful situation? To prove their omnipotence? To be the perfect parent? The perfect teacher? The perfect employee? To undo previous mistakes and failures? The need for challenging work? There is no value judgement to bearing the burden of burnout. It is as normal as apple pie, the American flag, and motherhood.

MAXIM: If you can't stand the heat get out of the kitchen.

ANSWER: Air-condition the kitchen.

A Brief Pause for a Doctor Story

Honesty Is Not Always The Best Policy. "This guy has to be fired. How do I do it?" growled Peter, the Cancer Center Director, grabbing my arm, obviously irritated, his frown a testimony to his annoyance.

The Center was functioning very well, research was progressing, finances were not a problem and morale was good. The Fellows-in-training were a dedicated group, offering only minimal and superficial complaints about menial medical chores and night call.

"So, Peter, who and why?"

"It's Jack. He comes to work late and even then he's lackadaisical. Doesn't follow through on assignments, procrastinates when the attendings tell him to do blood work on patients. I've had enough faculty complaints about him, how do I tell him he's out of the program?"

I demurred, "Peter, when he's asked why he's late, he says he overslept. The other Fellows use a 'flat tire' or 'wife is sick' excuse when they are late for rounds. When the Fellows don't follow up on assigned tasks, they defend by 'being busy.' Jack simply says, 'I forgot.' At least he's honest. The others might lie, but he never does."

"That's the problem! He has no damn imagination!"

Jack was not fired and today, years later, he is a well-known, well-respected oncologist. Go figure.

Choosing a Personal Doctor

The selective process dictates that there must be meaningful criteria for choosing a doctor—some objective, some subjective, ranging from appearances to whether or he or she is a "hand holder," an authoritarian or a "pussycat," easily controlled. Certainly, a sensible, responsible approach would involve verifying the physician's credentials: training, board certifications, and memberships and affiliations to various academic centers and medical societies. The usual and most frequent choice is made by "word of mouth" recommendations. This method, however, has constraints imposed by the managed care organization to which the patient is indentured. Despite the willingness by patient and doctor, they must share the same HMO.

A neglected, but successful, gratifying technique for selecting a personal doctor is to seek out a young, well-trained physician who has recently completed training and is now beginning to practice. He or she will not be famous, but certainly will not be too busy and therefore have plenty of time to spend with the patient, listening to problems, patiently explaining, and even being available for leisurely telephone calls—until he or she becomes popular and very busy.

Another pathway, which I heartily do *not* recommend, is the one taken by a lady I know. She related her impression of her first visit with her new doctor: He was thorough, but very aloof and abrupt. She had asked her friends about him and was told that he had a "terrible bedside manner." She said she had decided that he would be her doctor. Regarding her quizzically, I asked, "But, if he has such a terrible bedside manner, why would you want to use him?" She countered, her voice carrying a tone of triumph, "It's good that he's so bad that he has no patients. Now he'll have plenty of time for me."

How One Dies and How I (A Doctor) Learned About It

One Dies as One Has Lived. This sweet lady's husband, a doctor, was watching his wife die of breast cancer. Although he was a very responsible, highly esteemed, elderly, retired dermatologist, he was not interfering with his wife's care. Every day, however, he reported his wife's ups and downs to each of his medical friends. He carefully reported the frequency, quantity, and other aspects of his wife's urine and bowel movements, and also the physiology of each. Also, he reported what the tumor vascularization was doing.

All the while, his wife was demonstrating how people die: *One dies the way one has lived.* This particular patient had been very narcissistic, and this was the way she was dying. She mostly slept and would be dead in a few days. When she did awaken, she would ask where her husband and three grown children were. Upon being told that her husband was having lunch, she would state, "I don't want him to be eating lunch, I want him here." Also, if her sons or daughter were doing something else, making dinner or whatever, she was insistent that they were not to do that, they were to be with her. She then would immediate fall back to sleep. This was the way she had always behaved, like a queen "holding court." She may be dying, but she was keeping control of herself, her husband, and her children. She had cats to which she was seriously devoted. Once she asked me where her husband was. I said he was feeding the cats, and she shouted, "That's not important I want him here now!"

At one point, the family sought my advice, concerned that she was suffering, and that being deprived of quality of life, she would choose to die. I suggested to the husband and children that she not be offered nutrition, soup, oatmeal, water, or anything else, unless she asked for it. Then, she should be given water and food, but only if she could tolerate it. Also, they should be alert to inadequate medication so she wasn't under-sedated. They were not to deny her pain medication. I explained to the family that giving her hydration and nutrition may be prolonging her dying, which, suddenly, the family wanted her to do—a reversal. The patient herself, early on, wanted to expedite her dying, but now she wanted to "live forever," but most of the time, she was in and out of awareness.

Learning the Hard Way. This case above, a recent one, can be contrasted with an early experience I had when I was just an intern, before I learned what it really means to *be* a doctor. The National Cancer Institute was then a pilot organization at the U.S. Public Health Service Hospital in Baltimore. I can recall clearly the wife of a Coast Guard officer who was semi-comatose, dying of ovarian cancer, and receiving IV hydration. I was the lowly intern and the Chief of Medicine and his staff hovered over the patient during rounds. I was in the doorway behind the Chief and the residents when I heard the Chief say, "Discontinue the IVs," at which point I froze with my mouth open, stunned. Then the crowd passed me going up the hall. I started to run after them, shouting, "You can't do that, she's going to die, you can't do that, she's going to die." A resident grabbed me and muttered, "Don't—just be quiet."

This was before the time of chemotherapy, and the most merciful thing was to let the patient die. At that time, as a shiny new doctor, full of Hippocrates, I could not accept letting a patient die. This is in contrast to my suggestions to the preceding family to not give anything unless the patient asks for it. Of course, if the patient or family members ask for it, by all means give it to them. Fluids offer the patient comfort, not treatment.

The second example was also during that period when patients were left to die. When I was on hospital night call, I would hear dying cancer patients, those who failed their surgical venture, crying out that they were thirsty, moaning during the night. They could not have water, as they would vomit it or were unable to swallow because they were terminal. Feeling heavy with helplessness, I would wad up gauze sponges and soak them in water, squeeze out most of the water and put them in the mouths of those tormented souls, trying to get them some moisture, hoping to quench their thirst—and mostly, their moaning. Despite knowing that these patients were about to die, I did not appreciate that not prolonging dying was the most kind and merciful thing one could do. And here I am now, some 50 years later, doing just what I objected to when I started out early in my career. Being a slow learner, the patients had to work ever so much harder in their efforts to teach me how to be a real doctor.

A Conversation With John About AIDS. It was 1981 and the medical profession was confronted by a new phenomenon—AIDS. Its contagiousness and rapid fatality screamed a developing plague. Doctors, as well as the general population, were engulfed by the wave of fear. Many doctors, dentists, and nurses refused to care for AIDS patients. Fortunately, in short time, with education and research, doctors came to view AIDS as any other infectious disease—as a challenge.

A fifty-two year old man, admittedly homosexual, had been married for seventeen years before he became aware he was gay. He realized he was having homosexual feelings at a time when he was away from home giving a routine lecture. He had "wandered" into a homosexual bar, which was followed by an involvement, which convinced him he was gay. He discussed this with his wife. She was accepting, asking only that he have his contacts out of town. In fact, they continued living together until John was in the second year of his new relationship. Eventually, John's wife divorced him and they remained friends.

John's five-year relationship ended in the death of his lover. The loss sent John crashing into a frantic period he described as "wild and terrible." "I did everything, played every sex game, I took every drug, and went to hell with myself." He was convinced that he was exposed to the AIDS virus during that time. Fortunately, he met a man five years his junior and their relationship turned him around. They lived together for five years.

John's AIDS did not become evident until a year before his death. Blue lesions on his face and body alerted physicians to the diagnosis, Kaposi's sarcoma. He was philosophical about it, knowing full well that he was going to die. He wanted others to know about and profit from his experience. Though this was in the early '80s, the awareness of AIDS was not as it is today. He advocated safe sex, the good life, and that he wanted to tell everyone how grateful he was to have friends and other loving relationships. He knew he was going to die, but wanted to die in a way that it would be peaceful, surrounded by friends. He got his wish. He died at home and there were friends and near friends who came from across the country to support him physically, emotionally, and medically until he died. John demonstrated an acceptance of death that a rare few can equal. It is usually are the elderly and the very religious who can achieve this graceful, dignified parting from life.

Quality of Life:
The Doctor's and Patient's Shared Dilemma—An Essay

Today's physician is a scientist. This fact is supported by his or her dedication to research and computerized technology. In recent years, there has been a greater emphasis on the study of the total person (holistic medicine) and yet, perhaps unfortunately, at the same time we are experiencing an increase in specialization. As a byproduct of this paradox, the concept of a family doctor is blurred, and now a scientist cares for the patient. This in itself is not bad, but it is not enough. The physician has to approach his patient with a psychological awareness of himself as well as an awareness of what psychological factors go into the development of the patient. Today in medicine there is a movement toward the family practitioner brought about, not so much by an interest on the part of physicians in being a family physician, but more so by managed care. This is because the current concerns over health costs have dictated, if not mandated, that there be "gate-keepers" to decide what specialist a patient may be permitted to visit.

There has been much debate surrounding the issue of cure and care and their relative importance in healing. There are many who claim little attention is given to the latter while far too much is accorded the former, that the concern is more for cure than caring. The problems for medical personnel in caring for patients are nowhere more pronounced than with the terminally ill. But the question and concern is whether the focus remains on curative questions. And it does, despite the fact that a diagnosis for an incurable condition triggers a complex set of patient-family-physician reactions, which directly affect those individuals, their inter-relationships, and their roles. In such situations, the "quality of care" becomes crucial. If the medical helpers recognize these reactions, their roots and manifestations, they can offer the dying patient the support, strength, and dignity they need in this most difficult of times.

So much for the quality of care on the part of the medical helpers. Now what can the patient do to maintain his or her notion of quality of life, supported by the medical helpers' awareness of the patient's idea of quality of life. Today, despite the fact that the physicians have always been aware of caring for the patient's quality of life, there is a concern on the part of others to define the quality of life for the patient in terms of the idiom of the profession, i.e., the doctor needs to treat, to care.

I would define quality of life by asking the question, whose quality of life are we determining? Are we talking about my quality of life, or your quality of life, or his or her quality of life? The bottom line is, only each person can decide his or her own quality of life.

Hippocrates some 400 years ago wrote the following, "I will define what I conceive medicine to be. In general terms, it is to do away with the suffering of the sick, to lessen the violence of their diseases, *and to refuse to treat those who are overmastered by their diseases, realizing that in such cases medicine is powerless*" (emphasis mine). As an aside, Hippocrates is also invoked to argue against abortion and euthanasia because of the Hippocratic oath: "Do no harm."

Understandably, there is greater emphasis today on the patient's quality of life. Many research studies dealing basically with patients' medical care have quality-of-life studies tacked onto them. For the most part, the quality-of-life literature is becoming extensive, but it is primarily the work of psychologists with only limited physician participation. Interestingly, the emphasis in the quality-of-life literature is devoted to *measuring* the quality of life. There are well-intentioned attempts to assess changes in the well-being of the patient undergoing therapy of one kind or another. With the increasing number and variety of questionnaires that the patients participate in, there are understandable efforts to in some way make quality-of-life measurements into some kind of medicine that one can administer to a patient. The concern becomes rather "what" and "how." There is very little subjectivity on the part of the patient in filling out questionnaires so structured. In any kind of quality-of-life study, one has to somehow get around the problem of the "here" and "now" that the patient is experiencing because the fluctuations in "now" can change moment to moment, whether its nausea, or vomiting, or a pain in one's tooth.

In the efforts to measure the quality of life or to ascertain the well-being of the patients studied, there are various measurements that are utilized, sometimes referred to as dimensions, sometimes referred to as assessments. Much attention is paid to changes in one direction or another. Listed below are a few of the dimensions that are most frequently assessed. Physical functions address whether the person can walk, climb, etc. Another dimension is the psychological, whether the person is stress free or is constantly anxious or depressed. The sociological dimension concerns the patient's capacity to work, hold down a job, and participate in the community. Another considers symptoms, and whether is the symptom is disease specific, i.e., whether the disease is causing difficulty in swallowing, or difficulty in gaining weight, etc. Yet another dimension is spiritual, which is not necessarily religious, but can be what one thinks of life.

There are many arguments on both sides of the equation on how to use measurements for quality of life. They are sharply divided into two sides. One side believes very strongly that quality-of-life measurements are very necessary, while the other side feels the opposite. The proponents of quality-of-life measurements opine that from the medical point of view there is a better choice of different therapies. In other words, some therapies will cause havoc to patients, while some are only mildly toxic. Also they feel the quality-of-life measurements predict whether the patient will deteriorate as a result of a particular type of therapy. Another opinion is that the quality-of-life measurements are necessary to assess the harmful effect of the disease itself as well as assessing the therapy. There is also the conviction by the proponents that the measurements will help design clinical trial protocols. As an example, by adding a quality-of-life assessment onto a protocol investigating a particular drug as a therapy against cancer, the measurement will indicate whether this therapy will impinge overall on the patient's quality of life. (Side effects are well-known, prevalent in early trials, and generally predictable.)

Further, the proponents of quality-of-life measurements believe these measurements are necessary for making policy in terms of patient care. They point out that the quality-of-life measurements offer assurance that the patients' quality of life is enhanced. Also, they assert the quality-of-life measurements are useful to study quality of life. Lastly, they say policy decisions about using therapy versus no therapy, as well as whether the therapy is cost-effective, can be dictated by quality-of-life measurements.

On the other side of the equation are those people who not necessarily opponents of quality-of-life measurements, rather, they have many *questions* that immediately arise in terms of using quality-of-life measures. Their concern is how can these studies help the doctor and his or her patient. Many of these questions follow. Should the quality-of-life measurement be part of every study protocol? Does employing the quality-of-life measurement ensure the patient's compliance? Is a particular quality-of-life measurement oriented toward the diagnosis that is pointed to the disease, or is it oriented toward therapy, or are there two sets of measurements going in both directions simultaneously? A serious question arises out of the fact there are perhaps twenty or more questionnaires and there are new ones born every day. How does the oncologist know which one to use or in what combinations? The patient might find use of multiple questionnaires quite burdensome. Are the established guidelines to good patient care necessarily improved by quality-of life-questionnaires? Are the questionnaires an intellectualized way to determine whether the physician is going to have a better relationship with the patient rather than just allowing the doctor's personality to take on the manifestation of a concerned caretaker? Is the doctor sophisticated and caring enough to discern the patient's quality of life without the help of a questionnaire? Perhaps measurement should best be directed toward the physician. A good question, of course, would be is it cost-effective to give all these questionnaires to the patients? Is this somewhat like managed care? And, most importantly, does using the questionnaires and the quality-of-life measurements indeed advance medical knowledge?

There are more questions. Are the questionnaires useful in measuring quality of life versus the sanctity of life? Do the questionnaires measure the quality of life versus the quantity of life? Do they measure the subjectivity of the patient (which is paramount) or must they be objective to be reliable? In sum, is it the patient's quality of life versus the questioners' view of quality of life? Which brings us full circle to: Is it your quality of life or mine?

Setting aside for the moment the discussion of quality-of-life measurements to address the consumer, the patient. It is more important that we consider the quality of life, present and future, as it impinges on the patient, mainly regarding the patient's symptoms. There are problems that involve nausea and vomiting. Problems that involve pain, weight loss, and organ dysfunction and limitations. There are emotional problems, family and social issues, for example, whether the patient can involve himself or herself with the environment. There is that very important symptom, fatigue. The physician can address the problem of the patient's pain, nausea, and vomiting; there are medications such as morphine, radiation for pain, and other techniques. At the moment, however, there is no definitive therapy for

186

fatigue. We can tell the patient to rest and perhaps take vitamins, but the fatigue persists. It is the most difficult of the symptoms to treat.

Pain: Man's worst enemy, the purveyor of abject loneliness.

Pain certainly can manipulate the quality of life in different ways and in different spheres. Pain effects the quality of life from the physical point of view in that there is decreased functional capability and a diminution of strength and endurance. Psychologically, the quality of life is affected by a decrease in the capacity to experience enjoyment. There is increased anxiety, fear, and depression, and difficulty in concentration. In the social area, there is a diminished ability or capacity for social relationships. There is decreased social function, and at times the pain so intense that it is difficult for the person to relate to others or receive them with affection. Also, socially, there is the self-consciousness that goes with altered appearance, the loss of hair, weight or both. In the spiritual sphere, the intense pain can alter a patient's sense of the meaning of life. Pain, felt or anticipated, can be constant or intermittent, and quality of life ebbs and flows with it. Also, the intense suffering brought on by pain can sometimes motivate the patient to reevaluate his or her religious beliefs. Patients need denial, which equates with hope and is as useful as the narcotics necessary to relieve pain. Can a quality-of-life questionnaire keep up with the vacillating denial that resonates and dictates the patient's quality of life at any given moment?

Quality of life from the patient's point of view can be seen two ways, both negative and positive. Negative quality of life from the patient's standpoint is understandable, they may feel a sense of helplessness and the feeling of hopelessness, and the threat of dying and death. The pain, the self-absorption, the appearance—said without any value judgment—can make the patient so self-absorbed and feeling sorry for himself or herself. They may feel that friends, and sometimes even family, are not supportive. And those feelings may stretch into the patient feeling unloved. As a result of the negative feelings, the patient understandably begins to wallow in the bitterness of not only "Why me?" but also that the world is not fair, and also not very nice.

Yet, we have met patients who can perceive this onslaught to be contributing to a positive view of quality of life. There are those who use the illness to take inventory of what their life has been all about, and they find some meaning and purpose to it. There are those who become hopeful that some therapy in and of itself can enhance quality of life. For example, a patient with a painful metastatic lesion in a bony area may receive radiotherapy to the area, which relieves the patient's pain, and changes his or her perception of quality of life. Some patients may find creativity in this time of illness. We have met several patients who use humor to cope with their illness. One example is a woman, an artist, who chronicled her entire illness by drawing cartoons using known hospital characters and poking fun at the physicians. Some patients find that their illness allows them to accept not only the meaning of life, but also to accept their eventual ending of life. This acceptance is an intense, but very useful, denial. Some patients find that they not only receive, but also can give loving and caring to those in their environment. And not to be forgotten are those who profit by "It's an ill wind that does not blow some good." They seize upon their illness to manipulate and control their environment and everyone in it.

For many years I have thought that patients were "living with cancer" as a way of coping, implying that one is alive despite the fact that they have cancer. It has been my observation, however, that patients who are "living with cancer" are spending twenty-four hours a day preoccupied with their cancer. Thus, I have come to the view that patients, rather than "living with cancer," have a more useful way of coping by "living *along side* cancer." This mandates that patients go about their lives, their work, their relationships, and everything that they need to do and want to do. But when they have a symptom or concerns, they then do what is necessary: They see the doctor, or perhaps get more therapy, or do whatever is needed to improve their quality of life.

Having Cancer Demands Your Attention! Finally, of significance to quality of life, one must confront a possible answer to the question, "When is enough enough?" When does life no longer have quality? This is the burden weighing on the patient, and only the patient can answer this question. The patient's caretakers may have some ideas about their own quality of life, and perhaps what the patient is experiencing would be more than enough for them. However, it is a *patient decision!* The patient has to determine whether life is burdensome to him or her as well as to the family and whether there is a loss of control, not only of bodily functions, but in terms of what can be done for their future. Perhaps anti-cancer drugs are no longer an option. The patient must then consider hospice as an alternative, and whether hospice can be a guarantor of quality of life. Whether the patient wants to die at home or hospice or in the hospital must be decided. But today, in the era of managed care, the patient, as a rule, given financial restraints, cannot die in the hospital. Another quality-of-life concern the patient has to take into account is the possibility that palliation may no longer be effective. We have said elsewhere that pain control can be effective, but there are situations where pain control is most difficult and requires rather drastic therapy, for example, the use of neurosurgery. Also added to the pain can be relentless fatigue as well as severe body image changes.

But quality of life is not limited to living. *Quality of dying is part of the continuation of life.* The dying person is entitled to not be alone, in pain, or in fear. These words, sincerely and succinctly stated, faithfully express what the person facing death deserves. Why, then, is it necessary to utilize semantics and euphemisms? Using such terms as "good death," "dying well," and "healthy death" (!) to describe dying? Could it be that those who are presumed to care are using intellectualizations to put emotional distance between them and the person who needs their concern? Death cannot be denied, it will happen. But neither can personal control be denied.

So, finally, in the context of when is enough enough, the patient has to consider that technology can provide quantity of life, but not necessarily quality of life. Then the alternative, if not hospice, is euthanasia, whether it is done legally or whether the patient chooses it as a last effort in seeking personal control to find a dignified means to end the burdensome quality of life. In my experience, most patients who have made a personal choice for euthanasia, "wait one more day," thus exercising personal control and succumbing to a natural death. Having the option, the patient is free of the nagging fear of dying and death, and can relinquish the decision favoring euthanasia.

Even though it is highly controversial, euthanasia can be, at times, a supportive technique. Not "mercy killing," but death because the patient is convinced that he or she is no longer a *person*. The statement that euthanasia might be considered supportive may be seen by some as a most egregious and callous pronouncement. Not so when one stops to view the dyadic relationship between patient and survivors and the grieving that joins the diagnosis of cancer. The dying person can, in the process, suffer much and look to death as a relief. Survivors can take consolation that their loved one is no longer suffering. On the other hand, when a loved one dies suddenly through trauma or suicide, the survivors may experience anguish, guilt, or both. Palliative care is appropriate when aggressive therapy has been exhausted. This is humane—or is it? Is it humane when the consequence of palliation that is no longer effective is the prolongation of distress for the patient?

Again, quality of life: It is not yours or mine, it is the *patient's decision*!

And, What is in Store for Doctors of the Future?

The day may not be too far off when surgery, at least in the Western world, will be limited to trauma, transplantation, congenital defects, and cosmetic repair. The interventional radiologists will do more exotic, guided, therapeutic tours through the body. The infectious disease doctors will have even more sophisticated antibiotics to cleanse away our intrusive impurities.

A pill, a drink, a gene transfer; the practice of medicine, albeit gradually, will be more effectively changed, even more so than that attempted (or inflicted) by managed care.

The Doctor's Burden

You Just Don't Get Used To It:
She looked like Audrey Hepburn, somewhere between cute and beautiful.
He could pass as a young Cary Grant, somewhat classic looking.
Both in their twenties, their inner youth and beauty reflected in their outer charm.
Married, they were a natural together; full of life
(so the expression goes).

So, what's the problem?

Five years ago, David was diagnosed with leukemia.
Therapy had been aggressive and, it seemed, successful.
Heidi was one of his nurses and they had known each other.
You know the story, they spent time together, they fell deeply in love,
they married; he resumed his active professional career, she returned
to nursing; and they did their follow-up medical visits together, a practice
shared by his mother, sister and father.

The years were good despite occasional complications, which were usually
weathered well with routines resumed.
Now David was dying, a flood of complications were too overwhelming to
stem,
despite medical heroics and the family's hope and prayers.

The final hours: The air in the room was bittersweet with
the co-mingling of the love and somber sadness of the family.
The medical equipment, with its blinking eyes, and I bore silent witness.
Standing in the corner of the room, I felt as if I were viewing a tableau
fixed in time—resembling a five-pointed star.

The centerpiece was the sheet, a rectangle of white topped by David's now
peaceful
and accepting face. At midpoints of the respective sides of the white were

Heidi
and his sister, sitting at bedside, their heads bent to press their lips to David's hands.
At the bottom of the white were his parents, standing, each tenderly holding one of David's feet. No movement; not Heidi, not his sister, not his mother, not his father, not David. It was reminiscent of a Renaissance religious painting.

Time passed slowly until David, drawing his last breath, brought the still picture
abruptly to life. Now there was movement: tears, quiet sobbing and each in turn,
lovingly kissing David goodbye. Then the hugging each other, sharing their grief,
their relief of pain—his and, perhaps one day, theirs.

When the poignancy subsided, I took my turn to hug without words and left the room.
You just don't get used to it. *Never.*

VII.

THE WORLD OF CANCER: REVISITED

Introduction

This chapter gets pretty serious. Not because its orientation is the world of cancer, and not that the other chapters lack seriousness. Rather, here the approach is more tutorial—something like an introductory course in the "consequences of cancer." Yes, the articles, essays, and thoughts are indeed derived from what the patient's experiences have taught me. Here and there are anecdotes, but for the most part, they spell out the ideas their experiences have evoked in me. Coincidentally, many of these ideas can be translated into other areas of critical illness.

On the surface, the collection of topics may seem not to be connected, nonetheless, the reader will find them relevant. They are offered as insights for the reader who, hopefully, will find them useful in understanding patients as people in the broader sense. That is, the ramifications generated in and by the world they live in; the reciprocal effects that occur between them and their environment—family, friends, caretakers and caregivers, and the public.

Perhaps through an understanding of the world of the patient, the reader may find an opportunity to further share the patient's view of life at the various twists and turns in the road.

Now, take a deep breath and plunge in. The water is fine.

Drama: The Players and the Cancer Situation

Life's but a walking shadow, a poor player,
That struts and frets his hour on the stage,
And then is heard no more.
Shakespeare, Macbeth, Act V, Scene v, Line 24

Any illness, particularly a life-threatening one, has an aura of drama for the patient, the labile emotion, the conflict, and, unfortunately, the oppressive suspense. There are some verses in Shakespeare that would reflect the somewhat pessimistic ambiance of a cancer drama. Certainly, life has a temporal quality, but it need not be helpless or desperate. This fact will become evident by the coping techniques utilized by the three patients that follow. However, some basic understanding is required. In other words, a brief lecture.

Cancer is a life-threatening disease, as are fulminating and non-fulminating cardiovascular, renal, neurologic, pulmonary, and other systemic illnesses. The patient with cancer, however, serves well as a model for discussion of the emotional concomitants of life-threatening illnesses.

Subtle psychological concepts exert a powerful influence on all actors in this life-threatening drama. They are the unconscious, transference, and defenses. One sees the *unconscious* revealed in dreams, slips of the tongue and pen, hypnosis, and emotional symptoms. There are things we cannot tell our closest confidants (secrets), and, things we can only tell ourselves (fantasies), and things that we cannot even tell ourselves, they are out of our awareness (unconscious). The unconscious has little regard for reality and is timeless. If an experience is painful or shameful, the more likely it is that it will be repressed into the unconscious. This powerful source can determine an individual's behavior, compelling him or her to act in ways seemingly irrational to the current situation.

Transference is also unconscious and impels one to respond emotionally to important people as one once did to father, mother, and other significant persons in one's childhood. The phenomenon has ramifications in the patient-provider relationship.

Physical and physiological defenses are well known, but there are also emotional *defenses* against anxieties in one's inner and outer environment. In a situation where one experiences conflict or threat of personal injury or loss, or threat of loss of love, security, or self-esteem, anxiety signals the defensive process. The defenses can be utilized constructively or destructively, begin in early childhood, and develop experientially.

A few of the defense mechanisms relevant to the participants in the cancer drama are:

Repression: Unconscious forgetting.

Suppression: Conscious forgetting, e.g., Scarlett O'Hara saying, "I'll think about it tomorrow," but "tomorrow" comes too soon, proving the ineffectiveness of this defense.

Denial: Which is also unconscious and prevents one from seeing that which is unpleasant, particularly about oneself. This defense can spare one pain and preserve hope, as in the case of terminal illness. Conversely, denial can be used pathologically by patients who delay diagnosis and treatment. This is the most significant and prevalent defense. It is so powerful that the other mechanisms function in its service.

Displacement: A defense whereby the emotion remains the same, although it is now unconsciously transferred to a less anxiety-provoking object. The child who has a mask thrust upon his face, by an anesthesiologist, retaliates not to the anesthesiologist, but to a sibling or playmate.

Projection: A mechanism by which one's true feelings are unconsciously attributed to another. The patient may experience the side effects of chemotherapy and thus, resent the oncologist. In time, he or she wonders if these noxious reactions are necessary, or if they are deliberate punitive acts of the part of the oncologist who, "Doesn't like me."

Isolation: The de-emotionalizing of an affect. Intellectualization is frequently utilized in the service of isolation. An example: discussing all aspects of one's cancer and its treatment as if one were talking about another patient.

Three Patients

First: A brilliant scientist died at age 46 of melanoma. He was highly trained in the use of intellectual processes, and at the same time was given to macho endeavors, such as flying, mountain climbing, skiing, and scuba diving. Despite vigorous therapy, including chemotherapy and several surgical procedures, he continued his intellectual and physical pursuits. To himself he would not be "defeated by a melanoma" and to observers, he appeared to be successful. He too, believed this, for in his case, macho equated *denial*.

His wife's perceptions, however, were not in concurrence with his. His personality changed, according to her. He was quieter, at times withdrawn or irritable. He tried to maintain the "macho image" to the end. He flew, climbed mountains, and worked productively. A few days before he died, he attempted intercourse but was too weak. His wife tried to reassure him, "It's not important to me," and his macho reply, "But it is important to me!"

Second: A young, perky, attractive woman in her early thirties relapsed after a seven-year remission from Hodgkin's disease. It was not a simple process. For some time, she complained of backaches, but was reassured by her physician that these symptoms were "only housewifely complaints." She sought relief by buying a new mattress, sleeping on the floor, etc., to no avail. Finally, she asked her gynecologist to remove her IUD. He did, then ordered an intravenous pyelogram, and it soon became evident that a tumor was impinging on her right kidney. Active therapy was then initiated.

This experience was compounded with a similar previous one. When first diagnosed, she and her husband were given little information; they were not even told her diagnosis. She complained that she was treated like a child, at times given instructions resembling, according to her, "baby talk," even though she possessed two academic degrees.

These two experiences, both occurring with the awareness of illness, were available to her defensively. She became angry and bitter, but never verbally expressed these feelings to her doctors nor to the ancillary personnel, and at the same time, denied that the anger was directed at her illness. Anger was deflected (*displacement*) toward her husband, a professional, in that she felt he was not answering her questions, and not being responsive to her needs. She found it difficult to believe that her husband was not meeting her anger with anger out of deference to her illness. Both confessed to not admitting their anger toward their health care providers. They feared the staff may retaliate by withholding part or all of therapy. "We depend on them. We are in their hands."

Third: A woman in her forties, in remission from Hodgkin's disease, was a talented artist who drew humorous cartoons as a running diary of her experiences from the time of diagnosis on. She was popular with the staff, who found her likable, but at the same time, they were not cognizant of her anger and frustrations. Physicians, nurses, and therapists were portrayed in caricature. In the cartoons, the doctors reflect their fallibility, the nurses' caps had devil-like horns, the treatments were belittled to absurdity. The cartoons were a subtle sting cloaked in humor, which served as a vehicle of expression for her anger (*projection*).

Sexual innuendo was evident in almost all of her cartoons. The exceptions were significant. During the many complications of her illness, the patient was portrayed as a voluptuous, sexy, scantily clad female. When she was symptom free, she was somewhat plain and clothed decorously. During one period when she was asymptomatic, she drew a non-sexual cartoon as usual. But suddenly, while still presumed by the patient and staff to be asymptomatic, her cartoons took on an erotic coloring. Soon thereafter she became symptomatic. Her artwork had expressed the body image changes that were occurring without her own or the staff's conscious awareness.

These cases reflect the major characters poised at center stage in the cancer drama, the patient and his family. But there are other performers as well. Waiting in the wings are the supporting cast: the providers, the physicians, nurses, social workers, psychiatric consultants, and the non-medical staff in and out of the hospital. The responses of each are predicated on their individual personalities and previous experiences of themselves as providers.

> *All the world's a stage,*
> *And all the men and women merely players;*
> *They have their exits and their entrances...*
> *Shakespeare,* As You Like It
> *Act II, Scene vii, Line 139*

These three patients in their own way practiced different techniques of denial. The first patient practiced denial by way of intellectualization, the second patient by anger, and the third patient used humor as a technique for denial.

Consider each patient as an entity:

First Patient: He used the technique of intellectualization as well as machismo. He supported his denial with his highly honed capacity for intellectualization. As a scientist he functioned on an intellectual level. He discussed his "case" with great facility. By intellectualizing about his disease he obscured its reality and treated it as if it were another person's clinical history. Like many patients with cancer, he could speak of his symptoms, the prognosis, the blood counts, and the related data, but only as a subject somehow apart from him. His denial was apparent in the following example: His wife wanted to bring his comfortable office chair home the week before he died. At that time, his return to work was precluded by his terminal physical incapacitation. He demurred at the suggestion, saying, "What will I do for a chair when I go back to the office?"

In the same idiom he considered how he would terminate his life if he became incapacitated and no longer in control. He discussed with his wife overdosing on narcotics. When the time came for the decision, however, he postponed action for a day. He died naturally and quietly the next day.

Second Patient: This bright, young housewife denied any feelings of anger related to her Hodgkin's disease. Instead, she complained about, but not to, all the doctors and ancillary personnel who crossed her path as she relapsed. Her denunciation of them was bitter and vehement, and her husband was the sole recipient of this anger. When questioned about the intensity of her anger (not *why* she was angry) she would shout, "I'm not angry about my illness if that's what you're asking, I'm angry about everybody's stupidity!" (Which was not entirely without some substance.)

Anger for this patient reflected not a denial of relapse, but a denial of the possibility of helplessness. She was "fighting mad" and hope was on her side. Because the anger was displaced, the staff usually was oblivious to its presence, a result perhaps of the staff's need to be liked, or perhaps even because of their affection for the patient, a willingness to participate in her denial. In that sense, the staff also was practicing denial.

When patients complain to others about their professional caretakers and are advised to tell the particular staff person how they feel, they refuse and insist that the listener say nothing. Complaints are rare as patients feel their survival is in the hands of the helpers. The fear is that any antagonism will kindle anger and the patient will be abandoned. When the patient is obsequious or overly deferential, underlining anger should be suspected. A simple comment to the patient such as, "I wonder if you are feeling fed up with all this business?" usually evokes a critical vocalization.

Third Patient: Here denial is expressed, not as an intellectualization, not as anger, but as humor. The patient is laughing at herself—the cruel "joke" is on her. The reality of death "has lost its sting." Despite the humor in her cartoon captions, the sharp edge of her anger points toward her providers, but as with the second patient, the anger is never verbalized directly. In many of her cartoons, she criticizes the language of the oncologist, the use of acronyms, the protocols of therapy, the techniques of bone marrow and lumbar punctures, radiotherapy, and technological advances in general.

The dynamics of portraying herself as provocative and voluptuous during periods of symptomatic illness are of interest. Certainly with active disease there are bodily changes. Could the sexy quality of her drawings be a denial of unpleasant body image changes?

As with all of us, these three actors have practiced their roles since childhood. Personalities do not "just happen" nor are they a result of an accident of fate. They develop gradually, and with complexity, as a result of forces impinging from the individual's internal and external environments. Patterns of coping develop with experience. Patients, as with people generally, respond to stress in the ways they have always reacted to stress. Cancer is a most serious and severe stress.

"What's past is prologue," William Shakespeare, The Tempest

It is interesting how a person elects a technique, a defense mechanism, to practice his or her own kind of denial. The first patient was a scientist and intellectualization was his idiom. The second patient, always a kind of a maverick, used anger in her defensiveness to plead, "Why me?" For the third patient, an artist, cartooning was her own particular language style.

A phenomenon worthy of mention is the paradoxical response to "good news." Frequently, patients, when told that their CAT scan is negative or that they are now in "solid" remission, will feel a great sense of elation followed by a period of depression. A suggested explanation is that these patients have their defenses ("troops") always on the ready, only to find the effort is no longer necessary. Also they remain insecure, believing, "I'm okay now, but when will the axe fall? I have to sweat it out." An oncologist told one patient who had battled breast cancer and its recurrence and metastases for six years, that with a "new" treatment she could be "cured." After a day of high spirits she became severely depressed. Her way of life had been geared to a total commitment of time and effort to fighting cancer. Now she would no longer have anything to do and her life would be meaningless.

*"Life is a passing shadow," says Scripture. The
shadow of a tower or a tree? No: the shadow of a
bird—for when a bird flies away, there is neither
shadow nor bird.
Midrash: Genesis Rabbah, 80*

Death. It is feared, anticipated, denied, obsessed about, and even longed for. The patient, once feeling no different from anyone of us, but unlike us, is now under a temporal cloud—a judgment. The threatened, perhaps terminal, patient vacillates between intellectualizations and intense emotions, changing from moment to moment. I have observed terror (no hope of resolution), anger (for dying or for *not* dying soon enough), denial, pain, philosophical and clinical exhortation, and confusion ("What the hell is going on?") in dying patients. Some deny death, expecting to get better. Some are preoccupied with doctors and medications. Some resign and withdraw. Some are angry, and at times, destructive. Some regress to infantilism.

One is compelled to admire those patients who in their determination to survive—to live—will tolerate pain and painful and humiliating procedures and experiences. They die with pride, fighting to the end.

Equally admirable are those—a few—who seem to accept, not resigned to, the end of their lives. For the most part, these are the elderly, the religiously inclined. They die with calm dignity. And there are those whose acceptance is the ultimate manifestation of denial—with grace.

In short, individuals die in the style by which they have lived. Those of us who seem to fear the ever present possibility of death the most, may well fear life and living with the same intensity.

*Sun Journey
Hope is like the sun,
Which, as we journey toward it
Casts the shadow of our burden behind us.
Samuel Smiles
The Eternal Light, P. 130*

As Players in the Cancer Drama,
What Can the Patient or We Do to Help?

Patients need to be informed in a matter that is clear, unhurried, supportive and accepting of the fact that the patient will understandably utilize his defense mechanisms. The doctor or oncologist should not take personally his patient's dependency or demands or his therapeutic recalcitrance, but rather understand this is the patient's response to the emotional regression. The doctor, or staff, or helpers also should meet the family with calmness and a willingness to suppress any personal annoyance or restlessness.

This is not to suggest that the helpers be all-accepting and permissive, because this would not be in the patient's best interest. Because one has a life-threatening illness, or might be dying, or is aging does not mean that person is suddenly holy or good. One dies as one has lived. If one has been infantile or rigid, one will act the same during the process of the disease. If one has been flexible in one's coping one will be likewise with the illness. In some cases, the patient needs to be treated with concern, respect, and the appropriate therapy despite the fact that the patient is not a "good patient." He or she *is* a patient, as well as a person, and deserves the best of what we can do therapeutically.

The treating physician should not be patronizing when a sophisticated patient questions the details of therapy. It is important to permit and even encourage patients to retain some measure of personal control by offering them alternate choices of therapy whenever possible, honoring requests for second opinions. If the patient is actively involved in his or her treatment, this can soften or even prevent the patient's regression and improve compliance with therapy. The language of oncology often is confusing and frightening to the patient. When medical abbreviations and acronyms are discussed, they are often perceived as a foreign language and can easily provoke anger and frustration.

There comes a time when the efficacy of therapy is futile, painful, or harrowing and the result doubtful. The physician must then face the difficult but essential task of relating this to the patient, allowing the near-dying person the choice of refusing further active treatment. The helper's obligation is to relieve pain, alleviate discomfort, and, most importantly, to allay anxiety. The anxiety does not cease when a patient refuses to continue his specific treatment.

The most important function physicians can perform during this period is to give the patient the opportunity to talk. In the absence of a cure the real *art* of medicine is in amelioration. This can be achieved by actively listening and not gratuitously offering psychological or religious explanations. Listening is an art that can be time-consuming, tedious, and emotionally wearing, particularly the physician sees his or her power to cure failing. Nonetheless, listening can be extremely gratifying. When physicians manage to sublimate their need for omnipotence, the rewards are as great as for the surgeon who has successfully performed a difficult operation or the internist who nurses a coronary patient through the night. Listening enables patients to air their fears about life, death, the family, work—anything. And the involved physician permits his patients to talk freely and openly about very private matters. In this way, despite the absence of a cure, the patient's suffering is lessened. This is indeed the *art* of medicine in its ultimate sense. It also allows physicians to "hear" what their patients are really asking so they can guide them accordingly. Such guidance is best provided in the form of short, simple statements addressed to what the patient is asking, not by steering the patient away to another less charged topic. What is *really* being asked requires an answer, and it must be direct.

As time and treatments unfold, issues arise. Early on there are physical and emotional complications such as infections, pain, body image changes, and depression. But the providers, the helpers, are not without resources; there are medications to combat infections and elevate pain, and tranquilizers for anxiety, and anti-depressants when appropriate. Of course, requests for visits from clergy or lawyers are granted and at times even encouraged.

Most useful to the patient are his or her human contacts: family, friends, and helpers at all levels. Also important is the patient's use of denial. Denial equates with *hope* and as such, it is crucial to the patient's acceptance of therapy and all the potentially humiliating and painful side effects. For doctors to blatantly attack the use of denial is to deprive the patient of hope. Hope can be realistic; insulin and poliomyelitis vaccines give testimony to this fact. Skillful helpers will walk the thin line between repeatedly and consistently directing the patient toward reality, at the same time, permitting the patient the integrity of his denial. If there is insistence of reality, the patient will lose all hope. On the other hand, the overemphasis on denial leaves the patient feeling inadequate to deal with his or her illness and the demands that must be met. The families should be encouraged to listen to their ill relative. There are "death and dying" savants who advocate that families press the patient to discuss "feelings" about death. Most patients will discuss their thoughts and feelings about death (usually intellectualized denial) with their helpers, but not with their families. Most patients fear they would compound the family's experience of guilt by further burdening them with their illness.

I never ask patients to talk of dying. In my years of work with patients who are critically ill and actually in a terminal phase of their illness, very few have chosen to talk about their sense and feelings of dying. When this does happen, I listen without comment, but rarely do I hear anything other than the fact that, "Intellectually I know I'm dying, but I don't know what it *feels* like."

Physicians, out of necessity, go through training that emphasizes the medical-biological model of and for death. And recently there has evolved a popular intellectualized philosophical-psychological mode. Both are necessary for understanding of dying, grieving, and gaining insight into one's own feelings. But those who are experiencing losing and loss need ordinary, calm, unangry, unfrightened human contact, not parrot-like platitudes.

In the end, the listening continues, and at the very end, the doctor offers sadness as well as hope. Not tears, for they belong to the family, but the nonverbal sadness one friend feels for another on parting. Nor does the doctor bring hope in the religious sense, though where it seems appropriate, the physician may help patients accept a religious death without exerting his or her own convictions. The hope to be inferred here is concerned with self-dignity, which is achieved by working through the difficult process of dying as one feels a sense of accomplishment by working through the equally difficult process of living. A successful passage provides a sense of accomplishment.

A Moment for Musing

A question was raised at the home of a patient. She and her husband were talking about their marital relationship and the question was, "Is there any relationship that is perfect?" Of course the answer is "no." The next question then, is what in this world is perfect? There are those who would answer that the state of death might be considered perfect. Some believe that death evokes the day of judgment. Others might view this as perfection in that one is at rest, there is no longer pain, there are no longer any worries, no concerns about parents, siblings, friends, children, money, or whatever—that this is "perfect rest." And this is what some attempt to seek. These are those who will "let go," feeling that this life has been a veil of tears. There are those who fear death, *(in reality, this is a fear of life)*, and will fight vigorously not to let go. There are those who say early on, that if they're in pain, they will seek to be dead. As time goes by, however, we find that they fight very vehemently not to die, subjecting themselves to humiliation, painful procedures and embarrassment, perhaps viewing this battle as an act of courage. This is a subjective view of quality of life that for some of us could be considered terrible.

There are those who are dying who manage to be like opera's Traviata and have all their family and friends around. They demand that everyone be there, because should they die, they don't want to die alone. They become demanding, with the family hanging around, obeying every demand. In a way, this provides for them a quality of life, perhaps not what we would want, but not unlike the quadriplegics who say that they are satisfied with their life of dependency. As opposed to those who find gratification in their dependency, there are quadriplegics who would prefer to be "killed by a gun," a merciful escape from their prison. So quality of life is a very subjective thing.

Your life or mine?

Hospice: An Essay

Hospice (New Wine in Old Bottles). Is the hospice an alternative to euthanasia? In a word, no. As a concept, hospice is creditable, but not as an institution. Cicely Saunders was the guiding light of the current hospice movement. She resisted any form of euthanasia on religious grounds. So on the surface, it appears that hospice is indeed an alternative to euthanasia. But in practice, it rigidly fulfills the requirements for *passive* euthanasia.

The hospice movement has evolved from medieval times, beginning with shelters for travelers usually sponsored by a monastery. Then came hospitals with a church responsibility. Historically, hospitals were foreboding, usually considered a place to die. Even today, there are those who refuse to go the hospital because that is where people do go to die.

Today, the hospice movement reflects the past in its orientation, that is, church rather than medicine, comforters rather than medicine men. The literature on the hospice movement is written, for the most part, by non-physicians and usually is filled with well-intentioned catch phrases. Perhaps hospice is a testimonial to an assumed default on the part of the medical profession. Dying and death have come full circle. Once upon a time, people died at home. Later they died in hospitals, instilling a ubiquitous fear of the same. Today, they die in intensive care units. Now, there is an effort to again have people die at home—or at least in a simulated, home-like atmosphere. The rationale suggested for the hospice is that the terminally ill can be, and usually are abandoned by the medical profession, and usually are in pain. A further suggestion by the hospice movement is that the cancer patient, and other patients with chronic and degenerative diseases, should live his or her final months as productively and comfortably as possible: To die peacefully with dignity, and if the patient chooses, to die at home.

Certainly, there is no disagreement with these goals and objectives, but is it necessary to structure the concept in an edifice and call it hospice? As it is with the zeal and righteousness of ethicists, is it to be inferred that the medical profession only pays lip service to the concept? Does the movement require a physician figurehead for the group that needs to help the dying, much like the evangelist who needs sinners? Are we to believe that doctors feel that living and curing have meaning, but caring for the dying does not? Is it possible that there is no concern on the physicians' part for "quality of life"?

Prior to the era of chemotherapy, for patients with cancer, oncology units were places where patients with cancer came to be nursed and comforted until death. Today in the hospital setting, however, one can observe goals of hospice being carried out—not in one concentrated area, but within the diverse specialties and almost all units, whether general or specialized. The staff can be caring, visiting can be liberal, children can be welcomed, rooms are made homelike, dieticians, social workers, psychiatrists, occupational recreational therapists are often full-time workers and usually are as available as the oncologist. For example, at the University of Maryland Cancer Center, major holidays were celebrated jointly with patients, family, and friends. The holiday meal was an essential experience and was communal. Patients and families dined together in a solarium. The medical and nursing staff did the serving. This attitude on the part of the staff still prevails, not just during the holiday season, but throughout the year.)

There is something wrong with a patient-doctor relationship ending with a transfer to hospice, home, or facility. The patient now looks at new faces, feels a need for new trusts, a need to adjust to a new environment. A house does not make at home, nor does the hospice concept automatically imply the best or the most appropriate care for the dying. *People do make the difference.*

Whenever possible, dying at home is indeed to be preferred to dying in an institution. But there are pros and cons to dying at home. The patient and his family have an opportunity to cement and repair relationships. Guilt can be assuaged. On the other hand, nursing procedures can be difficult or repulsive. Some patients take too long to die, and some families fear finding the patient dead. When families talk with me about taking their relative home, I agree that it is a good idea if the patient does want to die at home. But I also tell the family, if at any time you find yourself checking the patient, your relative, every five minutes to see if he's dead, bring him back. Or if you find that the nursing procedures do upset you, bring him back. Or if you find that the process of watching him deteriorate physically, mentally, and even socially, disturbs you, bring him back.

A serious perspective on hospice can evoke the same emotional counterattack as is displayed toward one who might consider a pro-euthanasia posture. It is analogous to criticizing motherhood. The hospice concept is not new. It is no more or less effective or caring than any accredited group or institution. I remain apprehensive that the hospice movement will assume the faddish mantle that "death and dying" fervor carries: such euphemisms as death education, thanatology, healthy dying, peaceful death, and worst of all, "death with dignity." It should be remembered that the birth process is not particularly dignified. It is hoped that "hospice" does not become the buzzword with which good health care personnel are identified. The hospice concept, not the facility, should not be intellectualized because it is not an original one. The approach to the dying person should be to understand the person, not the topic, and certainly not the various models of terminally ill. The hospice movement does not have a corner on the market of palliative care. And, no, the hospice movement is not an alternative to euthanasia. It is passive euthanasia, "A rose by any other name."

There is hope. An encouraging sign is the recent plethora of articles, and in a few medical schools, courses and books on *palliative care.* Embodied in palliative care are end-of-life decisions and serious comfort measures. A caveat: While the concept of palliative care is meritorious, it should hold fast to patient *care* and not become another intellectual flag-waving.

Is This Hospice? One day, while performing my weekly house calls on my private, now-terminal patients, I visited with two who were home hospice patients. Both of them were in the care of their individual hospice nurse. Both were females. The first lady greeted me, saying, "That S.O.B. doctor of mine does not even call me to find out whether or not I'm dead. That so-and-so." I opined that if she wanted a call from him that she should talk with her hospice nurse. After some discussion, I left to visit the second lady. She, being less assertive, said in a wistful voice, "I never do hear from the doctor, I wonder if he thinks I'm already dead. You know he's busy and he really is such a fine person." I suggested that she discuss with her hospice nurse that she wanted to meet her doctor.

Well, the next week when I visited the first lady, I asked her if she had talked to the hospice nurse and she replied, "Yes I did, and she told me that I could not talk to my oncologist, that S.O.B. However, if I wanted to talk with the director of the hospice program, he would be glad to talk with me on the telephone. I told the hospice nurse, he can go @#!* himself." When I asked the second lady whether she had talked to her hospice nurse, she whispered, "Well, I didn't want..." Then she stuttered, "I really did not want to bother

her. She really is so pleasant to me. And she's just such a fine person."

Both were dealing with feelings of abandonment. The first patient was assertive and listened to her personality. She did not consider that it wasn't her right to complain. Also, she was furious about the fact that she was imminently dying. The second one, as with many patients, did not want to "bite the hand that was feeding her."

The next week, the first lady was dead, and within a few days, the second died. It is not hospice by and in itself, but *people who make the difference.*

Understanding Grief
(A Painful Yet Necessary Process)

Grief is sharp mental pain. Mourning is the expression of grief. Mourning is sadness combined with hurt. Depression is sadness plus a sense of futility. The futility encompasses one of the following factors or a combination thereof: guilt; the inability to find a replacement; refusal to separate or make a peace with the internalized person, now left with lost, hostile and conflicting feelings.

To every death there are two parties: the person who dies and his or her survivors—a dyad. In the process, the dying person can suffer much, but can look forward to death with its relief from pain. The survivors can take consolation that their suffering loved one is no longer in pain. Or, survivors can experience guilt, anguish, or both, when a loved one dies suddenly of trauma or suicide. In any case, grief and mourning seize the participants on both halves of the dyad. It goes without saying that families play an integral part as the patient moves through different phases of the disease. Their reactions directly and indirectly can and do affect the patient as well as the helpers.

While grief is the "normal" reaction to the loss of a loved one, it is the usual response to any loss or separation, including financial disaster, surgical amputation, graduation, family crisis, retirement, aging, and so forth.

What follows in the grief process applies equally to the patient and to the survivors: The family's immediate response is shock and anguish, which is shared by the patient, "Why me?" "Why him?" "Why her?" There are no answers to these questions. Nonetheless, patients and their families reach out to grasp at convincing explanatory fantasies: going out in the cold with wet hair, a neglected bee sting, a fall from a horse, an unforgiving attitude, frequent masturbation.

The initial shock response to the diagnosis introduces the *grief reaction* to the patient, his or her family, and friends. Death exacerbates the process for the survivors. The following "normal" symptoms are not *stages* but *phases* that overlap, or skip, or may be omitted, or proceed in sequence.

Initially, the response is shock, an expression of total disbelief, saying "It can't be true" or "I can't believe it." The grief-stricken person is stunned; emotion is suspended. This reaction happens regardless of whether the patient has been at end stage for some time or for the past few months. No matter when it happens, death is still perceived as a tremendous shock. It's not unlike the woman who visits her mother, who has had a stroke and is totally aphasic, every day in a nursing home. When the mother dies, however, the daughter still experiences the shock, perhaps with some guilt and relief, but shock nonetheless.

As a rule, but not always, shock is followed by emotional release, usually accompanied by covert hostility. There is the uncontrolled crying that occurs when the full impact of the loss has been realized. Hate and anger toward the lost person is expressed in the feeling of abandonment when the bereaved cries out, "Why did he have to die?" On a deeper level this may mean, "Why the *hell* did he have to die?!" "Why did he leave me? I'm so alone." "I have all these responsibilities." "Why didn't I die first?" While the feelings are powerful, they are not abnormal, but they can, unfortunately, inspire guilt. Emotion is no longer suspended, and now the full impact of the realization of the loss occurs. Now there is the emotional release, and usually tears, although there are some individuals who do have difficulty with the tears.

Coincidentally, there is also a sense of utter depression, and the sense of loneliness, despair, helplessness, hopelessness, and isolation may be experienced. There may be are physical (somatic) symptoms, such as anorexia, insomnia, or decreased libido. There can be a sense of panic when the individual feels that he or she cannot concentrate. They feel there is something wrong with themselves, in the sense of "What will become of me." Generally, somewhere in this experience of grief there is a sense of guilt, for the most part, unrealistic. The person turns on himself or herself, asking, "Why didn't I stay with her that afternoon," even though the deceased may have been bed-ridden and perhaps slowly dying for two years. Commonly, there is a sense of "I should have been more attentive." "I should have told her that I loved her." A recollection of being angry with the deceased relative can bring on an intense feeling of guilt. Perhaps of all the painful experiences following the loss of a loved one, the most painful is a sense of guilt.

It is not uncommon for the hostility to be expressed sometimes directly to the deceased, but usually the survivors' accusations are made against the doctors, hospital, "false friends," and others. From time to time, while a patient is in the hospital the family feels a great deal of gratitude, which they express freely and frequently to the staff, but then when the patient dies, the family becomes bitter and angry toward the staff. This anger is usually a manifestation of their sense of helplessness, melded with a twinge of guilt.

There are constant reminders for the survivor after the family member has died; there are split-second hallucinations that can be visual, auditory, or both, and can interfere with normal life, leading survivors to ask, "Am I going crazy?" There are frequent reminders, as when the widow expects her husband home at a specific time and he does not show. One widow provides a relevant, dramatic example. The widow had many very dear, caring, and attentive friends. So, about four months after her husband's death, she decided she would entertain for the first time. She invited her closest female friend and her friend's husband for dinner. After the friend and her husband arrived and while chatting the friend looked at the table setting. She saw that there were four place settings and said to the widow, "Are we expecting someone else?" The widow looked down at the table and burst into tears with the realization that she had set the table for her husband as well.

Then there is the waning of grief. Finally the grief and mourning begin to subside. The length of mourning varies from weeks to as much as two years. This follows a readjustment to society when one returns to one's "old self" again.

All of these symptoms can be summarized as *Shock, Turmoil,* and *Resolution.* One must keep in mind that mourning is a highly individualized process; everyone must mourn in his or her own way and in his or her own time. Most patients and their families begin the grieving process at the time of diagnosis. Other relatives may delay the process until the death of the patient.

Morbid or pathological grief reactions can be manifested in foolish behavior, over-dependency, delayed or chronic grieving, litigious behavior, suicide attempts, or the loss of capacity to feel emotion of any kind. Delayed grief may be manifested by the person who feels, "I can't afford to break down," a stoic who suffers many losses and then disintegrates when the cat dies, and has to be hospitalized for depression. In this reaction, the defenses of denial and repression are used generally to withhold hostility or ambivalent feelings toward the lost one. Delayed grief can move, unfortunately, into chronic grief. In this reaction, the grief process may last a lifetime. The mourner is frozen socially. This is usually a reflection of guilt and self-blame and is common in parents who have outlived their child or children. One can lose a parent, a relative, a friend, a sibling, and in time recover, but the loss of a child frequently is devastating. The child cannot be replaced. The parents can have *another* child, but not a replacement. When a parent, friend, or an older relative is lost, the *past* goes with them. A spouse or partner leaves and takes away the *present*. When a child dies, the *future* is lost. In each case, they leave behind memories—painful, angry, or "sweet sorrow."

As alluded to above, grief and mourning are normal processes subsequent to a loss. We also would include in the normality of grief that when we are bereft we grieve for ourselves as well as for the mental representative of the lost object or person.

There are certain factors that predispose individuals to severe pathological grief reactions. A long history of previous depressions, emotional disturbances, or both usually is elicited. A significant, and often irreplaceable, loss in early childhood is an important factor. Another factor is a markedly ambivalent relationship with a lost person, usually accented by a great dependency upon the lost person, the dependency fueling the ambivalence. Again, there are those seemingly stoic people who refuse to mourn after several losses, then pay the accumulated debt by falling apart after the loss of a pet or a distant relative. Another important dimension is the context of the loss: A sudden death can leave survivors without an opportunity for preparation, a suicide can bestow a legacy of shame and guilt on families and intimates. Suicides put skeletons in other people's closets.

Are grief and mourning normal or are they diseases? It can be argued either way. I have for the most part considered grief and mourning as very normal processes, and indeed they are. In contrast, however, if one chooses to view grief as a disease, the "etiology" would be a loss with the symptoms such as pain, suffering, and impairment of function. And, just as with organic trauma, with the trauma of grief, there evolves repair or complications. From this vantage point, one also could say that pregnancy is a disease of nine months duration with cure or complications, or that life itself is a disease ending in death.

Two other syndromes associated with grief, not necessarily pathological, are worthy of mention. In the "anniversary" reaction a survivor experiences a revival of mourning on the birth or death date of the lost one, usually without consciously recalling the date. There is a feeling of being "blue" or "under the weather" for a week or so until one associates the mood with a recall of the loss. The "Lazarus syndrome" may occur when a dying child is repeatedly taken to the hospital about to die, then again goes into remission. The parents alternate between mourning and relief, and some find adjusting difficult. It is conjectured, however, that the parents may begin to resent the recurrent, seemingly endless anxiety the child subjects them to. Their grief at the child's death is intensified by the guilt they feel for being angry with the child for putting them on that roller coaster. This phenomenon is not limited to the parents of the ill child. It is commonly seen in partner relationships where the patient is in and out of remission and relapse. The families or the partners wonder "how long is this going to go on," and then feel guilty. At times, they have a somewhat repressed feeling of anger for the travail the patient is putting them through, predisposing them to feel general irritability toward those in their environment.

There is another phenomenon experienced by some families. In an effort to preclude later feelings of guilt and loss, they move too close to the patient and overwhelm the patient, providers, the helpers, the staff. Other families go to the opposite extreme and abandon the patient to protect themselves from the pain of the anticipated loss. Both techniques fail as the mourning process comes regardless and is intense. It is incumbent upon the concerned friends and relatives to be alert to this patient-family interaction. It becomes their function to simply observe, intervening only when necessary, steering the family to a middle ground. This serves the patients' and families' best interests. Fortunately, most families, as it is with many patients, do cope with the crisis in a laudatory way.

Management of the Grief Reaction. Interference with the mourning process is useless and *can* be harmful! This awareness is the fundamental essential ingredient in the management of mourning. Since it is a "debt" that must be paid, the reaction is appropriate to a known loss. It is expected to follow its course to a spontaneous resolution. As suggested above, people will mourn in their own way, utilizing their individual styles of defense. It is also important to keep in mind that all mourning draws on previous losses, each subsequent loss stirs up the memories of earlier separations. (This generally goes on out of the person's awareness, i.e., unconsciously).

Tranquilizers inhibit the mourning process and contribute to confusion. If necessary, a mild bedtime sedative may be prescribed to soften the terror of the loneliness, which is enhanced by the muted darkness. The urge to suppress the mourning of others stems from one's need to allay one's own evoked anxiety.

Society and religion can impede or encourage the process of mourning, its resolution, or both. Memorials and funerals facilitate shared grief reactions.

Reassurance that mourning is appropriate by word and visit is helpful. The mourner's unrealistic guilt requires listening and understanding. Friends should not say, "Come to dinner some time," but rather should set a definite date for the invitation. This applies to the professional helpers (including the clergy) who should offer specific appointments instead of vague invitations. Certain groups, such as "widow to widow" programs, can be beneficial. There are some mourners who prefer to mourn in their own particular idiom, in their own way, privately. Others like to share their similar experiences with a group.

In reference to widows, a few words are appropriate relative to sex and guilt. As grief wanes and the widow begins to rekindle living, sexual feelings emerge as evidence. With these urges, however, guilt frequently is aroused. How can she make love without her former partner? The sexual feelings themselves give her pain as they remind her of her loss. Guilt and pain may manifest themselves in somatic symptoms. This phenomenon also is evident, but with lesser intensity, in widowers. Generally, it has been my practice when consoling a widow or widower soon after the loss of a partner to reassure the person that the crying and the shock and symptoms of mourning are quite normal. I counsel the individual not to make any decisions for at least six months, not to sell the house, not to change the job, and also wait at least a year and a half, preferably two years before getting married again. Usually, I am greeted by an angry retort that "Sex is the last thing on my mind!" when I give this recommendation. I agree with the patient that sex is not the issue. The issue I am concerned with is loneliness, and the fact we do very stupid and desperate things out of terrible loneliness. I urge the mourner to come in if they do decide to get married within the year and discuss it with me. Through the years, there has been only one person, a man, who was preparing to marry eight months after his loss. As he talked to me he changed his mind. In my experience, those widows and widowers, particularly the dependent individual, who marry very quickly because of loneliness, usually are divorced within two years. The relationship is a transitional one.

When guilt cannot be relieved or it is evident that one is faced with a pathologic grief reaction, referral to a psychotherapist is imperative. One can take some comfort from the words of a medieval writer on ethics, Ibn Gabirol, "Everything that grows begins small and then becomes big; but grief starts big and becomes small—and disappears." I would add that grief does not quite disappear, but rather it fades, and the loss and the feelings about the loss are quiet until awakened when the next loss occurs.

Quality of Life
and
Health Maintenance Organizations (HMOs)

A Double Whammy. Phyllis, was a thirty-four-year-old woman, but looked like she was eighty, as she was emaciated, weak, and had a staggering gait, products of her metastatic breast cancer. She had had her mastectomy about five years previously and subsequently received intensive chemotherapy and radiation. Metastases had spread to her skull, her hip, and to her leg. In spite of all of this, she was trying to eke out a taste of some quality of life acceptable to her. Almost two years after she was diagnosed, her husband came to her and said he wanted a divorce, that he "could not deal with this. With the throwing up, with the tiredness, I just can't handle it." Accordingly, they were divorced. She had an eleven-year-old and an eight-year-old, both daughters, who went down South with their father, and according to the patient, with the father's "friend." She knew her strength was ebbing and she would, even though she had full custody of the children, have to turn them over at Christmastime to her husband. She had been offered further chemotherapy, but raised the question whether of the treatment would give her "quantity of time or quality of time." She felt *if* the chemotherapy would, after a given period of side effects, offer her a better quality of life then what she had, she would take it, otherwise not. Her days were spent mostly in and out of bed with her "wishing it were over." We talked in terms of her getting more time out of bed though it was difficult. We talked about the things she could try for the nausea, which she had periodically during the day. Lorazepam seemed to help somewhat.

Sadly, her HMO became this patient's issue. The patient belonged to one HMO when she started her chemotherapy and had a doctor at one hospital. After her husband left her, she had to change to her mother's HMO. The patient then had to go to a new hospital and a different oncologist. It just so happens I knew both the oncologists, both good, both well trained. They have different personalities, however, both sincere, but in different ways. She was quite fortunate that she did manage to get an excellent physician, despite the transfer from one HMO to another. (Other patients have not been so lucky.) In her own words, "I had no choice and I did not know what I was going to get."

Phyllis offered to pay me for our visit, but I told her I was not going the charge her. After we talked, I contacted her doctor and discussed some of the things with him about further treatment. Another frustrating problem with the HMO was it would only pay for one consultation. She might want another visit with me, but she was entitled to only one official consult from her HMO. This would be feasible in the future if I would charge her then and not charge her for this visit. It was not to be. Her death intervened.

Another HMO Incident. HMOs require a "gatekeeper," a doctor who decides whether the patient can get this or that treatment. The "gatekeeper" decides where the patient should go and what consultations they might have. Not always. Here is Nancy, a bright, highly trained, responsible nurse who felt a breast lump. She called a well-known breast surgeon and made an appointment for a specific date. She then called the gatekeeper, who took offense, saying that she would have to cancel her appointment, that only he could make the appointment. He added, after he had met with her, he would then order a mammogram, look at the mammogram, and read the mammographer's report. He would then decide whether she should keep *her* appointment with *her* surgeon. This patient, however, told him that she was not going to take an appointment with him because it would be after the date of the confirmed appointment with the breast surgeon. She stood her ground and repeated that she was not going to spend weeks with anxiety over her breast lump. She wanted it looked at, diagnosed, and done with. After going back and forth with this particular doctor, he finally, in disgust, told her that she was a nuisance and she could go ahead and make her own arrangements.

So this is the way medicine is being practiced today. It is more of a business than a professional, medical relationship between the patient and his or her doctor. The thrust for HMOs and managed care is theoretically to save money. The assumption is this goal can be achieved by clamping down on unnecessary tests, procedures, and patient visits. Unfortunately, it is interfering, if not destroying, the doctor-patient relationship. It is my humble opinion that the day will come when instead of saving money there will be so many employees involved in managed care's upper and middle levels that it no longer will be cost-effective. Medicine will be practiced the way it was before. One can argue that today's technology is interfering with the doctor-patient relationship. There is some truth to this, but not to the extent that managed care will decide what patient will see what doctor and what care will be made available to what patient.

VIII.

A PERSONAL JOURNEY

Introduction

As I promised in this book's opening introduction, this chapter is about me—that is, about some personal experiences. As with the patients' stories, these are essentially true, but without any disguise. No camouflage.

They are not presented as a contribution toward an understanding of the deeper meanings of mankind's place in the next world, or even in this world.

Rather, think of this collection as dessert, as an after-dinner "sweet." You have dined mightily on heavy food for thought. You have come this far in your journey, sharing the travail of those who were or are ill. Now relax with a *leit motif.*

The stories are not meant to be unusual. You may have had similar experiences yourself. A "been there, done that" kind of thing.

So, thanks and enjoy!

A High-School Teacher Teaches. Teaches?

Medical school was somewhere in the future—I hoped. My fourth year of college still was available to me via the scholarship at Washington College, but I had no money for medical school despite having been accepted. I got smart, took education courses, qualified to be a teacher, made money, and then would go to medical school. After graduating from college, I took the qualifying high school teaching exams in Baltimore, and scored in math and science. Bingo! I was assigned to Baltimore City College High School as a science assistant. Three months later, the principal, a wonderful, tall, gray-haired, bespectacled, benign, and gentle man, Dr. Philip Edwards, came to me (he did not call me to come to him—what a *mensch*!). He informed me there was an opening at Patterson Park High School for a science teacher. Great! But Dr. Edwards quietly cautioned me that there was a disciplinary problem for that slot as three substitute teachers had come and gone, and besides that, the principal was a "stern" one. Dr. Edwards assured me that if the position did not work out, I should call him and he would find a place for me.

This was on a Thursday afternoon, I was to report on Monday. Here we go, I had just turned twenty-one, and had done some practice teaching while in college. I was scared, but armed with Dr. Edwards' insurance policy. I reported to Mr. Clark, the principal, at 7:30 a.m. on Monday. This short, bent, frowning, dour, dark man looked at this kid saying he was reporting for work. His response seemed like thunder to me.

"How long have you been teaching?!"

"Three months," I whispered.

"I asked for an experienced teacher, not a high school student!"

His whip–like words made me cringe. I pleaded, "Dr. Edwards recommended me."

"Your room is number thirteen, on the first floor, the keys are on the board," and he was gone.

Suppressing tears, I picked up the keys thinking, "Thirteen is an ominous omen," entered the room, and looked for lesson plans or some idea of what the students had been doing. I might as well have been trying to solve the riddle of the Sphinx.

Checking my class assignments, I discovered two ninth-, one eleventh- and one twelfth-grade class had been bestowed upon me. The science supervisor, a graying, motherly type, reinforced Dr. Edwards' evaluation of the disciplinary problem. She softened her message by telling me that one class could be rewarding, as the students there wanted to learn. Also, she gave me a syllabus of what the students should have been learning in the past few months, beginning with carbon and its uses.

Here they came! Our would-be scholars, our hope for the future. They were entering through the back door, tossing their books ahead of them, aiming for their desk tops with only moderate success. I leaned my buttocks on the edge of my desk and said nothing. Actually, truth be known, I did not know what to say. So I stood there, and stood there. After maybe ten minutes, which felt like ten years, the hubbub ceased. They looked at me and I looked at them. And, they looked at me and I looked at them. Still not knowing what to say, I continued to look at them, saying nothing. Thank God—the five-minute warning bell. Out of my mouth, me not really hearing what I was saying, "Today's lesson was on the uses of aluminum. Tomorrow, there will be a ten-minute quiz on today's work. That is all." There were reverberating guttural sounds, book banging, and out they went through the front door.

This continued, this "baby sitting," with the support of the science supervisor. The routine was not accomplished in one week; it was a constant redoing of the quiet, no real teaching, and here and there giving pop quizzes in an attempt to show them who was in charge.

Other incidents jump to my mind. The benevolent, understanding science supervisor was right. One ninth-grade class did want to learn and was eager to do so. What a joy! Evidence of the class that wanted to learn reemerged several years ago, and I was given a gift. A grown man introduced himself to me, saying he was now a successful, practicing lawyer. He told me how much he had enjoyed my teaching at Patterson Park High School. Ain't that something?

And how could I ever forget the day in the school elevator when one of the three gentle, women teachers in the elevator asked if I had a Patrol Leader badge, which would permit me to use the elevator. Before I could reply, another teacher blurted, "Oh, you're the new teacher." And the third counseled, "You're so young, why don't you grow a moustache?" I considered it, but did not.

Oh, and then there were the days when the teacher got taught. The classes were co-ed, the "students" were fifteen and sixteen. Three incidents have remained with me, refusing to be left in limbo. Once, early on, I decided to discipline one boy to set an example. I told him to stay after class in my homeroom. He sat there as I worked. When I finished, I sat next to him and said quietly, "The next time, you go to the principal, and the *next* time, your ass is out of here." He laughed and said, "Great! I'm only waiting 'till I'm sixteen and then I'm finished." I learned that lesson and never kept another student after school.

Another incident. Whether it was "quiet" day or a rare, actual Socratic day, my pattern was to walk up and down the aisles. I strolled toward the back of the room and turned to go forward into the next aisle, when up front a boy dropped a rolled condom out of his pocket, onto the floor. The girl to his left immediately put her foot on it. I discretely chose to turn and go down another aisle.

Which reminds me of yet another incident. "Incident?" The recollection makes the use of the word, seem overblown compared to today's classroom activities. One day, a "quiet" day, I was leaning against the edge of the desk facing the eleventh-grade class. To my chagrin and discomfort, the girls were tilting their chairs back, pushing the chair in front with their feet, and letting their skirts fall back. I walked to the back of the class, capitulating to their aim of making me uncomfortable. Wait. I'm not finished. Feeling some guilt, I guess maybe because I subconsciously enjoyed their provocative behavior, I went to the teacher's lounge to seek counsel from an older teacher. He had been one of my teachers many years ago at Poly High School. I described the incident to him. He smiled, "When they're in that mood, I give them something to write, and I sit down and enjoy it." A good lesson which, unfortunately, I was never able to apply, as the opportunity didn't present itself.

My second semester greeted me with an additional assignment. I was to have the responsibility of "study hall," *on the last two periods on Friday afternoon!* Inspired by naiveté, I suggested to the group that they use the time to do their homework so they would have the weekend free. This was met with such raucous laughter that the windows rattled. This unruly behavior continued through the next two weeks.

Suddenly, I had an idea. This happened during the era of television's Major Bowes Amateur Hour. I suggested to the Friday afternoon usual suspects that we have our own amateur hour. They went for it: single and group vocals, instruments from violins to washboards, magicians, ventriloquists, even stand-up comedians. Early on, there were a few disgruntled complainers who were promptly and authoritatively quieted by their peers. The overall enthusiasm was warm and joyous, and I not only shared it, I also reveled in it. The students judged themselves, indicating approval by applause—*loud* applause. During the first session, the applause was so vigorous, that it beckoned the principal out of his office, which was four doors away. He listened to my explanation and walked away without a comment. The amateur hour continued for the rest of the semester, then I was onto other things.

Except for high school, there has never been a time when I have not taught. I taught abnormal psychology in college, at Patterson Park High School, in the Army, in medical school, and as a physician in academia lecturing to the community and specialty disciplines. And I enjoyed every minute of it.

So, how did the Patterson Park experience close? Suddenly and quietly. World War II was on the horizon. Hitler was running fast and successfully. Here in the United States, a military draft was created to expedite preparedness. There was a lottery and every young male had a number. My number surfaced almost immediately. But what to do about teachers? Defer them and classify them to "2S." That was me. Then came the announcement that volunteer enlistment for one year would preclude being drafted for an indefinite time. I joined for the year, but my Army career lasted longer than one year (actually five years) thanks to the Japanese and their wake-up call at Pearl Harbor. When I informed Mr. Clark of my decision to enlist, he implored me not to do it, saying he would write a deferment letter for me. I thanked him, but said no thanks. Was he giving me a vote of confidence for a job well done, fearing the loss of faculty, or fearing the loss of a "baby sitter"?

Me and Eleazer—A Trip to Career Reality

It was 1965. I was excited, on an adrenaline high. As a faculty member of the Department of Psychiatry for the University of Maryland Medical School, I had just been invited to Israel to lecture on various aspects of psychiatry and psychoanalysis relevant to the practice of medicine. I jumped at the opportunity, feeling as if I was flying to Tel Aviv on my own power.

Once there, I taught at Tel HaShomer Hospital outside of Tel Aviv, at Hebrew University in Jerusalem, and at a community clinic, also in Jerusalem. From my point of view, the lectures went well and allowed me to meet with the faculty and their friends. It was pleasant for me socially, and provided me with a collegial opportunity.

One colleague in particular, was my host, Dr. Louis Miller, the Head of Mental Health for the state of Israel. We had several very cordial meetings and exchanged ideas and our histories. It turned out that he was an American and a child psychiatrist.

A later dilemma for Dr. Miller: In time, despite his personal reluctance, he was persuaded to pipe into the schools the broadcasts of the Eichman trial, the rationale was the children's need to *know* about the Holocaust. But there was a surprise fallout from the broadcasts. The children heard them as "horror stories," but the Holocaust victims in Israel had chosen to be mute about their experience in an effort to repress it. Hearing the broadcasts, they decompensated, suddenly flooding the clinics, now severely depressed.

Another sequel to the Holocaust was the loss of emotional trust by many survivors, so much so that mothers had difficulty bonding with their infants. Dr. Miller organized "orphanages" for the children where mothers and fathers could visit at any time, day or night in an effort to re-establish bonding. The children were raised with sights and smells that gave them a sense of home; even toddlers made cookies in the afternoon. Visitors were encouraged to pick up the children freely. When I visited, a little girl, about three years old, covered with flour, came toward me with her arms upraised. Of course, I picked her up. How sweet it was, raw flour never tasted so good.

Then came the zenith of my trip to Israel—an invitation from Dr. Miller to join the faculty at Hebrew University in Jerusalem for about $600 per month, half of which would probably go to taxes. I was beside myself, my insides boiling. Then I went to meet my guide, Beryl, a crusty *sabra*, whose parents had come from Poland during the early days of Palestine. We sat at a bar and I, in gushes, told him about the offer. Beryl thought for a moment, then, eyes intense, his words filtered through his Israeli accent:

"Dr. Schnaper, that's wonderful. We need educated young people like you. And I would be happy if you came. But I must tell you a story." He paused. "Eleazer was a venerable old Jew who had just died. The prophet Elijah came to him and said that God wanted Eleazer to decide his own resting place. Eleazer protested, 'I go wherever my God wants me to go.' Elijah shook his head. 'No, you have been a good and pious servant and He wants you to choose!' Eleazer, being the obedient and grateful one that God was concerned about, agreed. Elijah then said that there were two places from which to choose. Again, Eleazer protested that it was not necessary, but he bowed to God's will, and finally agreed to see the two places.

"The first one was a glorious panorama of lush, green land, a hundred vineyards, men happily making wine, many women dancing with timbrels. 'Fine,' laughed Eleazer. Elijah demurred; reminding Eleazer there was a second place. Elijah took Eleazer to the second place. It was much like the first, perhaps fewer vineyards, fewer men and women. Eleazer, again protested, 'I'll take either one, whichever God wants me to.' Elijah demanded that Eleazer pick one. Finally, the old man said, 'I'll go to the first one, praise the Lord.' Elijah then produced a document, a contract, for Eleazer to sign stating he was entering the first place."

Beryl paused, took a deep breath and quietly continued.

"Elijah opened the gate and in walked Eleazer. What a shock! The land was not green; it was barren, rocky, like the Negev. Men were sweating, working the earth with primitive tools. Eleazer, aghast, cried, 'What is this? This is not like either place that I saw!' 'Ah, but it is,' sighed Elijah, 'When you were here the first time you were a *tourist*. Now you are a *citizen*.'"

That night was one of the most difficult nights of my life. Tossing, turning, thinking of a possible life sea change, about family, thinking, thinking. I decided that I would remain a "citizen" of the United States. There have been moments of "what might have been," but no real regrets.

On Being a Doctor, or How I Ordered the Captain Off His Ship

In recent years, we in the medical profession have made an art of seeking relaxing diversions. This was not always so. Now, we golf, play tennis, fish, ski, hunt, jump out of airplanes, and engage in all sorts of unusual and interesting sports and hobbies. A favorite leisure endeavor for this physician is to travel, however, there are unexpected, potential perils for the physician traveler, as the following experience will testify. An experience that was in keeping with Robert Burns' words, "The best laid schemes o' mice and men gang aft a-gley" ("The best-laid plans of mice and men oft go astray).

It was May 1967. I was part of a group touring Israel. Suddenly, the country was in active military mobilization for the "Six Days War" to come. Our Israeli guide, a reserve captain, was called up to serve. He explained to me that I, as a doctor, and therefore "educated," would be responsible for the group's plane tickets and other pertinent material. (I was traveling as "Mr.," but somehow he knew otherwise.) Our tour was interrupted and we were being shunted off to Greece. He said he was wiring ahead to Athens, where a Greek courier would take over the tour. Indeed, when we deplaned in Athens, the young courier met our group asking for "The Doctor." He promised us an interesting and pleasant experience, which was an understatement, I was soon to discover.

The group was scheduled to visit Delphi and then go on to Piraeus to embark on a week's cruise of the Greek Islands. No sooner were we on the Aegean Sea, then the courier presented me with a problem. He had been in an auto accident the previous night, and now he was dizzy. He was given an immediate recommendation by me: see a doctor. But wasn't I a *medical* doctor? was his rebuttal. "I am a psychiatrist," I had said resolutely. "But you are a *medical* doctor," his rebuttal continued. "I am," but was there no ship's doctor? He was in Paris. Drawing on my neurology training from the distant past and without an opthalmoscope, I improvised a neurological examination. Constrained by my clinical limitations, it was nonetheless negative in all respects. He was given reassurance and an appointment for the next morning. The next day, I discharged him as my patient and also myself as a doctor and turned my energies to enjoying the cruise.

This freedom from medical responsibilities was brief. That afternoon, the young courier informed me that the ship's Captain was in distress with "stomach trouble," and asked if would I visit him. I ventured that there were other doctors among the 300 passengers—perhaps even a "stomach specialist." He conceded this possibility, but I was his choice. I reminded him that I was a psychiatrist, and that it had been years since my exposure to general medicine. This was totally irrelevant to him, as I was also a "medical" doctor, had treated him, and, most importantly, he had told the Captain that he "could trust this doctor." So, with noisy outward reluctance, but seduced by some inner stirring of adventure, I followed him to the Captain's cabin, a little room off the bridge.

The chain-smoking Captain had black, curly hair, not unlike that seen on early Greek sculptures. He was a handsome, pleasant man in his early forties, and appeared tense, but not acutely ill. He spoke English with some difficulty. Befitting his role of command responsibility, he was stoically indirect about giving the history of his illness and allowing the physical examination, minimizing his symptoms. He said he had had a six-month period of "stomach troubles" two years ago for which he had taken medication, but he had no bleeding then or now. Through the next several days, I apprehensively practiced a daily routine examination consisting of pulse taking, abdomen palpating, searching his conjunctiva—seeking evidence of possible bleeding. I found some anti-spasmodic capsules and a ship's officer who had a liquid antacid, and prescribed both of these, in addition to a strict diet—mostly warm milk and toast, hoping the trip would not end in crisis.

Being the Captain's physician brought some dividends blemished by embarrassment on my part. Respecting his privacy, I kept our relationship secret from the other passengers, however, the crew was fully aware of the goings-on. When I ordered drinks, stewards refused to let me sign the check. Bottles of gratis wine suddenly appeared at our table. If I was delayed with the Captain, a car or taxi would be assigned to join me to the off-ship island tour group, which showered me generously with suspicious or quizzical frowns. Throughout these experiences, I maintained a facade of nonchalance, as if I had business dealings on the islands and these perquisites were part of the "courtesy of the ship."

My journey into the area of internal medicine was not without hazards. One night, my secretiveness proved my undoing. I had examined the Captain at about 7 p.m. He appeared pale and somewhat drawn, and I suggested he stay off his feet. He protested that he could not, as he had to entertain in the main dining room. Fearing he might be bleeding internally, I said this was out of the question. He informed me that the Panamanian consul to Istanbul was aboard ship and, as Captain, he simply must entertain the consul, saying we were docking at Istanbul in the morning. I reluctantly agreed, suggested he have only warm consommé, push his food around his plate, fake his wine intake, and finish his hosting duties in half an hour.

I returned to my cabin and in short order, the phone rang. It was the Captain's secretary requesting the pleasure of my presence at the Captain's table at 8 p.m. How could I explain this invitation to the other seven passengers with whom I dined regularly? Simple: It was my custom to have a drink prior to dinner with a couple, a lawyer and his wife. I sought them out and told them about the invitation. They were pleased and surprised, and asked about the invitation. I fabricated the story that I had met this man who was the consul to Istanbul from Panama. I said that during World War II, I had spent some time in Panama (true), and this man and I had shared common experiences and reminiscences (not true). As consul, he had been invited to the Captain's table and, thoughtfully, had asked the Captain to include me (also, not true). My friend immediately shared this story with the other passengers. I joined the Captain's table and smiled pleasantly with each introduction until I came face to face with the consul. My chin fell—the consul was a *woman*! My lawyer friend later told me he had correctly surmised my secret role with the Captain.

Crisis! We were entering the Dardanelles and were to go up the Bosphorus to Istanbul the next morning. The Captain would have to be on the bridge all night—over my objections. At this point, I told him that if he used the toilet, he was not to flush it (which he had done daily against my instructions), and to call me. This he kindly acquiesced to the next morning. The bowl was filled with a large, black, tarry stool. His abdomen had slight guarding and tenderness on the left. His pulse was thready and had gone from 80 to 106, and his face, hands and conjuctiva were markedly pale, his skin clammy. He was bleeding in his intestinal tract!

Feeling uncomfortably audacious, I informed him that he would have to leave the ship and be hospitalized in Istanbul. He said he didn't trust the doctors there. He knew of an "American" hospital, but it was staffed by Turkish physicians. (There was also a "German" hospital and a "French" hospital, each named after the nationality of the rounding physician.) I insisted that he needed a thorough work-up, hematocrit, X-rays, blood pressure, and perhaps a transfusion and, worse, his life would be threatened if he remained on the ship after Istanbul, as we would be twenty hours at sea. Finally, he said he would go only if I went with him to the "American" hospital. I, of course, agreed.

Arrangements were wired ahead to the hospital and city authorities. A few hours later, the ship picked up a pilot and the shipping line's agent. Within moments of our conversation, the Captain's tiny cabin was filled to overflowing with ship's personnel of every age, size, shape, gender and rank. They washed him, dressed him. Some prayed quietly while others cried— also quietly. They tugged at my clothes, begging me to save him. Their concern for him and his welfare was most moving. It was as if death was pursuing their father and already had him at the banks of the River Styx.

In Istanbul, the police came aboard, coincident with docking, a routine procedure to check passports and issue landing passes. This process normally took some two hours, but as soon as they boarded, the chief purser obtained a landing pass for me. Immediately, we left the ship: the ship's agent, followed by the Captain in civilian clothes, followed by me in a blue sport shirt and white duck pants, and close behind me, the second officer in white dress uniform. The four of us descended the gangplank in single file, quickly and wordlessly—thump, thump, thump—into a waiting car, through the dock barricades rather than through the customs building, and off to the "American" hospital. Along the rails on every deck were the passengers, observing the landing procedure. Upon my return later, I heard the rumor: The Turkish police had come aboard and arrested a subversive American doctor. One woman, unknown to me, felt pressed to convey the information to me excitedly. I told her I was sorry to have missed it.

At the hospital waiting room we were greeted by flies, about one-half-inch in body diameter. This fact was called to the attention of the ship's agent, who shrugged his shoulders and commented that this was the "season." The examining room, however, was unexpectedly devoid of flies. After a short wait, an energetic young man in a tweed jacket, contrasting pants and striped tie entered. He was Dr. F., a Turk. The Captain sulkily deferred to me to answer the doctor's questions. Dr. F.'s English was excellent. When I complimented him on his command of the English language, he told me he had had lengthy training in the States. I asked where, and he gave me a tolerant look, and said quietly, "Mass General." With an audible sigh of relief, I gave an okay sign to the Captain, told him he was in good hands, and with mixed feelings, relinquished my position in general medicine to the savants, the appropriate authorities.

Epilogue. Subsequent correspondence revealed that the Captain had a radiographic diagnosis of duodenal ulcer. Gastro-intestinal bleeding also was confirmed. He was treated with transfusions, appropriate medications, and returned to Athens and bed rest. In several months, he was back on ship, eager to face the Hellespont and other assorted challenges.

The Captain and I corresponded every year or so. Twenty-five years subsequent to the episode, he informed me that he was the port captain in Piraeus, and as usual, asked when I was going to visit. In 1995 I did, and was treated as royalty—hotel suites, wine and fruit, a tour of the islands, reveling in the finest suite on the MTS Jason. The Captain was warm and in good health. He had aged well, as a seaman should. He was tanned, strong and wiry, and his face reflected "lines of character," trite but true.

Visiting Professor

Dumb Me and the Wedding. There I was during the last of November and part of December 1994 on an all-expense-paid trip to South America. The generous host and hostess for this marvelous trip were the representatives of the oncology society in Montevideo, Uruguay. My payment to enjoy this generosity was to give a series of lectures at an oncology conference. This was a bargain I couldn't refuse.

The trip began with an eight-day journey in a small boat going up the Peruvian Amazon River toward the Andes. A great trip, but that's another story.

Then I had ten days in Montevideo. In the United States, it is customary to play the national anthem at the beginning of a conference, a ball game or any kind of big-time public activity. Usually there follows a welcoming by the "important people," particularly representatives of the country or the host conference. It was quite different in Montevideo. The conference did not begin with their national anthem or with the usual introductions by the Dean of the Medical School and the president of the conference. No, instead, the morning began promptly at nine o'clock with the first lecture—and this was on a Monday morning. There were to be conferences and lectures Monday through Friday, inclusive. It was announced later, however, that on the evening of the first day, at eight o'clock, there would be the opening services for the conference.

So, after a day of lectures, conferences, and workshops, we met in this huge, huge auditorium where many local academic and political dignitaries sat on the stage. The ceremony began with the Uruguayan National Anthem. The music proceeded heroically with great crescendos for three or four minutes and then stopped. At this point, I sat down only to jump immediately back to my feet as the national anthem again went through high crescendos for two or three minutes and then stopped. This lasted for a total of about six or eight minutes. (Of course, I learned I needed to look around when the music stopped to make sure everyone else was starting to sit before taking my seat.) Then the assembled dignitaries made their speeches, including political leaders as well as officers of the sponsoring conference. Finally, the Dean of the medical school, without notes, talked in Spanish for a timed thirty minutes. (The lectures and conferences all had simultaneous translation of Spanish to English and reverse, but not for this particular occasion).

A cocktail party followed the lengthy introductions. There were many subsequent cocktail parties, home dinners, and spectacular side trips, all hosted by most gracious, wonderful people for the entire week. So there were late hours every night, the imperative routine, including lavish social functions to be enjoyed.

On the last day of the conference, Friday, it was announced that at 10 p.m., the closing ceremonies of the conference would be held at a local country club. About 9:30 in the evening, the van came to the hotel to collect members of the faculty who had been deposited there for the week. We boarded the van and drove out to the Montevideo countryside. The driver, who spoke Spanish, stopped the van in front of what was obviously a very fancy country club, and said something rapidly in Spanish as he pointed up ahead. Now, it helps to understand that the faculty at this conference were from the United States, Britain, Canada, Spain, France, and elsewhere. Thus, the remarks made by the driver were addressed to a Spanish-speaking gentleman, who was a professor from Madrid, Spain. Not understanding Spanish, I chose to look around. I was drawn to and wandered into this magnificent, lush building. The place was crowded with young people in fancy clothes, lots of food; it was just a great, happy party. Over in the corner, I saw the Dean of the Medical School, surrounded by people. He was the one who had given the long speech in Spanish at the opening service. I thought to myself, well, the closing ceremonies are going to include another long speech by this gentleman, but with enough drinks, everything would be okay. (In South America, drinks are not served at a bar, but rather by waiters with trays held aloft, each tray carrying a glass of scotch with ice cubes, a glass of wine, a glass of cola, a glass of water, and a glass of fruit juice. Waiters walked among the guests, who would help themselves. So for your second drink you need not stand in line at the bar, the waiter would soon come around and take your glass, and give you another drink. If you preferred a different drink, the waiter would be happy to oblige. This was the norm not only at cocktail parties, but also at dinner parties at private homes).

I was enthralled by the artwork in this magnificent country club. The waiter came by, and I helped myself to my second drink, which I was enjoying when one of the faculty members tugged on my sleeve, telling me that this was the "wrong place," that we belonged at the tennis club about 100 yards away from the country club. Obviously, this is what the driver was indicating to the Spanish professor, who did not feel it necessary to explain to everyone, or, in particular to me, because everyone else had gone ahead and I had naively wandered into the club.

There I was, a drink in hand, walking up to the tennis club. The hostess responsible for me, as well as the secretary of the conference, greeted me with, "Where were you!? And where did you get that drink?" I told her that I'd gone into the country club, unwittingly, and had gotten a drink. I was convinced that the closing ceremonies were going to be held there because I saw the Dean of the Medical School there, and I figured he was going to give us a speech concluding the conference. She began to laugh saying, "We don't have any closing ceremonies, we just have parties. And what's more, you saw the Dean there because you were at the wedding reception for his daughter!"

St. John's Abbey

A Journey Into Religion. During the late fifties and early sixties, I would spend a week every summer at the St. John's Abbey, a Benedictine Abbey in Collegeville, Minnesota, about ninety miles northwest of Minneapolis/St. Paul. Fifty priests, members of various religious orders, would assemble there for a week's psychosocial retreat, each year bringing a new, equally bright, group of clergy. The men would spend the week discussing a designated topic, which might be marital counseling, children, adolescence, or death and dying. I participated for a number of years and enjoyed the retreats tremendously. They were very stimulating and continued annually until it became obvious that every church, synagogue, and cleric was taking or giving courses with a psychological orientation. The campus also housed St. John's College (now St. John's University), a liberal-arts college for men, and a summer graduate program for priests, and nuns studying for their master's degree in theology.

The beauty of the campus is based solely in the realm of nature. Picture a serene, unblemished, green, rolling landscape of nearly twenty-five hundred acres, dotted here and there by prairie, wetlands, forests, and lakes, the latter each with its own undulating border design, some nourishing wild asparagus (which a Brother might harvest for one of our sumptuous meals). The texture formed by the trees and foliage was enhanced by the many colors of the wild flowers and fruits—so like an Impressionist painting. This was summer, but I am sure the view and feel are equally as beautiful when accented by winter's snow. Men of prominence have been known to visit and sit at lake's edge to take in its beauty and quietly meditate and refresh their souls.

Did the campus buildings infringe on this pastoral serenity? No, they did not. The college's academic buildings, The Liturgical Press (a leading publisher of religious materials), the dormitories, the library—all blended into the peaceful, park-like ambience that was peculiar to St. John's; many of the buildings have received of architectural awards.

The campus centerpiece was the St. John's Abbey University Church, a solid concrete edifice designed by the famous architect, Marcel Breuer. The sanctuary seated twenty-four hundred on wooden amphitheatre-style pews facing the white granite stone altar, which was embraced by a semicircle of wooden choir stalls. There were no columns; the altar was the center of attention. Thus, the faithful had an unobstructed view of the altar, no matter where they were seated, which imparted a sense of nearness. The lower level consisted of thirty-six Mass chapels, each with its own altar and a statue of a dedicated saint. The front façade, rising more than fifty feet was formed by connected hexagons superimposed on glass. The side walls included terra cotta tiles, which, when viewed from inside, changed earth tones, sometimes gold, sometimes hues of brown and burnt orange, sometimes shades of dark green—as demanded by the sun as it mixed shadows and sunlight during its travel toward the horizon.

The monastery, a flat red-brick building, the residence of the monks of St. John's Abbey, abutted the back of the church, accessing the lower level and the monks' private chapel, where our daily Masses were celebrated. The monks were the very fabric of the abbey. They were the teachers of theology, science, history, music, literature, and more. They were also administrators, editors, authors, laborers, carpenters, pastors, missionaries—the variety of their work was rich indeed.

Outside, separate from the church, was this huge, rectangular, solid-concrete banner, cantilevered on four large concrete arches that were joined at the top. The banner's body was interrupted by two open spaces: near the top, a vertical one embraced a wooden cross; below, a horizontal rectangular open space displayed a series of five bells. (I was told the banner was composed of 50,000 tons of poured cement, and I believe it.)

During the retreat, one of the four attending psychiatrists presented the morning lecture. We would rotate giving the lectures, and then break into four small groups, each with a psychiatrist and ten to fifteen members of the clergy. In the afternoon, one psychiatrist again would present, then the members would again separate into their small groups. In the evening, we four would sit as a panel for free-ranging discussion and then have friendship, which included food, beer, wine, and conversation. We were treated royally, despite being billeted in the college dorms. Lunches and dinners were feasts, attended by staff members eager to heed any request; and the campus religious community offered us many warm greetings.

The faculty psychiatrists were Catholics with one exception—me. My participation in the retreats began when a regular faculty psychiatrist became ill. Dr. Leo Bartemeier, who was then head of Seton Psychiatric Institute in Baltimore, a teacher and dear friend, invited me to come along as a replacement. When I reminded him I was Jewish, he assured me it was not a problem. He himself was a very religious man, a member of the Order of St. Gregory the Great—a highly regarded papal award. Then the annual pattern began. I would go to Collegeville, arriving on Sunday, returning home Friday night, usually emotionally exhausted, but exhilarated from the intellectual stimulation, and warmed by the freshly baked St. John's bread, the usual parting gift from the Benedictine sisters who lived in nearby St. Cloud.

My first day, my first year, began on a Sunday. I was joined by my inner companion: apprehensive anticipation. The next day, there was an opening faculty lecture on the subject for that week, which was marital counseling. Then we broke into small groups, and there I was with about twelve priests. As expected, they talked about things relevant to counseling for marital problems, and one priest bought up a pastoral experience for discussion. A man had come to him in the rectory asking what he should do about a troubling situation. He had attended a convention where women had been provided, and he had had a one-time sexual experience. The question was, "Should he tell his wife?" The priest presented this to me, asking for a suggestion. Trying to be a good group leader, I threw it out to the group, being the typical shrink, I asked, "What do you think?" They came up with some good answers, and I was pleased with their comments. One said, "That is a cruel thing to do to her if he only did it once," another said, "Well, he would just be expiating his own guilt."

There was more of this, and I was beginning to relax. Premature. Suddenly, one of the priests interjected, "Now wait a minute. He offended his wife personally, and she's entitled to a personal confession." My mind raced, I thought, what am I doing here? I'm Jewish. My brain was saying, "Now look you guys; if you want to talk theology, then talk theology. I'm here to talk *psychology,* and I'm ready to go back to Baltimore." All of this raced through my mind within the space of less than one second, although I said nothing. A loud voice interrupted my obsessing. On the other side of the table, I heard a priest saying, "You're full of shit." The priest continued, "Look, if you are driving down the street at night and your car hits another car and scrapes it, leave your insurance company's name and number. Let him know, because he will see that he has been personally offended. I'm not condoning the act, but this is not a personal offense, so you simply don't know what the hell you're talking about." Whew! I could have hugged him.

As I participated through the years, beginning in the late-fifties into the sixties, I saw some changes at St. John's. Early on, the nuns who were there for the summer master's work wore long habits. They would wish all of us a very pleasant "good morning" as we walked to Mass, and we would respond as cordially. Then, as years went by, the long habits gradually changed to short brown ones with pillbox hats. Then, near the end of the sixties, they were wearing shorts and halters—a reflection of the changing times.

At St. John's, the Benedictine Abbey, a leader in liturgical reform, had papal dispensation with permission to experiment with church procedure. It was there that the priest celebrant first faced the congregation, which has since become accepted usage. Also, the guitar Mass was the joyful routine at the St. John's monastery chapel. There were some die-hard priests, however, who objected to all this modern change.

I recall one year when there was a special Mass to celebrate graduation from the master's program. It was a dance Mass, where the graduates danced to prayers such as the Our Father. It was beautifully and gracefully done. Two priests, who had come for that retreat week, were upset with the very idea of a dance Mass, which to them bordered on heresy. I convinced them to come with me, which they did, albeit reluctantly. We sat there in the magnificent concrete chapel. They barely tolerated it until the very end when the Dean, who was the celebrant, said, "Go in peace the Mass is ended," and threw hand kisses to everybody. My two companions stormed out, huffing and puffing.

During my third year there, I was offered the privilege of giving the homily at the customary non-ecumenical Thursday morning Mass in the monastery chapel. This new tradition continued for the following years. For the homily, I would try to pick a theme relevant to the week's topic. That particular week's subject was marital counseling, and my topic was "A Few Kind Words for Infidelity." The topic was announced upon my arrival on Sunday, the usual procedure. There were appropriate readings chosen by me. The thrust of my homily was that unfaithfulness and disloyalty can take many forms, and I presented examples. To cite one, there is the man who gives materially to his wife and children, but not emotionally of himself. All the while, he devotes time and energy to the church, the community, or both. And when he dies, there is a two-column editorial eulogizing him. Finally, I pointed out that one cannot serve two masters or two mistresses, and "if this sound likes a pitch for celibacy, so be it." I sat down. Mass was over and we proceeded to breakfast as usual. There, I experienced a barrage of, "You no-good #$%@#! We thought you were going to present a defense of priests and pro-marriage."

More Religion. Strike That. Early on, I served as chairman of the Ritual Committee of my temple. The Rabbi was a bright, warm and clever person. There were twenty-four members on this committee, including the Rabbi. At our first meeting, I announced that the meetings would start promptly at eight p.m. and end promptly at ten, as we all had other meetings to attend during the week, as well as other responsibilities. We did not need a lot of late nights, and what was more, what we could not do in two hours was not worth doing. I also suggested that as a democratic process everyone should have an opportunity to speak, so we all needed to be brief. At quarter to ten, I would alert the group, to prepare them to end the meeting. What was left over in the agenda was carried to the next meeting.

There were several women on the committee who complained to the Rabbi that I was being autocratic, that their night out was too short. They felt that the meeting should last longer. The Rabbi informed them that they did not need an excuse to stay out to eleven or twelve. If they wanted to, they could go to the meeting, and afterwards they could all meet at some deli or a bar and enjoy themselves. And what's more, if they wanted to take it up with Dr. Schnaper, by all means they could do so. They never did.

When we would discuss a particular motion, the Rabbi would discuss his point of view, as would the other members. Then I would call for the vote. Not infrequently, the vote would go against whatever the Rabbi was favoring. I would then call for the next item on the agenda. The Rabbi often would pre-empt the agenda and give a lecture defending the vote he had just lost. I would say sternly, "Rabbi the motion has been discussed and carried. If you are eager to put this on next meeting's agenda, I would be glad to do so. There is no need to continue to discuss the previous motion." This happened quite a few times. One evening when we were alone together I asked him, "What the hell are you trying to do? The motion is carried and that's the end of it. Why do you keep bringing up the motion that has just carried and still try to discuss it?" He laughed and said, "Nathan, surely you watch the courtroom scenes on television. It's very obvious that even when the judge says 'Strike that from the record,' the jury has already heard it. So you see, the committee needs to hear it again even though the motion has been carried—unfortunately not to my great enjoyment."

Truly, he was a wise rabbi struggling to accept the democratic process.

A Doctor is Ill: Trials and Tribulations

It was 3 a.m. on a hot July night in 1964, yet I awoke shivering with cold, teeth chattering. My wife covered me with all the available blankets in the house. By dawn, the shaking had ceased, but I had a high fever and a sharp pain in my left chest with each inspiration. A physician examined me, diagnosed "pleurodynia," and gave me Demerol for pain. The next three days were vague. I slept most of the time, and I recall dreams of flying through forests, buildings and tunnels, all brightly lit. That weekend, we left to visit our children's camp with friends and I still slept—in the car, at the camp— and still had inspiratory pain.

On our return, I suggested to my wife that we take our vacation, leave Baltimore, and go to Florida so that I could convalesce from "this virus." I was practicing a massive denial, soon to be confronted.

Again, in Florida, I experienced the same pattern: sleeping almost continuously, eating only occasionally. On the third morning, I awoke with severe pain in my left testicle. Still denying, I attributed the pain to some abnormal position during sleep rather than to a systemic illness. The pain became unbearable, and calls to the two hotel physicians brought gratuitous suggestions; no house calls.

Fortunately, I remembered an internist who had trained at my hospital when I was a young staff member. He had since settled in Florida. He and his associates examined me very carefully, making small jokes in an effort to support me during the three hours they took to do their studies. Finally, he informed me that I had a friction rub on the left side, a generalized pleuritis, pericarditis, myocarditis, and epididmyitis; in short, all my serous membranes were affected. He could hospitalize me in Florida, but the Chief of Medicine at my home hospital was an authority on infectious diseases. He had already talked with both the Chief and the Chief of Cardiology, and they were expecting me for admission that day. I was flown out immediately.

Hospitalization was a lark, a new experience for the first few days. This was so despite severe pain in the other testicle and a pleural friction rub (the sound of leather rubbing against leather) audible for a distance of several feet. The hospitalization lasted thirty-one days, and the presumptive diagnosis was Coxsackie virus myocarditis. Treatment: absolute bed rest, no medications, careful monitoring of intake and output. Two years would pass before I could comprehend how seriously ill I was, and then only in retrospect.

In the beginning of my hospital stay, being on the staff, I was treated as a VIP. It was ego-building to have hordes of residents and medical students eager to examine me, nurses taking my fluctuating blood pressure every fifteen minutes, staff coming in to visit. But being a VIP and a physician had its disadvantages, for I had difficult convincing my attending physicians that I was a patient. Repeatedly, they would discuss the disease and other similar diseases, their therapy and its rationale, in detail—asking for my opinion, either overtly or tacitly. My standard response was that they were the doctors, and I was the patient.

As time went on, the fun evaporated. The examinations and visitors began to tire me, and I became inwardly very irritable, though I tried not to show it. The visitations were stopped, not by me but by my attendings. Each morning I would awaken around 4 a.m., deeply depressed, and a nurse would bring me a cup of coffee. I would feel ever so grateful to the nurse—nearly maudlin with gratitude for her magnificent gift. The same feeling extended to the orderlies for their routine services. By mid-morning, my mood would elevate.

I was discharged to home and more bed rest and sitting, which was to continue until late November. Like many others, I had always entertained the fantasy that given a restrictive illness, I would catch up on all my reading. But I found myself unable to do this, and spent much time in contemplation. On our living room wall is a large Chinese silk screen, depicting mountains, bushes, a stream, and a man on a bridge that crosses the stream. I spent hours studying this screen, seeing many variations and nuances in the panels. It was hypnotic. I wondered if the man, or I, was ever going to get to the other side.

In December, I returned to work for two or three hours a day, plus some individual tutoring for the residents at my home. I was overjoyed. Even though the friction rub was still there, I was alive and free again. Never had I felt such euphoria.

This feeling was soon shattered. New Year's Eve was approaching, and I told my wife to ask anyone who called to come over for a drink on their way to their celebrations. It would be festive; we would don formal attire. They would have to leave by 10 p.m., an hour past my regular bedtime. At 10:30,

I was sitting on the edge of my bed, taking off my shoes, saying that it was wonderful to have such warm friends, and that I'd never felt better. The next thing I knew, I was on the bed, still dressed, the inside of my lower lip cut. In the haze loomed two large state troopers. My wife had called the telephone operator to get an ambulance, shouting that I was in shock, and since it was New Year's Eve, the operator thought my wife had said "shot" and called the police was well as the fire department. Subsequently, I found out that I had had a seizure and had been unconscious.

I was taken to a nearby hospital where I was met by my physician and soon was diagnosed with a massive pleural effusion on the left. Another thirty days in the hospital at bed rest.

This time there was no period of adjustment; my feelings were, I am sure, akin to those of a prisoner of war. The door to my room was unlocked, but the pressure of incarceration was heavy. I began to badger the doctors for the date when I could return to work. The pattern of morning depression returned, but now it would last until mid-afternoon. Again, I over-evaluated any service, and many mornings I shed private tears of self-pity, wondering if it would not be easier if I would die. This seemed to me to be an *interminable* rather than a terminal illness. At no time, until now, did I reveal these feelings to anyone, although I am sure they were suspected by those close to me. Evenings would bring feelings of hope, and the imagined foreboding "giants" would seem to shrink to a more appropriate significance.

I returned home for another six months, then gradually worked toward putting in a full day's work. After a month at home, I read avidly for six weeks, then settled down to my old ways of sporadic reading.

Again, I spent much time thinking. In retrospect, a prolonged illness intensifies the regression that accompanies any illness. A person's thinking is an unconscious effort to stem, or at least cope with, the regression. One's concept of his place in the world is age-dependent—his perspective varies as he develops from childhood to maturity. So when regression takes place, his view of himself in relation to this environment will be proportionate to the degree of regression. The regression can be limited or permanent.

What activates regression and makes it so compelling? I would conjecture that in this situation, it is a defense against separation anxiety. Any illness brings with it the real or fancied threat of unpleasant body image changes. In an effort to cope with this threat, the patient gropes for a protecting, parental figure. The family and the professionals are there, but the illness persists. The more prolonged the illness, the more severe the physical injury, the more the patient feels abandoned. As the feeling of separation intensifies, the patient regresses to even earlier stages of childhood development, becoming increasingly clinging, frightened, and dependent.

When regression is severe, two choices are present: either total capitulation to regression to an infantile stage, or resistance through thought, behavior, or both. In either case, a massive alteration in outlook occurs.

As a corollary to the process of regression, it is important that physicians be aware of the paradox that may ensue with a regressed patient. On the surface, the patient becomes very dependent and apparently grateful. The physician's power blends with that of the patient's parents, and all the patient's needs have the promise of being magically gratified. But in actuality, the patient, feeling this great need for the doctor and seeing himself so passive and vulnerable, becomes resentful. This resentment is followed by guilt for resenting the physician who is being so "nice." At this point, the physician sees an irritable, demanding, or withdrawn patient. It is incumbent upon the physician to be aware of this process and not regard the patient's behavior as directed personally toward him or her.

In my case, although outwardly I appeared somewhat withdrawn, my mind was busy. My thinking resulted in a reassessment of values and a reordering of priorities. Relationships and teaching became more important, money less. Above all, death no longer was a threat. I was, and am, on bonus time. All this could well be denial again, but I feel not that I am looking forward to dying, but rather that death can be approached philosophically as part of living.

The basis for this philosophy rests on overall experience, as it must with those suffering imprisonment, severe illness of all kinds, and other overwhelming emotional experiences. The pain was the least of the problems. More important were the feelings of helplessness, the indignity of the hospital procedures, wanting something from others but not knowing what or how to ask. The helplessness engenders feelings of desperation that border on futility. A person in this situation unrealistically compares himself with his former active self, and it is a painful conflict to see himself as incapacitated, helplessly dependent on others for gratification of needs, when he had been self-sufficient and responsible for the needs of others. I would suspect that this role-reversal dynamic applies to other active people, and is not limited to physicians. Perhaps it is more painful to those who are in the care-taking professions. A similar sequence may occur following retirement; the loss here is the active self, and compounding the loss is, again, the comparison to one's former active self. Regression then ensues.

A comment on the attitudes of the people in my environment when I was a patient: There were those whose concern was real and evident; then there were those who were pressing to tell of their own or another's illnesses. Many truly were concerned about me, but were uncomfortable in expressing it. Some talked unusually quickly, others were unusually tongue-tied. And some just stared. At the time, their reactions puzzled and annoyed me. Subsequently, I came to understand that they were uncomfortable with the possibility that I might be dying.

A second trial came nine years later. Glaucoma had been progressing in my right eye over several years and was not responding to medication. The recommendation was cryogenics to the ciliary body. The ophthalmologist also discussed the possibility of enucleation, the surgical removal of the eye, as cryogenics was a temporizing procedure, and I had only pinpoint light vision in the eye. I told him I was the patient and he was the doctor. He suggested I see a consultant prior to surgery. I had been seen by quite a few consultants, each hinting at enucleation, but avoiding the word. One highly respected, elderly ophthalmologist went so far as to say that Wiley Post flew around the world with one eye, and that it was legal to drive a car with one eye, but offered no recommendations.

Then came a most-upsetting incident. During a routine preoperative examination, a senior resident who was looking in on the proceedings commented that he would not remove the eye, although he knew this was being considered. The eye, although without vision, could pick up light, and further, he thought the mandated consultant tomorrow was very experienced and would not go along with enucleation. I said nothing, but went back to my room, angry, frightened, and again helpless. I had accepted the enucleation six months prior, knowing it was coming. It was a matter of the doctor and myself each waiting for the other to put it into words.

The next morning, the consultant recommended enucleation, saying in his experience people who have an eye that picks up distracting sparkles of light want it removed. The enucleation was performed.

The day prior to my discharge, I called in the senior resident and explained that he had upset me, and that I wanted to speak to him as a patient, but also as a doctor. As a patient, I felt he was doing me great emotional harm by recommending a particular course of action after I had been prepared in another direction by my own physician. As a doctor, I did not think it would please him very much if a resident usurped him as the responsible doctor to one of his patients. He was humbly apologetic, saying that his only excuse was he had been speaking to me as "doctor to doctor." I told him that I had not discussed this matter with my doctor or the consultant (his chief), and hoped that he would consider this part of his training.

What I learned, then, from both illnesses was a new awareness of the feelings of others. Following my first illness, patients varied in their approach to my absence. Some complained about the separation, some were concerned, some, defensively, were totally unconcerned. Two who had early childhood losses unrealistically assumed responsibility for my illness. A similar distribution occurred after the enucleation. Most assumed, after seeing me with an eye bandage, that I had had some kind of eye surgery. After seeing my prosthesis, they made further assumptions, saying they were "glad that your operation went well and you can see better." If they did not ask what was done, I did not tell them.

With all this in mind, it seems appropriate to take note not only of the feelings of hopeless frustration connected with being a patient, but also the increased frustration of being a physician-patient. No longer is the doctor the god-like healer. The physician is now stripped of the omnipotence and objectivity he or she usually employs in dealing with illness, for this illness is the doctor's own. The doctor can approach the disease clinically, as if it belongs to another, as did a colleague with terminal multiple sclerosis as he discussed the progression of his symptoms. Or the doctor can minimize and dismiss his or her illness, as I tried to do. In either situation, the defense of denial is working. Denial can be pathological if one is avoiding proper treatment, but it is constructive if it permits one hope where the possibility of cure is absent. In other words, denial can help a person function when the emotional ramifications of an illness could render the patient dysfunctional.

It is frequently said, sometime facetiously, sometimes in anger, that "doctors and nurses make the worst patients." Omnipotence is fighting off regression. The physician, now a patient, may insist on participating actively in all treatment decisions concerning his illness. It is unfortunate that some physicians-in-charge encourage this behavior, to the detriment of the patient. I would suspect that it reflects the helper's insecurity or his unconscious identification with the physician-patient's omnipotence.

Regardless of profession or trade, if we can accept regression as temporary, secure in the knowledge that we can "come back," we make a contribution to our treatment. Of course, this is easier said then done. But having had the experience, we should then be able to draw on it when needed.

As physicians, if we can relinquish our omnipotence, conceding that we are not the best doctor for ourselves, our prospects for being healed are enhanced.

We do not have to seek illness or trouble, they overtake us in the course of living. Coming to grips with adversity gives us muscle. Perhaps the trials and tribulations that accompany illness provide us with a glimmer of insight into ourselves and others, giving us the quiet will to go on.

Why I Quit Smoking

Here's Rover, this man's best friend. Rover was alert and perky with piercing yellow and black eyes, a white belly, a palette of colors, sky blue and turquoise tropical sea gracing his back and tail feathers. What a parakeet, and could he talk! He was a birthday gift from my children, which I accepted reluctantly, protesting most ungraciously that it would be "too much work." Was I dumb.

Rover's training was easy. I taught him to fly to my finger while in his cage, then to my finger while out of his cage. His world was the kitchen, which he royally surveyed from the top curtain rod. In the beginning, he resisted leaving his throne to return to my finger on command. One day, in frustration, I yelled, "Get your ass down here!" He did, and that sentence became his favorite expletive. One day, my teenage son was entertaining a girlfriend in the kitchen. I was upstairs. Suddenly, Rover yelled—in my voice—"Get your ass down here!" She screamed, nearly falling off her chair, thinking it was me. I ran downstairs to reassure her it was not. I guess she, as with me, never forgot Rover.

Rover had other phrases and sentences in his vocabulary: "I wanna dance," meaning he wanted to be on your shoulder while you gyrated. "Nathan Schnaper, Nathan Schnaper!" which translated into "Come here." He learned my name from hearing me give it over the kitchen telephone. And if anyone was talking on the phone, he would interrupt his preening, jump on a shoulder, and attempt distraction by pulling on an individual hair. As soon as the conversation ended, he would return to his perch—like a small child seeking attention. Some words he learned from radio songs. Most remarkable for this little brain of his was his ability to obey commands. If I ordered, "Go to your cage," he would go. "Take a bath," he would fly to the sink and I would turn on the water. And, the best, "Give me a kiss," and he would. My scientist friends were in awe of his performance.

But, most importantly, above all, were the intimate moments we shared every morning and every evening. In the morning, I would have my coffee, newspaper, and two cigarettes. Rover would sit on my shoulder, peck on the paper's edge, *and it was good*. After work, I would have a scotch and water with lemon, some pretzels, two cigarettes, and watch the news on television. Rover would sit on the edge of the glass, either pecking at the lemon peel or talking into the glass to hear his echo. Of course, he also would eat at the same pretzel as I. At times, I would put a pretzel on the table to steer him away from mine. He would peck at it, suddenly become aware that I was not on the other end of it, would fly up to my mouth, *and it was good*.

Now, the moment of truth. One evening, two friends came to dinner. The three of us were in the kitchen smoking and simultaneously let out a puff of smoke. I watched it rise—*DIRECTLY TOWARD ROVER!* My immediate association was to the days when miners would take a canary down into the mine to monitor lethal gases. I quickly ushered my friends out of the kitchen, threw away my cigarettes, and never smoked again. Nor did I ever have the desire to smoke again.

Rover lived for some eight years thereafter. He was never sick, but died quietly one night of old age. It was a terrible shock, and I still miss him, my best friend.

Memories

Memories course through my brain like a river. At times they meander peacefully or whirl in eddies, at times they are rushing, trying to get safely beyond the blocking rocks, and sometimes the memories are stagnant, painfully polluting my mind—and I desperately wish they would move out to sea.